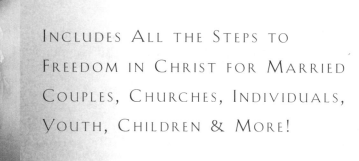

MINISTERING *the* STEPS *to* FREEDOM IN CHRIST

INCLUDES ALL THE STEPS TO
FREEDOM IN CHRIST FOR MARRIED
COUPLES, CHURCHES, INDIVIDUALS,
YOUTH, CHILDREN & MORE!

DR. NEIL T. ANDERSON

Gospel Light

Gospel Light is an evangelical Christian publisher dedicated to serving the local church. We believe God's vision for Gospel Light is to provide church leaders with biblical, user-friendly materials that will help them evangelize, disciple and minister to children, youth and families.

We hope this Gospel Light resource will help you discover biblical truth for your own life and help you minister to adults. God bless you in your work.

For a free catalog from Gospel Light please contact your Christian supplier or contact us at 1-800-4-GOSPEL.

PUBLISHING STAFF
William T. Greig, Publisher
Dr. Elmer L. Towns, Senior Consulting Publisher
Dr. Gary S. Greig, Senior Consulting Editor
Jill Honodel, Editor
Pam Weston, Assistant Editor
Kyle Duncan, Associate Publisher
Bayard Taylor, M.Div., Editor, Theological and Biblical Issues
Barbara LeVan Fisher, Cover Design
Debi Thayer, Designer

How to Make Clean Copies from This Book

YOU MAY MAKE COPIES OF PORTIONS OF THIS BOOK WITH A CLEAN CONSCIENCE IF:

- you (or someone in your organization) are the original purchaser;
- you are using the copies you make for a noncommercial purpose (such as teaching or promoting your ministry) within your church or organization;
- you follow the instructions provided in this book.

HOWEVER, IT IS **ILLEGAL** FOR YOU TO MAKE COPIES IF:

- you are using the material to promote, advertise or sell a product or service other than for ministry fund-raising;
- you are using the material in or on a product for sale;
- you or your organization are **not** the original purchaser of this book.

By following these guidelines you help us keep our products affordable.
Thank you,
Gospel Light

Contents

Introduction

When I was pastor of a local church, many people came to see me for help with a myriad of problems. While I was able to help some with prayer and counsel based on the Word of God, coupled with some good old common sense, many were not helped in a life-changing way, and I wasn't satisfied with just helping them cope. I never questioned that Christ was the answer and that the truth of God's Word would set them free, but then I didn't know how to help them resolve their conflicts in a comprehensive way.

When the Lord called me to teach at Talbot School of Theology, I offered an elective class titled "Spiritual Conflicts and Counseling." Every year the class grew dramatically as I learned how we are to submit to God and resist the devil (see James 4:7). As a result, I started to see dramatic changes as people were set free from eating disorders, sexual addictions, panic attacks, chronic depression, bitterness, pride and many other serious problems. From this important time of learning and ministering, the Steps to Freedom in Christ slowly evolved into these current versions.

You will find eight reproducible versions of the Steps to Freedom in Christ in this one volume or you may prefer securing the Steps in individual versions (especially when large quantities are needed for seminars or group studies). Carefully read the introductory comments and familiarize yourself with each step, as well as the important aftercare issues. Additional resources are listed at the beginning of each version and these are available from your local Christian bookstore or Freedom in Christ Ministries. A complete training schedule for studying these resources is described at the end of this introduction.

This volume includes the following versions of the Steps to Freedom in Christ:

> **Steps to Freedom in Christ for Adults**
> **Steps to Freedom in Christ for Young Adults**
> **Steps to Freedom in Christ for Youth**
> **Steps to Setting Your Child Free—for ages 9–12**
> **Steps to Setting Your Child Free—for ages 0–8**
> **Steps to Setting Your Marriage Free**
> **Steps to Beginning Your Marriage Free—for engaged couples**
> **Steps to Setting Your Ministry Free—for churches, ministries and organizations**

Please understand that the Steps to Freedom in Christ don't set you free. It is *Christ* who sets you free and your response to Him in repentance and faith is *what* sets you free. The Steps to Freedom are just tools, but like most tools, they can be used in a right way or a wrong way.

The discipleship counseling process, which serves as the basis for this approach, understands that the wonderful Counselor is Christ, because only He can grant repentance leading to a knowledge of the truth which sets captives free (see 2 Timothy 2:24-26). I elaborate on this entire discipleship counseling process in my book, *Helping Others Find Freedom in Christ*, a prerequisite for using these Steps to Freedom.

A parenting book I coauthored with Peter and Sue Vander Hook titled *Spiritual Protection for Your Children* has Steps to Setting Your Child Free for children twelve years and younger. Peter and Sue are a committed evangelical pastor and his wife who suddenly found themselves in a spiritual battle. In the process of helping their children, they found their own freedom in Christ which led to helping many others, including the leaders of their church.

The youth and young adult versions of the Steps were coauthored by Dave Park and Rich Miller. Rich and I also coauthored a youth version of *Helping Others Find Freedom in Christ* titled *Leading Teens to Freedom in Christ*.

Dr. Charles Mylander and I have sought to show how *corporate* freedom may be found in our books *The Christ-Centered Marriage* and *Setting Your Church Free*. I believe that Jesus is the wonderful Counselor and the ultimate church consultant! A very similar approach for counseling individuals is also used for resolving corporate conflicts in marriages and in churches. Personal freedom in Christ must be established first, however, before corporate issues can be resolved. Couples or ministry leaders need to use the adult version of the Steps to Freedom in Christ individually before going on to the marriage or ministry steps.

If you have a church full of people with unresolved conflicts, you have a church in bondage, and no church can be any stronger than the marriages and families that make up the congregation. The whole cannot be any greater than the sum of its parts. We encourage you to discover the joyful process of establishing Christ at the center of your marriage and ministry.

Churches and missionary groups of many denominations are using this process all over the world. It is not a condemning or finger-pointing process because there is no condemnation for those who are in Christ Jesus (see Romans 8:1); nor is it one of helping to cope or manage conflicts. Rather, it is a process of resolving conflicts *in Christ*. There is no way to fix our pasts, but we can be free from them by genuinely repenting and putting our faith in God.

Every church should be able to establish their people alive and free in Christ. To do this, leaders must be adequately equipped to do the work of ministry. There are no shortcuts to helping others find their freedom.

How to Establish an Ongoing Freedom Ministry in Your Church

Crystal Evangelical Free Church in Minneapolis hosted our "Living Free in Christ" conference, then immediately began training encouragers to develop their own freedom ministry. Within four years, over 1,500 hurting and desperate people—struggling with panic attacks, eating disorders, depression, addictive behaviors and a multitude of other problems—were led to freedom in Christ! Crystal has even hosted its own conference to show other churches how to do it and they are networking with many other churches in the Minneapolis area.

Ninety-five percent of Crystal's trained encouragers are laypeople. Training lay people has to happen if we're going to see our churches and ministries come alive. The reason for this is that there aren't enough professional pastors or counselors in our country to reach more than five percent of our population, even if that were all they did! We have to equip the saints to do the work of ministry (see Ephesians 4:12).

Suppose your church carefully chose 20 people and trained them as outlined below. Further suppose that each trained person agreed to help just one other person every other week. By the end of one year, your church would have helped 520 people and the ministry wouldn't stop there! These people, now free in Christ, would become witnesses without even trying! Your church would become known in the community as a place that really cares for people and has answers for the real-life problems people face. After all, what kind of witness does a person have if he or she is living in bondage? However, when children of God are established free in Christ, they will naturally (or supernaturally) be witnesses glorifying God and bearing fruit.

A variety of material is available for training encouragers, including books, study guides and both video and audiotape series. Each tape series has a corresponding workbook. The best training takes place when the trainees watch the videos, read the books and complete the corresponding study guides. Study guides greatly increase the learning process and help personalize and internalize the message. Some groups minimize training costs by eliminating use of the videos. Many others purchase library copies of the videos and encourage their trainees to cover the cost of their own training materials.

Use the following Basic and Advanced Training Schedules as guidelines for your freedom ministry. The materials are listed in the order they should be taught.

BASIC LEVEL TRAINING
(16-Week Schedule)

FIRST FOUR WEEKS	
Purpose	To understand who we are in Christ, how to walk by faith, win the battle for our minds, and to understand our emotions and biblical insights for our relationships.
Video/Audio Series	"Resolving Personal Conflicts"
Books	*Victory over the Darkness* and *Study Guide*
Youth Edition	*Stomping Out the Darkness* and *Study Guide*
Supplemental Reading	*Living Free in Christ*: The purpose of this book is to establish the believer complete in Christ and show how He meets our most critical needs of life, identity, acceptance, security and significance. This is the first book a person should read after going through the Steps to Freedom or when he or she has prayed to receive Christ.

SECOND FOUR WEEKS	
Purpose	To understand the nature of the spiritual world; the position, authority, protection and vulnerability of the believer, and how to set captives free in Christ.
Video/Audio Series	"Resolving Spiritual Conflicts"
Books	*The Bondage Breaker* and *Study Guide*
Youth Edition	*The Bondage Breaker Youth Edition* and *Study Guide*
Supplemental Reading	*Released from Bondage:* This book has chapter-length personal testimonies of finding freedom in Christ from depression, incest, lust, panic attacks, eating disorders, etc. with explanatory comments by Neil Anderson.

Note: *Breaking Through to Spiritual Maturity* is an adult group study for teaching the above material ("Resolving Personal and Spiritual Conflicts"). *Busting Free* is the youth group study for teaching the above youth editions.

THIRD AND FOURTH WEEKS	
Purpose	To understand both the theology and practical means by which we can help others find freedom in Christ with a true discipleship counseling approach.
Video/Audio Series	"Spiritual Conflicts and Counseling" and "Helping Others Find Freedom in Christ"
Reading	*Helping Others Find Freedom in Christ* and the *Training Manual and Study Guide:* The study guide also details how your church can establish a discipleship counseling ministry, and it has answers for the most commonly asked questions.
Youth Edition	*Leading Teens to Freedom in Christ*
Supplemental Reading	*Daily in Christ*: This is a 365-day devotional that we encourage individuals, as well as families, to go through for one year. There are also four forty-day devotionals for youth, entitled *Ultimate Love, Awesome God, Extreme Faith* and *Reality Check*.

To successfully complete the basic training each person should…

- Have gone through the *Steps to Freedom in Christ* personally with another encourager.
- Have participated in two or more freedom appointments as a prayer partner.
- Be recommended by the director of your freedom ministry and meet the qualifications established by your church.

Note: For a more detailed listing of these resources, turn to the bibliography at the end of this book.

In addition to basic training, Freedom in Christ Ministries also has powerful materials for advanced training dealing with specific areas of ministry. These advanced topics can be offered in special or regularly scheduled encourager meetings. We strongly suggest that your team of encouragers meet regularly for prayer, instruction and feedback because it is our experience that as the group matures, needs and cases become more difficult.

On-the-job training is essential for any ministry. None of us have fully arrived. Just about the time you think you've heard it all, along comes a case that shatters all stereotypes and doesn't fit into any mold! However, this keeps us from falling into patterns of complacency and relying on our own cleverness instead of on God.

ADVANCED LEVEL TRAINING
(16 Weeks or More)

FIRST FOUR WEEKS	
Purpose	To discern counterfeit guidance from divine guidance, explain fear and anxiety, how to pray in the Spirit, and how to walk by the Spirit.
Book	*Walking in the Light*
Youth Edition	*Know Light, No Fear*

SECOND FOUR WEEKS	
Purpose	To understand the culture that our children are being raised in, what is going on in their minds, how to be the parent they need, and how to lead them to freedom in Christ.
Book and Video Series	*The Seduction of Our Children*
Supplemental Reading	*Spiritual Protection for Your Children*
For Youth	*To My Dear Slimeball*

THIRD FOUR WEEKS	
Purpose	To understand how people get into sexual bondage and how they can be free in Christ.
Book	*A Way of Escape*
Youth Edition	*Purity Under Pressure*

FOURTH FOUR WEEKS	
Might include one of the following:	
Book and Video Series	*Freedom from Addiction* and *Workbook:* This book and video series teaches the nature of substance abuse and how the addictions can be broken in Christ.
Book and Video Series	*Setting Your Church Free*: This book and video series is for Christian leaders. It teaches a biblical pattern of leadership and shows how churches can resolve their corporate conflicts and establish Christ as the Head of their ministry.
Book and Video Series	*The Christ-Centered Marriage* and *Study Guide*
Book	*Spiritual Warfare*
Video/Audio Series	"Resolving Spiritual Conflicts and Cross-Cultural Ministry"
Book and Study Guide	*The Common Made Holy* and *Study Guide:* This book is a comprehensive study on positional and progressive sanctification in Christ. It explains who we are in Christ and how we are conformed to His image.

Note: For a more detailed listing of these resources, turn to the bibliography at the end of this book.

SCHEDULES FOR BASIC LEVEL TRAINING

A 16-week format would require a two- to three-hour meeting one night each week. It will take about 12 weeks to complete the first three video series if two video lessons are viewed each night. The last four weeks of training works best by using "Helping Others Find Freedom in Christ" Video Training Program. This series has four sessions, each 45 minutes long. Show one video session each evening and allow ample time for discussion. This schedule does not include much time for discussing the books, study guides or the content of the video series. Groups that have provided for additional discussion time at another meeting or on a Sunday, etc., have experienced the most dramatic growth and training.

Weeks 1 through 4	Weeks 5 though 8	Weeks 9 through 16
"Resolving Personal Conflicts"	"Resolving Spiritual Conflicts"	"Spiritual Conflicts and Counseling" & "Helping Others Find Freedom in Christ"
Two video lessons each meeting	Two video lessons each meeting—the last tape has the Steps to Freedom which can be done as a group in the class or separately with an encourager.	Two video lessons each meeting for four weeks, then one hour per meeting for four weeks.

Although your meetings can be open to all who will commit the time, you should make it clear that attending the training does not automatically qualify a person to participate in your freedom ministry. Each church needs to insure that only mature people are available for this vital discipleship counseling ministry.

A Modified Schedule Summary for Basic Training

Another possible schedule would be showing one whole video series on a weekend (two lessons on Friday night and six on Saturday). If several leaders were available, it would require only one facilitator giving one weekend each month, allowing you to cover all the material in four weekends. There is less time for discussion of the videos in this schedule, but you could meet Sunday morning or one night a week to discuss the videos, the books and the study guides.

Weekend One	Weekend Two	Weekend Three
"Resolving Personal Conflicts"	"Resolving Spiritual Conflicts"	"Spiritual Conflicts and Counseling"
Friday Night: Video lessons 1 and 2	Friday Night: Video lessons 1 and 2	Friday Night: Video lessons 1 and 2
Saturday: Video lessons 3 through 8	Saturday: Video lessons 3 through 7 and *The Steps to Freedom in Christ* booklet	Saturday: Video lessons 3 through 8

The fourth weekend could be completed on Saturday only, using the shorter video series "Helping Others Find Freedom in Christ" Video Training Program. We realize there's a lot of material to cover, but you'll experience great rewards as people and families are established free in Christ. All of the "Resolving Personal and Spiritual Conflicts" material is covered at our church conferences. God bless you as you begin your ministry.

Note: For a more detailed listing of these resources, turn to the bibliography at the end of this book.

To purchase materials, ask questions or schedule a Freedom in Christ conference contact:

Freedom in Christ Ministries
491 East Lambert Road
La Habra, California 90631
(562) 691-9128
Fax: (562) 691-4035
or visit us at www.freedominchrist.com

It is my deep conviction that the finished work of Jesus Christ and the presence of God in our lives are the only means by which we can resolve our personal and spiritual conflicts. Christ in us is our only hope (see Colossians 1:27), and He alone can meet our deepest needs of life: acceptance, identity, security and significance. The discipleship counseling process upon which these steps are based should not be understood as just another counseling technique that we learn. It is an encounter with God. He is the Wonderful Counselor. He is the One who grants repentance that leads to a knowledge of the truth which sets us free (see 2 Timothy 2:25,26).

The Steps to Freedom in Christ do not set you free. *Who* sets you free is Christ, and *what* sets you free is your response to Him in repentance and faith. These Steps are just a tool to help you submit to God and resist the devil (see James 4:7). Then you can start living a fruitful life by abiding in Christ and becoming the person He created you to be. Many Christians will be able to work through these steps on their own and discover the wonderful freedom that Christ purchased for them on the cross. Then they will experience the peace of God which surpasses all comprehension, and it shall guard their hearts and their minds (see Philippians 4:7, *NASB*).

BEFORE YOU BEGIN

The chances of that happening and the possibility of maintaining that freedom will be greatly enhanced if you read *Victory over the Darkness* and *The Bondage Breaker* first. Many Christians in the western world need to understand the reality of the spiritual world and our relationship to it. Some can't read these books or even the Bible with comprehension because of the battle that is going on for their minds. They will need the assistance of others who have been trained. The theology and practical process of discipleship counseling is given in my book, *Helping Others Find Freedom in Christ,* and the accompanying *Training Manual and Study Guide* and Video Training Program. The book attempts to biblically integrate the reality of the spiritual and the natural world so we can have a whole answer for a whole person. In doing so, we cannot polarize into psychotherapeutic ministries that ignore the reality of the spiritual world or attempt some kind of deliverance ministry that ignores developmental issues and human responsibility.

YOU MAY NEED HELP

Ideally, it would be best if everyone had a trusted friend, pastor or counselor who would help them go through this process because it is just applying the wisdom of James 5:16: "Therefore confess your sins to each other and pray for each other so that you may be healed. The prayer of a righteous man is powerful and effective." Another person can prayerfully support you by providing objective counsel. I have had the privilege of helping many Christian leaders who could not process this on their own. Many Christian groups all over the world are using this approach in many languages with incredible results because the Lord desires for all to come to repentance (see 2 Peter 3:9), and to know the truth that sets us free in Christ (see John 8:32).

APPROPRIATING AND MAINTAINING FREEDOM

Christ has set us free through His victory over sin and death on the cross. However, appropriating our freedom in Christ through repentance and faith and maintaining our life of freedom in Christ are two different issues. It was for freedom that Christ set us free, but we have been warned not to return to a yoke of slavery which is legalism in this context (see Galatians 5:1) or to turn our freedom into an opportunity for the flesh (see Galatians 5:13). Establishing people free in Christ makes it possible for them to walk by faith according to what God says is true, to live by the power of the Holy Spirit and to not carry out the desires of the flesh (see Galatians 5:16). The true Christian life avoids both legalism and license.

If you are not experiencing freedom, it may be because you have not stood firm in the faith or actively taken your place in Christ. It is every Christian's responsibility to do whatever is necessary to maintain a right relationship with God and mankind. Your eternal destiny is not at stake. God will never leave you nor forsake you (see Hebrews 13:5), but your daily victory is at stake if you fail to claim and maintain your position in Christ.

YOUR POSITION IN CHRIST

You are not a helpless victim caught between two nearly equal but opposite heavenly superpowers. Satan is a deceiver. Only God is omnipotent, omnipresent and omniscient. Sometimes the reality of sin and the presence of evil may seem more real than the presence of God, but that's part of Satan's deception. Satan is a defeated foe and we are in Christ. A true knowledge of God and knowing our identity and position in Christ are the greatest determinants of our mental health. A false concept of God, a distorted understanding of who we are as children of God, and the misplaced deification of Satan are the greatest contributors to mental illness.

Many of our illnesses are psychosomatic. When these issues are resolved in Christ, our physical bodies will function better and we will experience greater health. Other problems are clearly physical and we need the services of the medical profession. Please consult your physician for medical advice and the prescribing of medication. We are both spiritual and physical beings who need the services of both the church and the medical profession.

WINNING THE BATTLE FOR YOUR MIND

The battle is for our minds, which is the control center of all that we think and do. The opposing thoughts you may experience as you go through these steps can control you only if you believe them. If you are working through these steps alone, don't be deceived by any lying, intimidating thoughts in your mind. If a trusted pastor or counselor is helping you find your freedom in Christ, he or she must have your cooperation. You must share any thoughts you are having in opposition to what you are attempting to do. As soon as you expose the lie, the power of Satan is broken. The only way that you can lose control in this process is if you pay attention to a deceiving spirit and believe a lie.

YOU MUST CHOOSE

The following procedure is a means of resolving personal and spiritual conflicts which have kept you from experiencing the freedom and victory Christ purchased for you on the cross. Your freedom will be the result of what *you* choose to believe, confess, forgive, renounce and forsake. No one can do that for you. The battle for your mind can only be won as you personally choose truth. As you go through this process, understand that Satan is under no obligation to obey your thoughts. Only God has complete knowledge of your mind because He is omniscient—all-knowing. So we can submit to God inwardly, but we need to resist the devil by reading aloud each prayer and by verbally renouncing, forgiving, confessing, etc.

This process of reestablishing our freedom in Christ is nothing more than a fierce moral inventory and a rock-solid commitment to truth. It is the first step in the continuing process of discipleship. There is no such thing as instant maturity. It will take you the rest of your life to renew your mind and conform to the image of God. If your problems stem from a source other than those covered in these steps, you may need to seek professional help.

May the Lord grace you with His presence as you seek His face and help others experience the joy of their salvation.

Neil T. Anderson

PRAYER

Dear Heavenly Father,

We acknowledge Your presence in this room and in our lives. You are the only omniscient (all-knowing), omnipotent (all-powerful), and omnipresent (always-present) God. We are dependent upon You, for apart from You we can do nothing. We stand in the truth that all authority in heaven and on earth has been given to the resurrected Christ, and because we are in Christ, we share that authority in order to make disciples and set captives free. We ask You to fill us with Your Holy Spirit and lead us into all truth. We pray for Your complete protection and ask for Your guidance. In Jesus' name, amen.

DECLARATION

In the name and authority of the Lord Jesus Christ, we command Satan and all evil spirits to release _____(name)_____ in order that _____(name)_____ can be free to know and choose to do the will of God. As children of God seated with Christ in the heavenlies, we agree that every enemy of the Lord Jesus Christ be bound to silence. We say to Satan and all your evil workers that you cannot inflict any pain or in any way prevent God's will from being accomplished in _____(name's)_____ life.

Preparation

Before going through the Steps to Freedom, review the events of your life to discern specific areas that might need to be addressed. For a more detailed review of your life, complete the Confidential Personal Inventory in the appendix.

Family History

❑ Religious history of parents and grandparents

❑ Home life from childhood through high school

❑ History of physical or emotional illness in the family

❑ Adoption, foster care, guardians

Personal History

❑ Eating habits (bulimia, bingeing and purging, anorexia, compulsive eating)

❑ Addictions (drugs, alcohol)

❑ Prescription medications (what for?)

❑ Sleeping patterns and nightmares

❑ Rape or any other sexual, physical, emotional abuse

❑ Thought life (obsessive, blasphemous, condemning, distracting thoughts, poor concentration, fantasy)

❑ Mental interference during church, prayer or Bible study

❑ Emotional life (anger, anxiety, depression, bitterness, fears)

❑ Spiritual journey (salvation: when, how, and assurance)

Now you are ready to begin. The following are seven specific steps to process in order to experience freedom from your past. You will address the areas where Satan most commonly takes advantage of us and where strongholds have been built.

If your problems stem from a source other than those covered in these steps, you have nothing to lose by going through them. If you are sincere, the only thing that can happen is that you will get very right with God!

STEP 1

Counterfeit vs. Real

The first Step to Freedom in Christ is to renounce your previous or current involvement with satanically-inspired occult practices and false religions. You need to renounce any activity or group that denies Jesus Christ, offers guidance through any source other than the absolute authority of the written Word of God or requires secret initiations, ceremonies or covenants.

In order to help you assess your spiritual experiences, begin this step by asking God to reveal false guidance and counterfeit religious experiences.

> **Dear Heavenly Father,**
> I ask You to guard my heart and my mind and reveal to me any and all involvement I have had either knowingly or unknowingly with cultic or occult practices, false religions or false teachers. In Jesus' name, I pray. Amen.

Using the Non-Christian Spiritual Experience Inventory on the following page, carefully check anything in which you were involved. This list is not exhaustive, but it will guide you in identifying non-Christian experiences. Add any additional involvement you have had. Even if you innocently participated in something or observed it, you should write it on your list to renounce, just in case you unknowingly gave Satan a foothold.

NON-CHRISTIAN SPIRITUAL EXPERIENCE INVENTORY

Please check all those that apply

- ❑ Astral-projection
- ❑ Ouija board
- ❑ Table or body lifting
- ❑ Dungeons and Dragons
- ❑ Speaking in trance
- ❑ Automatic writing
- ❑ Magic Eight Ball
- ❑ Telepathy
- ❑ Using spells or curses
- ❑ Seance
- ❑ Materialization
- ❑ Clairvoyance
- ❑ Spirit guides
- ❑ Fortune-telling
- ❑ Tarot cards
- ❑ Palm reading
- ❑ Astrology/horoscopes
- ❑ Rod/pendulum (dowsing)
- ❑ Self-hypnosis
- ❑ Mental manipulations or attempts to swap minds
- ❑ Black and white magic
- ❑ New Age medicine
- ❑ Blood pacts or self-mutilation
- ❑ Fetishism (objects of worship, crystals, good-luck charms)
- ❑ Incubi and succubi (sexual spirits)
- ❑ Other _____

- ❑ Christian Science
- ❑ Unity
- ❑ The Way International
- ❑ Unification Church
- ❑ Mormonism
- ❑ Church of the Living Word
- ❑ Jehovah's Witnesses
- ❑ Children of God (Love)
- ❑ Swedenborgianism
- ❑ Masons
- ❑ New Age
- ❑ The Forum (EST)
- ❑ Spirit worship
- ❑ Other _____

- ❑ Buddhism
- ❑ Hare Krishna
- ❑ Bahaism
- ❑ Rosicrucianism
- ❑ Science of the Mind
- ❑ Science of Creative Intelligence
- ❑ Transcendental Meditation (TM)
- ❑ Hinduism
- ❑ Yoga
- ❑ Echkankar
- ❑ Roy Masters
- ❑ Silva Mind Control
- ❑ Father Divine
- ❑ Theosophical Society
- ❑ Islam
- ❑ Black Muslim
- ❑ Religion of martial arts
- ❑ Other _____

1. Have you ever been hypnotized, attended a New Age or parapsychology seminar, consulted a medium, spiritist or channeler? Explain.

2. Do you or have you ever had an imaginary friend or spirit guide offering you guidance or companionship? Explain.

3. Have you ever heard voices in your mind or had repeating and nagging thoughts condemning you or that were foreign to what you believe or feel, as if there were a dialogue going on in your head? Explain.

4. What other spiritual experiences have you had that would be considered out of the ordinary?

5. Have you ever made a vow, covenant or pact with any individual or group other than God?

6. Have you been involved in satanic ritual or satanic worship in any form? Explain.

When you are confident that your list is complete, confess and renounce each involvement whether active or passive by praying aloud the following prayer, repeating it separately for each item on your list:

> **Lord,**
> **I confess that I have participated in _____, and I renounce _____.**
> **Thank You that in Christ I am forgiven.**

If there has been any involvement in satanic ritual or heavy occult activity, you need to state aloud the following special renunciations which apply. Read across the page, renouncing the first item in the column of the

Kingdom of Darkness and then affirming the first truth in the column of the Kingdom of Light. Continue down the page in this manner.

All satanic rituals, covenants and assignments must be specifically renounced as the Lord allows you to recall them. Some who have been subjected to satanic ritual abuse may have developed multiple personalities in order to survive. Nevertheless, continue through the Steps to Freedom in order to resolve all that you consciously can. It is important that you resolve the demonic strongholds first. Every personality must resolve his/her issues and agree to come together in Christ. You may need someone who understands spiritual conflict to help you maintain control and not be deceived into false memories. Only Jesus can bind up the brokenhearted, set captives free and make us whole.

Kingdom of Darkness	Kingdom of Light
I renounce ever signing my name over to Satan or having had my name signed over to Satan.	I announce that my name is now written in the Lamb's Book of Life.
I renounce any ceremony where I might have been wed to Satan.	I announce that I am the bride of Christ.
I renounce any and all covenants that I made with Satan.	I announce that I am a partaker of the New Covenant with Christ.
I renounce all satanic assignments for my life, including duties, marriage and children.	I announce and commit myself to know and do only the will of God and accept only His guidance.
I renounce all spirit guides assigned to me.	I announce and accept only the leading of the Holy Spirit.
I renounce ever giving of my blood in the service of Satan.	I trust only in the shed blood of my Lord Jesus Christ.
I renounce ever eating of flesh or drinking of blood for satanic worship.	By faith I take Holy Communion which represents the body and the blood of the Lord Jesus.
I renounce any and all guardians and satanist parents who were assigned to me.	I announce that God is my Father and the Holy Spirit is my Guardian by which I am sealed.
I renounce any baptism in blood or urine whereby I am identified with Satan.	I announce that I have been baptized into Christ Jesus and my identity is now in Christ.
I renounce any and all sacrifices that were made on my behalf by which Satan may claim ownership of me.	I announce that only the sacrifice of Christ has any hold on me. I belong to Him. I have been purchased by the blood of the Lamb.

STEP 2
Deception vs. Truth

Truth is the revelation of God's Word, but we need to acknowledge the truth in the inner self (see Psalm 51:6). When David lived a lie, he suffered greatly. When he finally found freedom by acknowledging the truth, he wrote: "Blessed is the man…in whose spirit is no deceit" (Psalm 32:2). We are to lay aside falsehood and speak the truth in love (see Ephesians 4:15,25). A mentally healthy person is one who is in touch with reality and relatively free of anxiety. Both qualities should characterize the Christian who renounces deception and embraces the truth.

Begin this critical step by expressing aloud the following prayer. Don't let the enemy accuse you with thoughts such as: *This isn't going to work* or *I wish I could believe this, but I can't* or any other lies in opposition to what you are proclaiming. Even if you have difficulty doing so, you need to pray the prayer and read the Doctrinal Affirmation.

> Dear Heavenly Father,
>
> I know that You desire truth in the inner self and that facing this truth is the way of liberation (see John 8:32). I acknowledge that I have been deceived by the father of lies (see John 8:44) and that I have deceived myself (see 1 John 1:8). I pray in the name of the Lord Jesus Christ that You, Heavenly Father, will rebuke all deceiving spirits by virtue of the shed blood and resurrection of the Lord Jesus Christ. By faith I have received You into my life and I am now seated with Christ in the heavenlies (see Ephesians 2:6). I acknowledge that I have the responsibility and authority to resist the devil, and when I do, he will flee from me. I now ask the Holy Spirit to guide me into all truth (see John 16:13). I ask You to "search me, O God, and know my heart; try me and know my anxious thoughts; and see if there be any hurtful way in me, and lead me in the everlasting way" (Psalm 139:23,24, *NASB*). In Jesus' name, I pray. Amen.

You may want to pause at this point to consider some of Satan's deceptive schemes. In addition to false teachers, false prophets and deceiving spirits, you can deceive yourself. Now that you are alive in Christ and forgiven, you never have to live a lie or defend yourself. Christ is your defense. How have you deceived or attempted to defend yourself according to the following? Please check any of the following that apply to you:

Self-Deception
❑ Hearing God's Word but not doing it (see James 1:22; 4:17)
❑ Saying you have no sin (see 1 John 1:8)
❑ Thinking you are something when you aren't (see Galatians 6:3)
❑ Thinking you are wise in your own eyes (see 1 Corinthians 3:18,19)
❑ Thinking you will not reap what you sow (see Galatians 6:7)
❑ Thinking the unrighteous will inherit the kingdom (see 1 Corinthians 6:9)
❑ Thinking you can associate with bad company and not be corrupted (see 1 Corinthians 15:33)

Self-Defense
(Defending ourselves instead of trusting in Christ)
❑ Denial (conscious or subconscious refusal to face the truth)
❑ Fantasy (escaping from the real world)
❑ Emotional insulation (withdrawing to avoid rejection)
❑ Regression (reverting back to a less threatening time)
❑ Displacement (taking out frustrations on others)
❑ Projection (blaming others)
❑ Rationalization (making excuses for poor behavior)

For each of those things that you have checked, pray aloud:

> **Lord, I agree that I have been deceiving myself in the area of** _____. **Thank You for forgiving me. I commit myself to know and follow Your truth. Amen.**

Choosing the truth may be difficult if you have been living a lie (being deceived) for many years. You may need to seek professional help to weed out the defense mechanisms you have depended upon to survive. The Christian needs only one defense—Jesus. Knowing that you are forgiven and accepted as God's child is what sets you free to face reality and declare your dependence on Him.

Faith is the biblical response to the truth and believing the truth is a choice. When someone says, "I want to believe God, but I just can't," they are being deceived. Of course you can believe God. Faith is something you decide to do, not something you feel like doing. Believing the truth doesn't make it true. It's true; therefore, we believe it. The New Age movement is distorting the truth by saying we create reality through what we believe. We can't create reality with our minds; we face reality. It is what or who you believe in that counts. Everybody believes in something, and everybody walks by faith according to what he or she believes. But if what you believe isn't true, then how you live (walk by faith) won't be right.

Historically, the Church has found great value in publicly declaring its beliefs. The Apostles' Creed and the Nicene Creed have been recited for centuries. Read aloud the following affirmation of faith, and do so again as often as necessary to renew your mind. Experiencing difficulty in reading this affirmation may indicate where you are being deceived and under attack. Boldly affirm your commitment to biblical truth.

DOCTRINAL AFFIRMATION

I recognize that there is only one true and living God (see Exodus 20:2,3) who exists as the Father, Son and Holy Spirit and that He is worthy of all honor, praise and glory as the Creator, Sustainer and Beginning and End of all things (see Revelation 4:11; 5:9,10; 22:13; Isaiah 43:1,7,21).

I recognize Jesus Christ as the Messiah, the Word who became flesh and dwelt among us (see John 1:1,14). I believe that He came to destroy the works of Satan (see 1 John 3:8), that He disarmed the rulers and authorities and made a public display of them, having triumphed over them (see Colossians 2:15).

I believe that God has proven His love for me because when I was still a sinner, Christ died for me (see Romans 5:8). I believe that He delivered me from the domain of darkness and transferred me to His kingdom, and in Him I have redemption—the forgiveness of sins (see Colossians 1:13,14).

I believe that I am now a child of God (see 1 John 3:1-3) and that I am seated with Christ in the heavenlies (see Ephesians 2:6). I believe that I was saved by the grace of God through faith, that it was a gift, and not the result of any works on my part (see Ephesians 2:8,9).

I choose to be strong in the Lord and in the strength of His might (see Ephesians 6:10). I put no confidence in the flesh (see Philippians 3:3) for the weapons of warfare are not of the flesh (see 2 Corinthians 10:4). I put on the whole armor of God (see Ephesians 6:10-20), and I resolve to stand firm in my faith and resist the evil one.

I believe that apart from Christ I can do nothing (see John 15:5), so I declare myself dependent on Him. I choose to abide in Christ in order to bear much fruit and glorify the Lord (see John 15:8). I announce to Satan that Jesus is my Lord (see 1 Corinthians 12:3), and I reject any counterfeit gifts or works of Satan in my life.

I believe that the truth will set me free (see John 8:32) and that walking in the light is the only path of fellowship (see 1 John 1:7). Therefore, I stand against Satan's deception by taking every thought captive in obedience to Christ (see 2 Corinthians 10:5). I declare that the Bible is the only authoritative standard (see 2 Timothy 3:15,16). I choose to speak the truth in love (see Ephesians 4:15).

I choose to present my body as an instrument of righteousness, a living and holy sacrifice, and I renew my mind by the living Word of God in order that I may prove that the will of God is good, acceptable and perfect (see Romans 6:13; 12:1,2). I put off the old self with its evil practices and put on the new self (see Colossians 3:9,10), and I declare myself to be a new creature in Christ (see 2 Corinthians 5:17).

I trust my heavenly Father to fill me with His Holy Spirit (see Ephesians 5:18), to lead me into all truth (see John 16:13), and to empower my life that I may live above sin and not carry out the desires of the flesh (see Galatians 5:16). I crucify the flesh (see Galatians 5:24) and choose to walk by the Spirit.

I renounce all selfish goals and choose the ultimate goal of love (see 1 Timothy 1:5). I choose to obey the two greatest commandments: to love the Lord my God with all my heart, soul and mind, and to love my neighbor as myself (see Matthew 22:37-39).

I believe that Jesus has all authority in heaven and on earth (see Matthew 28:18) and that He is the Head over all rule and authority (see Colossians 2:10). I believe that Satan and his demons are subject to me in Christ since I am a member of Christ's Body (see Ephesians 1:19-23). Therefore, I obey the command to submit to God and to resist the devil (see James 4:7), and I command Satan in the name of Christ to leave my presence.

STEP 3

Bitterness vs. Forgiveness

We need to forgive others in order to be free from our pasts and to prevent Satan from taking advantage of us (see 2 Corinthians 2:10,11). We are to be merciful just as our heavenly Father is merciful (see Luke 6:36). We are to forgive as we have been forgiven (see Ephesians 4:31,32). Ask God to bring to mind the names of those people you need to forgive by expressing the following prayer aloud:

Dear Heavenly Father,

I thank You for the riches of Your kindness, forbearance and patience, knowing that Your kindness has led me to repentance (see Romans 2:4). I confess that I have not extended that same patience and kindness toward others who have offended me, but instead I have harbored bitterness and resentment. I pray that during this time of self-examination You would bring to my mind those people whom I need to forgive in order that I may do so (see Matthew 18:35). I ask this in the precious name of Jesus. Amen.

As names come to mind, list them on a separate sheet of paper. At the end of your list, write "myself." Forgiving yourself is accepting God's cleansing and forgiveness. Also, write "thoughts against God." Thoughts raised up against the knowledge of God will usually result in angry feelings toward Him. Technically, we don't forgive God because He cannot commit any sin of commission or omission. But we do need to specifically renounce false expectations and thoughts about God and agree to release any anger we have toward Him.

Before you pray to forgive these people, stop and consider what forgiveness is, what it is not, what decision you will be making and what the consequences will be. In the following explanation, the main points are in bold print:

Forgiveness is not forgetting. People who try to forget find they cannot. God says He will remember our sins no more (see Hebrews 10:17), but God, being omniscient, cannot forget. Remember our sins no more means that God will never use the past against us (see Psalm 103:12). Forgetting may be the result of forgiveness, but it is never the means of forgiveness. When we bring up the past against others, we are saying we haven't forgiven them.

Forgiveness is a choice, a crisis of the will. Since God requires us to forgive, it is something we can do. However, forgiveness is difficult for us because it pulls against our concept of justice. We want revenge for offenses suffered. However, we are told never to take our own revenge (see Romans 12:19). You say, "Why should I let them off the hook?" That is precisely the problem. You are still hooked to them, still bound by your past. **You can let them off your hook, but they are never off God's.** He will deal with them fairly—something we cannot do.

You say, "You don't understand how much this person hurt me!" But don't you see, they are still hurting you! How do you stop the pain? **You don't forgive someone for their sake; you do it for your own sake so you can be free. Your need to forgive isn't an issue between you and the offender; it's between you and God.**

25

Forgiveness is agreeing to live with the consequences of another person's sin. Forgiveness is cost- ly. You pay the price of the evil you forgive. You're going to live with those consequences whether you want to or not; your only choice is whether you will do so in the bitterness of unforgiveness or the freedom of forgiveness. Jesus took the consequences of your sin upon Himself. All true for- giveness is substitutionary because no one really forgives without bearing the consequences of the other person's sin. God the Father "made Him who knew no sin to be sin on our behalf, that we might become the righteousness of God in Him" (2 Corinthians 5:21, *NASB*). Where is the justice? It's the cross that makes forgiveness legally and morally right: "For the death that He died, He died to sin, once for all" (Romans 6:10, *NASB*).

Decide that you will bear the burdens of their offenses by not using that information against them in the future. This doesn't mean that you tolerate sin. You must set up scriptural boundaries to pre- vent future abuse. Some may be required to testify for the sake of justice but not for the purpose of seeking revenge from a bitter heart.

How do you forgive from your heart? You acknowledge the hurt and the hate. If your forgiveness doesn't visit the emotional core of your life, it will be incomplete. Many feel the pain of interperson- al offenses, but they won't or don't know how to acknowledge it. Let God bring the pain to the surface so He can deal with it. This is where the healing takes place.

Don't wait to forgive until you feel like forgiving; you will never get there. Feelings take time to heal after the choice to forgive is made and Satan has lost his place (see Ephesians 4:26,27). Freedom is what will be gained, not a feeling.

As you pray, God may bring to mind offending people and experiences you have totally forgotten. Let Him do it even if it is painful. Remember, you are doing this for your sake. God wants you to be free. Don't rational- ize or explain the offender's behavior. Forgiveness is dealing with your pain and leaving the other person to God. Positive feelings will follow in time; freeing you from the past is the critical issue right now.

Don't say, "Lord, please help me to forgive" because He is already helping you. Don't say, "Lord, I want to forgive," because you are bypassing the hard-core choice to forgive which is your responsibility. Focus on each individual until you are sure you have dealt with all the remembered pain—what they did, how they hurt you, how they made you feel: rejected, unloved, unworthy, dirty, etc.

You are now ready to forgive the people on your list so you can be free in Christ, with those people no longer having any control over you. For each person on your list, pray aloud:

Lord, I forgive _____ (name the person) _____ for _____ (verbally share every hurt and pain the Lord brings to your mind and how it made you feel) _____.

After you have forgiven every person for every painful memory, then finish this step by praying:

Lord, I release all these people to You, and I release my right to seek revenge. I choose not to hold on to my bitterness and anger, and I ask You to heal my damaged emotions. In Jesus' name, I pray. Amen

STEP 4
Rebellion vs. Submission

We live in rebellious times. Many believe it is their right to sit in judgment of those in authority over them. Rebelling against God and His authority gives Satan an opportunity to attack. As our commanding General, the Lord tells us to get into ranks and follow Him; He will not lead us into temptation, but will deliver us from evil (see Matthew 6:13).

We have two biblical responsibilities regarding authority figures: Pray for them and submit to them. The only time God permits us to disobey earthly leaders is when they require us to do something morally wrong before God or attempt to rule outside the realm of their authority. Pray the following prayer:

Dear Heavenly Father,

You have said that rebellion is like the sin of witchcraft and insubordination is like iniquity and idolatry (see 1 Samuel 15:23). I know that in action and attitude I have sinned against You with a rebellious heart. Thank You for forgiving my rebellion, and I pray that by the shed blood of the Lord Jesus Christ all ground gained by evil spirits because of my rebelliousness will be canceled. I pray that You will shed light on all my ways that I may know the full extent of my rebelliousness. I now choose to adopt a submissive spirit and a servant's heart. In the name of Christ Jesus, my Lord, amen.

Being under authority is an act of faith. You are trusting God to work through His established lines of authority. There are times when employers, parents and husbands are violating the laws of civil government which are ordained by God to protect innocent people against abuse. In these cases, you need to appeal to the state for your protection. In many states, the law requires such abuse to be reported.

In difficult cases, such as continuing abuse at home, further counseling help may be needed. And, in some cases, when earthly authorities have abused their position and are requiring disobedience to God or a compromise in your commitment to Him, you need to obey God, not man.

We are all admonished to submit to one another as equals in Christ (see Ephesians 5:21). However, there are specific lines of authority in Scripture for the purpose of accomplishing common goals:

Civil government (see Romans 13:1-7; 1 Timothy 2:1-4; 1 Peter 2:13-17)
Parents (see Ephesians 6:1-3)
Husbands (see 1 Peter 3:1-4) or wives (see Ephesians 5:21; 1 Peter 3:7)
Employers (see 1 Peter 2:18-23)
Church leaders (see Hebrews 13:17)
God (see Daniel 9:5,9)

Examine each area and confess those times you have not been submissive by praying:

Lord, I agree I have been rebellious toward _____. I choose to be submissive and obedient to your Word. In Jesus' name, amen.

STEP 5
Pride vs. Humility

Pride is a killer. Pride says, "I can do it! I can get myself out of this mess without God or anyone else's help." Oh no, we can't! We absolutely need God, and we desperately need each other. Paul wrote: "For it is…we who worship by the Spirit of God, who glory in Christ Jesus, and who put no confidence in the flesh" (Philippians 3:3). Humility is confidence properly placed. We are to be "strong in the Lord and in his mighty power" (Ephesians 6:10). James 4:6-10 and 1 Peter 5:1-10 reveal that spiritual conflict follows pride. Use the following prayer to express your commitment to live humbly before God:

> Dear Heavenly Father,
> You have said that pride goes before destruction and an arrogant spirit before stumbling (see Proverbs 16:18). I confess that I have lived independently and have not denied myself, picked up my cross daily and followed You (see Matthew 16:24). In so doing, I have given ground to the enemy in my life. I have believed that I could be successful and live victoriously by my own strength and resources. I now confess that I have sinned against You by placing my will before Yours and by centering my life around myself instead of You. I now renounce the self-life and by so doing cancel all the ground that has been gained in my members by the enemies of the Lord Jesus Christ. I pray that You will guide me so that I will do nothing from selfishness or empty conceit, but with humility of mind I will regard others as more important than myself (see Philippians 2:3). Enable me through love to serve others and in honor prefer others (see Romans 12:10). I ask this in the name of Christ Jesus, my Lord. Amen.

Having made that commitment, now allow God to show you any specific areas of your life where you have been prideful, such as:

- ❑ Having a stronger desire to do my will than God's will;
- ❑ Being more dependent upon my strengths and resources than God's;
- ❑ Too often believing that my ideas and opinions are better than others';
- ❑ Being more concerned about controlling others than developing self-control;
- ❑ Sometimes considering myself more important than others';
- ❑ Having a tendency to think that I have no needs;
- ❑ Finding it difficult to admit that I was wrong;
- ❑ Having a tendency to be more of a people-pleaser than a God-pleaser;
- ❑ Being overly concerned about getting the credit I deserve;
- ❑ Being driven to obtain the recognition that comes from degrees, titles and positions;
- ❑ Often thinking I am more humble than others;
- ❑ These other ways: _____

For each of these that has been true in your life, pray aloud:

> Lord, I agree I have been prideful by _____. I choose to humble myself and place all my confidence in You. Amen.

STEP 6

Bondage vs. Freedom

The next Step to freedom deals with habitual sin. People who have been caught in the trap of sin-confess-sin-confess may need to follow the instructions of James 5:16, "Confess your sins to each other and pray for each other so that you may be healed. The prayer of a righteous man is powerful and effective." Seek out a righteous person who will hold you up in prayer and to whom you can be accountable. Others may only need the assurance of 1 John 1:9: "If we confess our sins, He is faithful and righteous to forgive us our sins and to cleanse us from all unrighteousness" (*NASB*). Confession is not saying "I'm sorry"; it's saying "I did it." Whether you need the help of others or just the accountability to God, pray the following prayer:

Dear Heavenly Father,
   You have told us to put on the Lord Jesus Christ and make no provision for the flesh in regard to its lust (see Romans 13:14, *NASB*). I acknowledge that I have given in to fleshly lusts which wage war against my soul (see 1 Peter 2:11). I thank You that in Christ my sins are forgiven, but I have transgressed Your holy law and given the enemy an opportunity to wage war in my physical body (see Romans 6:12,13; Ephesians 4:27; James 4:1; 1 Peter 5:8). I come before Your presence to acknowledge these sins and to seek Your cleansing (see 1 John 1:9), that I may be freed from the bondage of sin. I now ask You to reveal to my mind the ways that I have transgressed Your moral law and grieved the Holy Spirit. In Jesus' precious name, I pray. Amen.

The deeds of the flesh are numerous. Many of the following issues are from Galatians 5:19-21. Check those that apply to you and any others you have struggled with that the Lord has brought to your mind. Then confess each one with the concluding prayer.

Note: Sexual sins, eating disorders, substance abuse, abortion, suicidal tendencies, perfectionism and fear will be dealt with later in this Step, beginning on page 30.

❑ Stealing   ❑ Complaining   ❑ Procrastinating
❑ Lying   ❑ Criticizing   ❑ Swearing
❑ Fighting   ❑ Lusting   ❑ Greediness
❑ Jealousy   ❑ Cheating   ❑ Laziness
❑ Envying   ❑ Gossiping   ❑ Divisiveness
❑ Outbursts of anger   ❑ Controlling   ❑ Gambling
   ❑ Other_____

Dear Heavenly Father,
   I thank You that my sins are forgiven in Christ, but I have walked by the flesh and therefore sinned by _____. Thank You for cleansing me of all unrighteousness. I ask that You would enable me to walk by the Spirit and not carry out the desires of the flesh. In Jesus' name, I pray. Amen.

It is our responsibility not to allow sin to reign in our mortal bodies by not using our bodies as instruments of unrighteousness (see Romans 6:12,13). If you are struggling or have struggled with sexual sins (pornography, masturbation, sexual promiscuity, etc.) or are experiencing sexual difficulty in your marriage, pray as follows:

> Lord,
> I ask You to reveal to my mind every sexual use of my body as an instrument of unrighteousness. In Jesus' precious name, I pray. Amen.

As the Lord brings to your mind every sexual misuse of your body, whether it was done to you—rape, incest or other sexual abuse—or willingly by you, renounce every occasion:

> Lord,
> I renounce _____ (name the specific misuse of your body) _____ with _____ (name the person) _____ and ask You to break that bond.

Now commit your body to the Lord by praying:

> Lord,
> I renounce all these uses of my body as an instrument of unrighteousness and by so doing ask You to break all bondages Satan has brought into my life through that involvement. I confess my participation. I now present my body to You as a living sacrifice, holy and acceptable unto You, and I reserve the sexual use of my body only for marriage. I renounce the lie of Satan that my body is not clean, that it is dirty or in any way unacceptable as a result of my past sexual experiences. Lord, I thank You that You have totally cleansed and forgiven me, that You love and accept me unconditionally. Therefore, I can accept myself. And I choose to do so, to accept myself and my body as cleansed. In Jesus' name, amen.

SPECIAL PRAYERS FOR SPECIFIC PROBLEMS

Homosexuality

> Lord,
> I renounce the lie that You have created me or anyone else to be homosexual, and I affirm that You clearly forbid homosexual behavior. I accept myself as a child of God and declare that You created me a man (woman). I renounce any bondages of Satan that have perverted my relationships with others. I announce that I am free to relate to the opposite sex in the way that You intended. In Jesus' name, amen.

Abortion

> Lord,
> I confess that I did not assume stewardship of the life You entrusted to me. I choose to accept your forgiveness, and I now commit that child to You for Your care in eternity. In Jesus' name, amen.

Suicidal Tendencies

Lord,

I renounce suicidal thoughts and any attempts I have made to take my own life or in any way injure myself. I renounce the lie that life is hopeless and that I can find peace and freedom by taking my own life. Satan is a thief and he comes to steal, kill and destroy. I choose to be a good steward of the physical life that You have entrusted to me. In Jesus' name, I pray. Amen.

Eating Disorders or Self-Mutilation

Lord,

I renounce the lie that my value as a person is dependent upon my physical beauty, my weight or size. I renounce cutting myself, vomiting, using laxatives or starving myself as a means of cleansing myself of evil or altering my appearance. I announce that only the blood of the Lord Jesus Christ cleanses me from sin. I accept the reality that there may be sin present in me due to the lies I have believed and the wrongful use of my body, but I renounce the lie that I am evil or that any part of my body is evil. My body is the temple of the Holy Spirit and I belong to You, Lord. I receive Your love and acceptance of me. In Jesus' name, amen.

Substance Abuse

Lord,

I confess that I have misused substances (alcohol, tobacco, food, prescription or street drugs) for the purpose of pleasure, to escape reality or to cope with difficult situations—resulting in the abuse of my body, the harmful programming of my mind and the quenching of the Holy Spirit. I ask Your forgiveness. I renounce any satanic connection or influence in my life through my mis-use of chemicals or food. I cast my anxiety onto Christ Who loves me, and I commit myself to no longer yield to substance abuse, but to the Holy Spirit. I ask You, Heavenly Father, to fill me with Your Holy Spirit. In Jesus' name, amen.

Drivenness and Perfectionism

Lord,

I renounce the lie that my self-worth is dependent upon my ability to perform. I announce the truth that my identity and sense of worth are found in who I am as Your child. I renounce seeking the approval and acceptance of other people, and I choose to believe that I am already approved and accepted in Christ because of His death and resurrection for me. I choose to believe the truth that I have been saved, not by deeds done in righteousness, but according to Your mercy. I choose to believe that I am no longer under the curse of the law because Christ became a curse for me. I receive the free gift of life in Christ and choose to abide in Him. I renounce striving for perfection by living under the law. By Your grace, Heavenly Father, I choose from this day forward to walk by faith according to what You have said is true by the power of Your Holy Spirit. In Jesus' name, amen.

Plaguing Fears

Dear Heavenly Father,

I acknowledge You as the only legitimate fear object in my life. You are the only omnipresent (always-present) and omniscient (all-knowing) God and the only means by which all other fears can be expelled. You are my sanctuary. You have not given me a spirit of timidity, but of power and love and discipline. I confess that I have allowed the fear of man and the fear of death to exercise control over my life instead of trusting in You. I now renounce all other fear objects and worship You only. I pray that You would fill me with Your Holy Spirit that I may live my life and speak your Word with boldness. In Jesus' name, I pray. Amen.

After you have confessed all known sin, pray:

Dear Heavenly Father,

I now confess these sins to You and claim my forgiveness and cleansing through the blood of the Lord Jesus Christ. I cancel all ground that evil spirits have gained through my willful involvement in sin. I ask this in the wonderful name of my Lord and Savior, Jesus Christ. Amen.

STEP 7

Acquiescence vs. Renunciation

Acquiescence is passively giving in or agreeing without consent. The last step to freedom is to renounce the sins of your ancestors and any curses which may have been placed on you. In giving the Ten Commandments, God said: "You shall not make for yourself an idol, or any likeness of what is in heaven above or on the earth beneath or in the water under the earth. You shall not worship them or serve them; for I, the LORD your God, am a jealous God, visiting the iniquity of the fathers on the children, on the third and the fourth generations of those who hate Me" (Exodus 20:4,5, *NASB*).

Familiar spirits can be passed on from one generation to the next if not renounced and if your new spiritual heritage in Christ is not proclaimed. You are not guilty for the sin of any ancestor, but because of their sin, Satan may have gained access to your family. This is not to deny that many problems are transmitted genetically or acquired from an immoral atmosphere. All three conditions can predispose an individual to a particular sin. In addition, deceived people may try to curse you, or satanic groups may try to target you. You have all the authority and protection you need in Christ to stand against such curses and assignments.

Ask the Lord to reveal to your mind the sins and iniquities of your ancestors by praying the following prayer:

Dear Heavenly Father,

I thank You that I am a new creation in Christ. I desire to obey Your command to honor my mother and my father, but I also acknowledge that my physical heritage has not been perfect. I ask you to reveal to my mind the sins and iniquities of my ancestors in order to confess, renounce and forsake them. In Jesus' name, I pray. Amen.

Now claim your position and protection in Christ by making the following declaration verbally, and then by humbling yourself before God in prayer.

DECLARATION

I here and now reject and disown all the sins and iniquities of my ancestors, including _____ (name them) _____. As one who has been delivered from the power of darkness and translated into the kingdom of God's dear Son, I cancel out all demonic working that has been passed on to me from my ancestors. As one who has been crucified and raised with Jesus Christ and who sits with Him in heavenly places, I renounce all satanic assignments that are directed toward me and my ministry, and I cancel every curse that Satan and his workers have put on me. I announce to Satan and all his forces that Christ became a curse for me (see Galatians 3:13) when He died for my sins on the cross. I reject any and every way in which Satan may claim ownership of me. I belong to the Lord Jesus Christ who purchased me with His own blood. I reject all other blood sacrifices whereby Satan may claim ownership of me. I declare myself to be eternally and completely signed over and committed to the Lord Jesus Christ. By the authority I have in Jesus Christ, I now command every spiritual enemy of the Lord Jesus Christ to leave my presence. I commit myself to my heavenly Father to do His will from this day forward.

PRAYER

Dear Heavenly Father,

I come to You as Your child purchased by the blood of the Lord Jesus Christ. You are the Lord of the universe and the Lord of my life. I submit my body to You as an instrument of righteousness, a living sacrifice, that I may glorify You in my body. I now ask You to fill me with Your Holy Spirit. I commit myself to the renewing of my mind in order to prove that Your will is good, perfect and acceptable for me. All this I do in the name and authority of the Lord Jesus Christ. Amen.

Once you have secured your freedom by going through these seven steps, you may find demonic influences attempting reentry, days or even months later. One person shared that she heard a spirit say to her mind, "I'm back," two days after she had been set free. "No, you're not!" she proclaimed aloud. The attack ceased immediately. One victory does not constitute winning the war. Freedom must be maintained. After completing these steps, one jubilant lady asked, "Will I always be like this?" I told her that she would stay free as long as she remained in right relationship with God. "Even if you slip and fall," I encouraged, "you know how to get right with God again."

One victim of incredible atrocities shared this illustration: "It's like being forced to play a game with an ugly stranger in my own home. I kept losing and wanted to quit, but the ugly stranger wouldn't let me. Finally I called the police (a higher authority), and they came and escorted the stranger out. He knocked on the door trying to regain entry, but this time I recognized his voice and didn't let him in."

What a beautiful illustration of gaining freedom in Christ. We call upon Jesus, the ultimate authority, and He escorts the enemy out of our lives. Know the truth, stand firm and resist the evil one. Seek out good Christian fellowship, and commit yourself to regular times of Bible study and prayer. God loves you and will never leave or forsake you.

Aftercare

Freedom must be maintained. You have won a very important battle in an ongoing war. Freedom is yours as long as you keep choosing truth and standing firm in the strength of the Lord. If new memories should surface or if you become aware of lies that you have believed or other non-Christian experiences you have had, renounce them and choose the truth. Some have found it helpful to go through the steps again. As you do, read the instructions carefully.

For your encouragement and further study, read *Victory over the Darkness* (or the youth version *Stomping Out the Darkness*), *The Bondage Breaker* (adult or youth version) and *Released from Bondage*. If you are a parent, read *Spiritual Protection for Your Children. Walking in the Light* was written to help people understand God's guidance and discern counterfeit guidance. Also, to maintain your freedom, we suggest the following:

1. Seek legitimate Christian fellowship where you can walk in the light and speak the truth in love.

2. Study your Bible daily. Memorize key verses.

3. Take every thought captive to the obedience of Christ. Assume responsibility for your thought life, reject the lie, choose the truth and stand firm in your position in Christ.

4. Don't drift away! It is very easy to get lazy in your thoughts and revert back to old habits or patterns of thinking. Share your struggles openly with a trusted friend. You need at least one friend who will stand with you.

5. Don't expect another person to fight your battle for you. Others can help, but they can't think, pray, read the Bible or choose the truth for you.

6. Continue to seek your identity and sense of worth in Christ. Read *Living Free in Christ* and the devotional, *Daily in Christ*. Renew your mind with the truth that your acceptance, security and significance is in Christ by saturating your mind with the following truths. Read the entire list of who you are "In Christ" (p. 38) and the Doctrinal Affirmation (in Step 2) aloud morning and evening over the next several weeks (and look up the verses referenced).

7. Commit yourself to daily prayer. You can pray these suggested prayers often and with confidence:

DAILY PRAYER

Dear Heavenly Father,

I honor You as my sovereign Lord. I acknowledge that You are always present with me. You are the only all-powerful and wise God. You are kind and loving in all Your ways. I love You and thank You that I am united with Christ and spiritually alive in Him. I choose not to love the world, and I crucify the flesh and all its passions.

I thank You for the life that I now have in Christ, and I ask You to fill me with Your Holy Spirit, that I may live my life free from sin. I declare my dependence upon You, and I take my stand against Satan and all his lying ways. I choose to believe the truth and I refuse to be discouraged. You are the God of all hope, and I am confident that You will meet my needs as I seek to live according to Your Word. I express with confidence that I can live a responsible life through Christ who strengthens me.

I now take my stand against Satan and command him and all his evil spirits to depart from me. I put on the whole armor of God. I submit my body as a living sacrifice and renew my mind by the living Word of God in order that I may prove that the will of God is good, acceptable and perfect. I pray these things in the precious name of my Lord and Savior, Jesus Christ. Amen.

BEDTIME PRAYER

Thank You, Lord, that You have brought me into Your family and have blessed me with every spiritual blessing in the heavenly realms in Christ. Thank You for providing this time of renewal through sleep. I accept it as part of Your perfect plan for Your children, and I trust You to guard my mind and my body during my sleep. As I have meditated on You and Your truth during this day, I choose to let these thoughts continue in my mind while I am asleep. I commit myself to You for Your protection from every attempt of Satan or his emissaries to attack me during sleep. I commit myself to You as my Rock, my Fortress and my Resting Place. I pray in the strong name of the Lord Jesus Christ. Amen.

CLEANSING HOME/APARTMENT
After removing all articles of false worship from home/apartment, pray aloud in every room if necessary:

Heavenly Father,

We/I acknowledge that You are Lord of heaven and earth. In Your sovereign power and love, You have given us/me all things richly to enjoy. Thank You for this place to live. We/I claim this home for our/my family as a place of spiritual safety and protection from all the attacks of the enemy. As children/a child of God seated with Christ in the heavenly realm, we/I command every evil spirit claiming ground in the structures and furnishings of this place, based on the activities of previous occupants, to leave and never return. We/I renounce all curses and spells utilized against this place. We/I ask You, Heavenly Father, to post guardian angels around this home (apartment, condo, room, etc.) to guard it from attempts of the enemy to enter and disturb Your purposes for us/me. We/I thank You, Lord, for doing this, and pray in the name of the Lord Jesus Christ. Amen.

LIVING IN A NON-CHRISTIAN ENVIRONMENT
After removing all articles of false worship from your room, pray aloud in the space allotted to you:

Thank You, Heavenly Father, for my place to live and be renewed by sleep. I ask You to set aside my room (portion of my room) as a place of spiritual safety for me. I renounce any allegiance given to false gods or spirits by other occupants, and I renounce any claim to this room (space) by Satan based on activities of past occupants or me. On the basis of my position as a child of God and a joint-heir with Christ who has all authority in heaven and on earth, I command all evil spirits to leave this place and never to return. I ask You, Heavenly Father, to appoint guardian angels to protect me while I live here. I pray this in the name of the Lord Jesus Christ. Amen.

Additional resources to be used with the Steps for adults:
See the bibliography for complete information on each resource.
Books:
Victory over the Darkness
Living Free in Christ
Daily in Christ
Breaking Through to Spiritual Maturity
The Bondage Breaker and *Study Guide*
Spiritual Warfare
Walking in the Light
Helping Others Find Freedom in Christ with *Training Manual and Study Guide*
Released from Bondage
Freedom from Addiction and *Workbook*

Audio/Visual Series:
"Free in Christ"
"Resolving Personal Conflicts"
"Resolving Spiritual Conflicts"
"Helping Others Find Freedom in Christ Video Training Program"
"Spiritual Conflicts and Counseling"
"Freedom from Addiction Video Study"

In Christ

I Am Accepted

John 1:12	I am God's child.
John 15:15	I am Christ's friend.
Romans 5:1	I have been justified.
1 Corinthians 6:17	I am united with the Lord, and I am one spirit with Him.
1 Corinthians 6:20	I have been bought with a price. I belong to God.
1 Corinthians 12:27	I am a member of Christ's Body.
Ephesians 1:1	I am a saint.
Ephesians 1:5	I have been adopted as God's child.
Ephesians 2:18	I have direct access to God through the Holy Spirit.
Colossians 1:14	I have been redeemed and forgiven of all my sins.
Colossians 2:10	I am complete in Christ.

I Am Secure

Romans 8:1,2	I am free from condemnation.
Romans 8:28	I am assured that all things work together for good.
Romans 8:31-34	I am free from any condemning charges against me.
Romans 8:35-39	I cannot be separated from the love of God.
2 Corinthians 1:21,22	I have been established, anointed and sealed by God.
Colossians 3:3	I am hidden with Christ in God.
Philippians 1:6	I am confident that the good work God has begun in me will be perfected.
Philippians 3:20	I am a citizen of heaven.
2 Timothy 1:7	I have not been given a spirit of fear, but of power, love and a sound mind.
Hebrews 4:16	I can find grace and mercy to help in time of need.
1 John 5:18	I am born of God and the evil one cannot touch me.

I Am Significant

Matthew 5:13,14	I am the salt and light of the earth.
John 15:1,5	I am a branch of the true vine, a channel of His life.
John 15:16	I have been chosen and appointed to bear fruit.
Acts 1:8	I am a personal witness of Christ.
1 Corinthians 3:16	I am God's temple.
2 Corinthians 5:17-21	I am a minister of reconciliation for God.
2 Corinthians 6:1	I am God's coworker (see 1 Corinthians 3:9).
Ephesians 2:6	I am seated with Christ in the heavenly realm.
Ephesians 2:10	I am God's workmanship.
Ephesians 3:12	I may approach God with freedom and confidence.
Philippians 4:13	I can do all things through Christ who strengthens me.

Galatians 5:1 says, "It is for freedom that Christ has set us free. Stand firm, then, and do not let yourselves be burdened again by a yoke of slavery." If you have received Christ as your Savior, He has already set you free through His victory over sin and death on the cross. The question is: Are you living victoriously in Christ's freedom or are you still living in slavery?

How can you tell if you are living free in Christ? Freedom in Christ is having the desire and power to know, love, worship and obey God. It is the joyful liberty of knowing God's truth and walking according to God's truth in the power of the Holy Spirit. It is not a *perfect* life, for that is impossible this side of heaven. But it is a growing, *abundant life* in Christ (see John 10:10)!

If you are not experiencing that kind of freedom, it may be because you have not stood firm in the faith or lived according to who you are *in Christ*. Somehow you have allowed a yoke of slavery to put you back into bondage.

It is your responsibility, however, to do whatever is needed to walk in your freedom in Christ. If you are a Christian already, your eternal life is not at stake; you are safe and secure in Christ. But your daily victory is at stake if you choose not to walk according to the truth.

No matter how tough things might be for you spiritually right now, we've got great news for you! You are not a helpless victim caught in a tug-of-war match between two nearly equal but opposite heavenly superpowers—God and Satan. Only God is all-powerful, always present and all-knowing. Satan was defeated by Christ the Victor at the cross, so don't believe the lie that your situation is hopeless or that you are helpless against the devil's attacks.

Satan knows you have authority over him in Christ, but he doesn't want you to know it. He is a liar and the only way he can have power over you is if you believe his lies.

The battle is for your mind. During this session you may experience nagging thoughts such as, *This isn't going to work* or *God doesn't love me*, etc. Don't believe the devil's lies. If you believe Satan's deceptions, you will really struggle with making it through the Steps to Freedom in Christ.

If you are working through the Steps by yourself, don't pay any attention to accusing or threatening thoughts. If you are working through this with a trusted friend, pastor or counselor (which we heartily encourage), then tell him/her any thoughts you are having that are in opposition to what you are trying to do.

Remember, the only power Satan has over you is the power of the lie. Expose the lie by getting it out in the open; then choose the truth and the power of that lie is broken.

In that way you will be able to maintain control during this session.

You must cooperate with the person who is trying to help you by sharing what is going on inside your mind. Also, if you experience any physical discomfort such as headache, nausea, tightness in the throat, etc., don't be alarmed. Just tell the person you are with so that he/she can pray for you. Don't let the devil set the agenda during this time; let the Holy Spirit call the shots.

As believers in Christ, we can pray with authority to stop any interference by Satan. Here is a prayer and declaration to get you going. Read these and all the prayers and declarations aloud.

OPENING PRAYER

Dear Heavenly Father,

We know that You are right here in this room with us and that You are present in our lives right now. You are the only all-knowing, all-powerful, and ever-present God. We are completely dependent upon You because without Jesus Christ we can do nothing. We choose to stand in the truth of Your Word and we refuse to believe the devil's lies. We thank You that the risen Lord Jesus has all authority in heaven and on earth. Father, thank You that because we are in Christ we share His authority in order to make disciples and set captives free. We ask You to protect our minds and bodies during this time. Please fill us with the Holy Spirit so that He can guide us into all truth. We choose to submit to His guidance alone during this time. Please reveal to our minds everything that You want us to deal with today. We ask for and trust in Your wisdom. We pray all this in faith, in the name of Jesus. Amen.

DECLARATION

In the name and authority of the Lord Jesus Christ we command Satan and all evil spirits to release their hold on _____(name)_____ in order that _____(name)_____ can be free to know and choose to do the will of God. As children of God, raised up and seated with Christ in the heavenly places, we agree that every enemy of the Lord Jesus Christ be bound. We say to Satan and all his evil workers that you cannot inflict any pain or in any way prevent God's will from being done today in _____(name's)_____ life.

Before going through the Steps to Freedom, review the events of your life to discern specific areas that might need to be addressed. For a more detailed review of your life, complete the Confidential Personal Inventory in the appendix.

Family History	**Personal History**

❏ Religious history of parents and grandparents

❏ Home life from childhood through high school

❏ History of physical or emotional illness in the family

❏ Adoption, foster care, guardians

❏ Eating habits (bulimia, bingeing and purging, anorexia, compulsive eating)

❏ Addictions (drugs, alcohol)

❏ Prescription medications (what for?)

❏ Sleeping patterns and nightmares

❏ Rape or any other sexual, physical or emotional abuse

❏ Thought life (obsessive, blasphemous, condemning, distracting thoughts, poor concentration, fantasy)

❏ Mental interference during church, prayer or Bible study

❏ Emotional life (anger, anxiety, depression, bitterness, fears)

❏ Spiritual journey (salvation: when, how, and assurance)

Now you are ready to start going through the Steps to Freedom in Christ. The following seven steps will help you experience freedom from your past. You will address the areas in which Satan commonly takes advantage of believers and where strongholds are often built.

Remember that the Lord Jesus Christ has already purchased your freedom over sin and Satan on the cross. Experiencing that freedom will be the result of what *you* choose to believe, confess, renounce and forgive. No one can do that for you, not even God. The battle for your mind will only be won as you personally choose the truth.

During each Step, it is very important that you submit to God inwardly while resisting the devil outwardly. Do this by praying each prayer and making each declaration *aloud*. The prayers and declarations are all in bold type to remind you to do that.

You will be taking a very thorough inventory of your life in order to make a rock-solid commitment to the truth. If your problems stem from another source not covered in these steps, you will have lost nothing by going through them. If you are open and honest during this time, you will greatly benefit by becoming right with God and close to Him once again.

May the Lord greatly touch your life during this time. He alone can and will give you the grace to make it through. Lean on His strength and wisdom, not on your own. It is crucial that you work through *all* seven Steps during this session. Take short breaks as you need them, but don't allow yourself to become discouraged and give up.

Remember, the freedom that Christ purchased for all believers on the cross is meant for *you*!

Counterfeit vs. Real

The first Step toward experiencing your freedom in Christ is to renounce—verbally reject—all past or present involvement with occult practices, cult teachings and rituals, as well as non-Christian religions.

You must renounce any activity or group that denies Jesus Christ, or offers guidance through any source other than the absolute authority of the Bible. Any group that requires dark, secret initiations, ceremonies, promises or pacts should also be renounced. Begin this step by praying aloud:

> **Dear Heavenly Father,**
> I ask You to bring to my mind anything and everything that I have done knowingly or unknowingly that involves occult, cult or non-Christian teachings or practices. I want to experience Your freedom by renouncing these things right now. In Jesus' name, I pray. Amen.

Even if you took part in something and thought it was just a game or a joke, you need to renounce it. Satan will try to take advantage of anything he can in our lives, so it is always wise to be as thorough as possible. Even if you were just standing by and watching others do it, you need to renounce your passive involvement. You may not have even realized at the time that what was going on was evil. Still, go ahead and renounce it.

If something comes to your mind and you are not sure what to do about it, trust that the Spirit of God is answering the prayer you just prayed, and go ahead and renounce it.

Note the Non-Christian Spiritual Checklist. This inventory covers many of the more common occult, cult and non-Christian religious groups and practices. It is not a complete list, however. Feel free to add others with which you were personally involved.

Following the checklist, there are some additional questions designed to help you become aware of other things you may need to renounce. Below those questions is a short prayer of confession and renunciation. Pray it *aloud*, filling in the blanks with the groups, teachings or practices that the Holy Spirit has prompted you to renounce during this time of personal evaluation.

NON-CHRISTIAN SPIRITUAL CHECKLIST

Check all those in which you have participated.

- ❑ Out-of-body experience (astral-projection)
- ❑ Ouija Board
- ❑ Bloody Mary
- ❑ Light-as-a-Feather (or other occult games)
- ❑ Table lifting
- ❑ Magic Eight Ball
- ❑ Spells or curses
- ❑ Mental telepathy or mental control of others
- ❑ Automatic writing
- ❑ Trances
- ❑ Spirit guides
- ❑ Fortune-telling/divination (i.e., tea leaves)
- ❑ Tarot cards
- ❑ Levitation
- ❑ Witchcraft/sorcery
- ❑ Satanism
- ❑ Palm reading
- ❑ Astrology/horoscopes
- ❑ Hypnosis (amateur or self-induced)
- ❑ Seances
- ❑ Black or white magic
- ❑ Dungeons & Dragons (and similar games such as Magic)
- ❑ Blood pacts or cutting yourself on purpose
- ❑ Objects of worship/crystals/good luck charms
- ❑ Sexual spirits
- ❑ Martial arts (mysticism/devotion to sensei)
- ❑ Superstitions
- ❑ Occult or violent video or computer games. List them:

- ❑ New Age (books, objects, seminars, medicine)
- ❑ Mormonism (Latter Day Saints)
- ❑ Jehovah's Witnesses (Watchtower)
- ❑ Masons
- ❑ Christian Science
- ❑ Mind science cults
- ❑ The Way International
- ❑ Unification Church (Moonies)
- ❑ The Forum (EST)
- ❑ Church of the Living Word
- ❑ Children of God (Children of Love)
- ❑ Church of Scientology
- ❑ Unitarianism/Universalism
- ❑ Roy Masters
- ❑ Silva Mind Control
- ❑ Transcendental Meditation (TM)
- ❑ Yoga
- ❑ Hare Krishna
- ❑ Bahaism
- ❑ Native American spirit worship
- ❑ Islam
- ❑ Hinduism
- ❑ Buddhism (including Zen)
- ❑ Black Muslim
- ❑ Rosicrucianism
- ❑ Other non-Christian religions:

- ❑ Movies, TV shows, music, books, magazines or comics that the Lord is bringing to your mind—*especially those that glorified Satan, caused fear or nightmares, were gruesomely violent or stimulated the flesh*. List them:

1. Have you ever seen, heard or felt a spiritual being in your room?

2. Do you have recurring nightmares? Specifically renounce any accompanying fear.

3. Do you now have, or have you ever had, an imaginary friend, spirit guide or "angel" offering you guidance or companionship? (If it has a name, renounce it by name.)

4. Have you ever heard voices in your head or had repeating, nagging thoughts such as, *I'm dumb, I'm ugly, Nobody loves me, I can't do anything right*, etc. as if there were a conversation going on inside your head? List any specific nagging thoughts.

5. Have you ever consulted a medium, spiritist or channeler?

6. Have you ever seen or been contacted by beings you thought were aliens?

7. Have you ever made a secret vow or pact?

8. Have you ever been involved in a satanic ritual of any kind or attended a concert in which Satan was the focus?

9. What other spiritual experiences have you had that would be considered out of the ordinary?

Once you have completed your checklist, confess and renounce each item you were involved in by praying the following prayer *aloud*:

Lord,
I confess that I have participated in _____. I know that it was evil and offensive in Your sight. Thank You for Your forgiveness. I renounce any and all involvement with _____, and I cancel out any and all ground that the enemy gained in my life through this activity. In Jesus' name, amen.

We were created to worship the true and living God. In fact, the Father seeks those who will worship Him in spirit and in truth (see John 4:23). As children of God, "We know also that the Son of God has come and has given us understanding, so that we may know him who is true. And we are in him who is true—even in his Son Jesus Christ. He is the true God and eternal life" (1 John 5:20).

Who or what is most important to us becomes that which we worship. Our thoughts, love, devotion, trust, adoration and obedience are directed to this object above all others. This object of worship is truly our God or god.

The apostle John follows the above passage with a warning, "Little children, guard yourselves from idols" (1 John 5:21, *NASB*). An idol is a false god, any object of worship other than the true God.

Though we may not bow down to statues, it is easy for people and things of this world to subtly become more important to us than the Lord Himself. The following prayer expresses the commitment of a heart that chooses to "worship the Lord [our] God, and serve him only" (Matthew 4:10).

Dear Lord God,
I know how easy it is to allow other things and other people to become more important to me than You. I also know that this is terribly offensive to Your Holy eyes as You have commanded that I shall have no other gods before You (see Exodus 20:3).
I confess to You that I have not loved You with all my heart and soul and mind (see Matthew 22:37) and as a result I have sinned against You, violating the first and greatest commandment. I repent of and turn away from this idolatry and now choose to return to You, Lord Jesus, as my first love once again (see Revelation 2:4).
Please reveal to my mind now any and all idols in my life. I want to renounce each of them and in so doing cancel out any and all ground Satan may have gained in my life through my idolatry. In the name of Jesus, the true God, amen.

As the Holy Spirit brings to your mind the things or people that have become more important to you than the true God, Jesus Christ, use the prayer following the checklist to renounce them. The checklist may be a help to you in recognizing those areas. Notice that most, if not all, of the areas listed below are not evil in themselves; they become idols when they usurp God's rightful place as Lord of our lives.

- ❑ Ambition
- ❑ Food or any substance
- ❑ Money/possessions
- ❑ Computers/games/software
- ❑ Financial security
- ❑ Rock stars/media celebrities/athletes
- ❑ Church activities
- ❑ TV/movies/music/other media
- ❑ Sports or physical fitness
- ❑ Fun/pleasure
- ❑ Ministry

- ❑ Appearance/image
- ❑ Work
- ❑ Busyness/activity
- ❑ Friends
- ❑ Power/control
- ❑ Boyfriend/girlfriend
- ❑ Popularity/opinion of others
- ❑ Spouse
- ❑ Knowledge/being right
- ❑ Children
- ❑ Hobbies
- ❑ Parents

In the name of the true and living God, Jesus Christ, I renounce my worship of the false god of _____ (name the idol) _____. I choose to worship only You, Lord, and ask You, Father, to enable me to keep this area of _____ (name the idol) _____ in its proper place in my life.

If you have been involved in satanic rituals or heavy occult activity (or you suspect it because of blocked memories, severe and recurring nightmares or sexual bondage or dysfunction), you need to say aloud the Special Renunciations for Satanic Ritual Involvement on the following page.

Read across the page, renouncing the first item in the column under "Kingdom of Darkness" and then announcing the first truth in the column under "Kingdom of Light." Continue down the page in this manner.

SPECIAL RENUNCIATIONS FOR SATANIC RITUAL INVOLVEMENT

Kingdom of Darkness	Kingdom of Light
I renounce ever signing my name over to Satan or having my name signed over to Satan.	I announce that my name is now written in the Lamb's Book of Life.
I renounce any ritual where I was wed to Satan.	I announce that I am the Bride of Christ.
I renounce any and all covenants, agreements or promises that I made to Satan.	I announce that I have made a new covenant with Christ.
I renounce all satanic assignments for my life, including duties, marriage and children.	I announce and commit myself to know and do only the will of God and I accept only His guidance for my life.
I renounce all spirit guides assigned to me.	I announce and accept only the leading of the Holy Spirit.
I renounce ever giving of my blood in the service of Satan.	I trust only in the shed blood of my Lord Jesus Christ.
I renounce ever eating of flesh or drinking of blood for satanic worship.	By faith I take Holy Communion which represents the body and the blood of the Lord Jesus.
I renounce all guardians and satanist parents who were assigned to me.	I announce that God is my heavenly Father and the Holy Spirit is my Guardian by whom I am sealed.
I renounce any baptism whereby I am identified with Satan.	I announce that I have been baptized into Christ Jesus and my identity is now in Him.
I renounce any sacrifice made on my behalf by which Satan may claim ownership of me.	I announce that only the sacrifice of Christ has any claim on me. I belong to Him. I have been purchased by the blood of the Lamb.

In addition to the lists above, all other satanic rituals, covenants, promises and assignments must be specifically renounced as the Lord brings them to your mind.

Some people who have been subjected to Satanic Ritual Abuse (SRA) develop multiple personalities (alters) in order to cope with their pain. If this is true in your case, you need someone who understands spiritual conflict to help you work through this problem.

For now, walk through the rest of the Steps to Freedom in Christ as best you can. It is important that you remove any demonic strongholds in your life first before trying to integrate the personalities.

Eventually, every alter personality (if this is the case with you) must be identified and guided into resolving the issues that caused its formation. Then, all true alters can agree to come together in Christ.

STEP 2

Deception vs. Truth

God's Word is true and we need to accept His truth in the innermost part of our being (see Psalm 51:6). Whether or not we *feel* it is true, we need to *believe* it is true!

Since Jesus is the truth (see John 14:6), the Holy Spirit is the Spirit of truth (see John 16:13), and the Word of God is truth (see John 17:17), we ought to speak the truth in love (see Ephesians 4:15).

The believer in Christ has no business deceiving others by lying, exaggerating, telling white lies, stretching the truth or anything relating to falsehoods. Satan is the father of lies (see John 8:44), and he seeks to keep people in bondage through deception (see Revelation 12:9; 2 Timothy 2:26), but it is the truth in Jesus that sets us free (see John 8:32-36).

We will find real joy and freedom when we stop living a lie and walk openly in the truth. After confessing his sin, King David wrote, "Blessed [happy] is the man...in whose spirit is no deceit" (Psalm 32:2).

How can we find the strength to walk in the light (see 1 John 1:7)? When we are sure that God loves and accepts us, we can be free to own up to our sin, face reality, and not run and hide from painful circumstances.

Start this step by praying the following prayer aloud. Don't let any opposing thoughts such as *This is a waste of time* or *I wish I could believe this stuff but I just can't* keep you from praying and choosing the truth. Even if this is difficult for you, work your way through this step. God will strengthen you as you rely on Him.

> **Dear Heavenly Father,**
>
> I know that You want me to know the truth, believe the truth, speak the truth and live in accordance with the truth. Thank You that it is the truth that will set me free. In many ways I have been deceived by Satan, the father of lies, and I have deceived myself as well.
>
> Father, I pray in the name of the Lord Jesus Christ, by virtue of His shed blood and resurrection, asking You to rebuke all of Satan's demons that are deceiving me.
>
> I have trusted in Jesus alone to save me, and so I am Your forgiven child. Therefore, since You accept me just as I am in Christ, I can be free to face my sin and not try to hide. I ask the Holy Spirit to guide me into all truth. I ask You to "search me, O God, and know my heart; test me and know my anxious thoughts. See if there is any offensive way in me, and lead me in the way everlasting" (Psalm 139:23,24). In the name of Jesus, Who is the Truth, I pray. Amen.

There are many ways in which Satan, the god of this world (see 2 Corinthians 4:4), seeks to deceive us. Just as he did with Eve, the devil tries to convince us to rely on ourselves and to try to get our needs met through the world around us, rather than trusting in the provision of our Father in heaven.

The following exercise will help open your eyes to the ways you have been deceived by the world system around you. Check each area of deception that the Lord brings to your mind and confess it, using the prayer following the list.

WAYS YOU CAN BE DECEIVED BY THE WORLD

- ❑ Believing that acquiring money and things will bring lasting happiness (see Matthew 13:22; 1 Timothy 6:10)
- ❑ Believing that consuming food and alcohol excessively will make you happy (see Proverbs 20:1; 23:19-21)
- ❑ Believing that a great body and personality will get you what you want (see Proverbs 31:10; 1 Peter 3:3,4)
- ❑ Believing that gratifying sexual lust will bring lasting satisfaction (see Ephesians 4:22-24; 1 Peter 2:11)
- ❑ Believing that you can sin and get away with it and not have it affect your heart (see Hebrews 3:12,13)
- ❑ Believing that you need more than what God has given you in Christ (see 2 Corinthians 11:2-4,13-15)

- ❑ Believing that you can do whatever you want and no one can touch you (see Proverbs 16:18; Obadiah 3; 1 Peter 5:5)
- ❑ Believing that people can live a life of sin and still go to heaven (see 1 Corinthians 6:9-11)
- ❑ Believing that you can hang around bad company and not become corrupted (see 1 Corinthians 15:33,34)
- ❑ Believing that there are no consequences on earth for your sin (see Galatians 6:7,8)
- ❑ Believing that you must gain the approval of certain people in order to be happy (see Galatians 1:10)
- ❑ Believing that you must measure up to certain standards in order to feel good about yourself (see Galatians 3:2,3; 5:1)

Lord, I confess that I have been deceived by _____. I thank You for Your forgiveness and I commit myself to believing only Your truth. In Jesus' name, amen.

It is important to know that in addition to being deceived by the world, false teachers and deceiving spirits, we can also deceive ourselves. Now that you are alive in Christ, completely forgiven and totally accepted, you don't need to defend yourself the way you used to. Christ is now your defense. Confess the ways the Lord shows you that you have deceived yourself or defended yourself wrongly by using the lists and prayers of confession below:

WAYS YOU CAN DECEIVE YOURSELF

- ❑ Hearing God's Word but not doing what it says (see James 1:22)
- ❑ Saying you have no sin (see 1 John 1:8)
- ❑ Thinking you are something you're really not (see Galatians 6:3)
- ❑ Thinking you are wise in this worldly age (see 1 Corinthians 3:18,19)
- ❑ Thinking you can be truly religious but not bridle your tongue (see James 1:26)

Lord, I confess that I have deceived myself by _____. Thank You for Your forgiveness. I commit myself to believing only Your truth. In Jesus' name, amen.

WAYS YOU CAN WRONGLY DEFEND YOURSELF

- ❑ Denial of reality (conscious or unconscious)
- ❑ Fantasy (escaping reality through daydreaming, TV, movies, music, computer or video games, etc.)
- ❑ Emotional insulation (withdrawing from people or keeping people at a distance to avoid rejection)
- ❑ Regression (reverting back to a less threatening time)
- ❑ Displaced anger (taking out your frustrations on innocent people)
- ❑ Projection (blaming others for your problems)
- ❑ Rationalization (making excuses for your own poor behavior)

Lord, I confess that I have defended myself wrongly by _____. Thank You for Your forgiveness. I now commit myself to trusting in You to defend and protect me. In Jesus' name, amen.

Choosing the truth may be hard for you if you have been believing lies for many years. You may need some ongoing counseling to help weed out any defense mechanisms that you have relied on to cope with life. Every Christian needs to learn that Christ is the only defense he or she needs. Realizing that you are already forgiven and accepted by God through Christ will help free you to place all your dependence on Him.

Faith is the biblical response to the truth and believing what God says is a choice we all can make. If you say, I wish I could believe God, but I just can't, you are being deceived. Of course you can believe God, because what God says is always true.

Sometimes we are greatly hindered from walking by faith in our Father God because of lies we have believed about Him. We are to have a healthy fear of God—awe of His holiness, power and presence—but we are not to be afraid of Him. Romans 8:15 says, "For you did not receive a spirit that makes you a slave again to fear, but you received the Spirit of sonship. And by him we cry, 'Abba, Father.'" The following exercise will help break the chains of those lies and enable you to begin to experience that intimate Abba Father relationship with Him.

Work your way down the following lists, one by one, left to right. Begin each one with the statement in bold print at the top of that list. Read through the list *aloud*.

I renounce the lie that my Father God is ...	I joyfully accept the truth that my Father God is ...
Distant and disinterested.	Intimate and involved (see Psalm 139:1-18).
Insensitive and uncaring.	Kind and compassionate (see Psalm 103:8-14).
Stern and demanding.	Accepting and filled with joy and love (see Romans 15:7; Zephaniah 3:17).
Passive and cold.	Warm and affectionate (see Isaiah 40:11; Hosea 11:3,4).
Absent or too busy for me.	Always with me and eager to be with me (see Hebrews 13:5; Jeremiah 31:20; Ezekiel 34:11-16).
Never satisfied with what I do; impatient or angry.	Patient and slow to anger (see Exodus 34:6; 2 Peter 3:9).
Mean, cruel or abusive.	Loving, gentle and protective of me (see Jeremiah 31:3; Isaiah 42:3; Psalm 18:2).
Trying to take all the fun out of life.	Trustworthy and wants to give me a full life; His will is good, perfect and acceptable for me (see Lamentations 3:22,23; John 10:10; Romans 12:1,2).
Controlling or manipulative.	Full of grace and mercy, and He gives me freedom to fail (see Hebrews 4:15,16; Luke 15:11-16).
Condemning or unforgiving.	Tenderhearted and forgiving; His heart and arms are always open to me (see Psalm 130:1-4; Luke 15:17-24).
Nitpicking, exacting or perfectionistic.	Committed to my growth and proud of me as His growing child (see Romans 8:28,29; Hebrews 12:5-11; 2 Corinthians 7:4).

I Am the Apple of His Eye!
Deuteronomy 32:9,10

A central part of walking in the truth and rejecting deception is to deal with the fears that plague our lives. First Peter 5:8 says that our enemy, the devil, prowls around like a roaring lion, seeking people to devour. Just as a lion's roar strikes terror into the hearts of those who hear it, so Satan uses fear to try to paralyze Christians. His intimidation tactics are designed to rob us of faith in God and drive us to try to get our needs met through the world or the flesh.

Fear weakens us, causes us to be self-centered, and clouds our minds so that all we can think about is the thing that frightens us. But fear can only control us if we let it.

God, however, does not want us to be mastered by anything, including fear (see 1 Corinthians 6:12). Jesus Christ is to be our only Master (see 2 Timothy 2:21; John 13:13). In order to begin to experience freedom from the bondage of fear and the ability to walk by faith in God, pray the following prayer from your heart:

> **Dear Heavenly Father,**
> I confess to You that I have listened to the devil's roar and have allowed fear to master me. I have not always walked by faith in You but instead have focused on my feelings and circumstances (see 2 Corinthians 4:16-18; 5:7). Thank You for forgiving me for my unbelief. Right now I renounce the spirit of fear and affirm the truth that You have not given me a spirit of fear but of power, love and a sound mind (see 2 Timothy 1:7). Lord, please reveal to my mind now all the fears that have been controlling me so I can renounce them and be free to walk by faith in You.
> I thank You for the freedom You give me to walk by faith and not by fear. In Jesus' powerful name, I pray. Amen.

The following list may help you recognize some of the fears the devil has used to keep you from walking by faith. Check the ones that apply to your life. Write down any others that the Spirit of God brings to your mind. Then, one by one renounce those fears aloud, using the suggested renunciation below.

- ❑ Fear of death
- ❑ Fear of Satan
- ❑ Fear of failure
- ❑ Fear of rejection by people
- ❑ Fear of disapproval
- ❑ Fear of becoming/being homosexual
- ❑ Fear of financial problems
- ❑ Fear of never getting married
- ❑ Fear of the death of a loved one
- ❑ Fear of being a hopeless case
- ❑ Fear of losing my salvation
- ❑ Fear of having committed the unpardonable sin
- ❑ Fear of not being loved by God
- ❑ Fear of never loving or being loved by others
- ❑ Fear of embarrassment

- ❑ Fear of being victimized by crime
- ❑ Fear of marriage
- ❑ Fear of divorce
- ❑ Fear of going crazy
- ❑ Fear of pain/illness
- ❑ Fear of the future
- ❑ Fear of confrontation
- ❑ Fear of specific individuals; list them:

- ❑ Other specific fears that come to mind now:

I renounce the _____(name the fear)_____ because God has not given me a spirit of fear (see 2 Timothy 1:7). I choose to live by faith in the God who has promised to protect me and meet all my needs as I walk by faith in Him (see Psalm 27:1; Matthew 6:33,34).

After you have finished renouncing all the specific fears you have allowed to control you, pray the following prayer from your heart:

> Dear Heavenly Father,
> I thank You that You are trustworthy. I choose to believe You, even when my feelings and circumstances tell me to be fearful. You have told me not to fear, for You are with me; to not anxiously look about me, for You are my God. You will strengthen me, help me and surely uphold me with Your righteous right hand (see Isaiah 41:10). I pray this with faith in the name of Jesus my Master. Amen.

Faith is choosing to believe and act upon what God says, regardless of our feelings or circumstances. Believing something, however, does not make it true. *It's true; therefore, we choose to believe it.*

The New Age movement has twisted the concept of faith by saying that we make something true by believing it. No, we can't create reality with our minds; only God can do that. We can only *face* reality with our minds.

Just "having faith" is not enough. The key question is whether the object of your faith is trustworthy. If the object of your faith is not reliable, then no amount of believing will make it reliable. That is why our faith must be on the solid rock of God Himself and His Word. That is the only way to live a responsible and fruitful life. On the other hand, if what you believe in is not true, then the way you end up living will not be right.

For generations, Christians have known the importance of publicly declaring what they believe. Read aloud the following Statements of Truth, thinking about what you are saying. You may find it very helpful to read it daily for several weeks to renew your mind with the truth and replace any lies you might be believing.

STATEMENTS OF TRUTH

I recognize that there is only one true and living God (see Exodus 20:2,3) who exists as the Father, Son and Holy Spirit. He is worthy of all honor, praise and glory as the One who made all things and holds all things together (see Colossians 1:16,17).

I recognize that Jesus Christ is the Messiah, the Word who became flesh and dwelt among us (see John 1:1,14). I believe that He came to destroy the works of the devil (see 1 John 3:8), and that He disarmed the rulers and authorities and made a public display of them, having triumphed over them (see Colossians 2:15).

I believe that God has proven His own love for me because when I was still a sinner, Christ died for me (see Romans 5:8). I believe that He has delivered me from the domain of darkness and transferred me to His kingdom, and in Him I have redemption—the forgiveness of sins (see Colossians 1:13,14).

I believe that I am now a child of God (see 1 John 3:1-3) and that I am seated with Christ in the heavenlies (see Ephesians 2:6). I believe that I was saved by the grace of God through faith, and that it was a gift and not a result of any works on my part (see Ephesians 2:8,9).

I choose to be strong in the Lord and in the strength of His might (see Ephesians 6:10). I put no confidence in the flesh (see Philippians 3:3), for the weapons of warfare are not of the flesh but are divinely powerful for the destruction of strongholds (see 2 Corinthians 10:4). I put on the full armor of God (see Ephesians 6:10-20). I resolve to stand firm in my faith and resist the evil one.

I believe that apart from Christ I can do nothing (see John 15:5), so I declare my complete dependence on Him. I choose to abide in Christ in order to bear much fruit and glorify my Father (see John 15:8). I announce to Satan that Jesus is my Lord (see 1 Corinthians 12:3), and I reject any and all counterfeit gifts or works of Satan in my life.

I believe that the truth will set me free (see John 8:32) and that Jesus is the truth (see John 14:6). If He sets me free, I will be free indeed (see John 8:36). I recognize that walking in the light is the only path of true fellowship with God and man (see 1 John 1:3-7). Therefore, I stand against all of Satan's deception by taking every thought captive in obedience to Christ (see 2 Corinthians 10:5). I declare that the Bible is the only authoritative standard for truth and life (see 2 Timothy 3:15-17).

I choose to present my body to God as a living and holy sacrifice (see Romans 12:1) and the members of my body as instruments of righteousness to God (see Romans 6:13). I choose to renew my mind by the living Word of God in order that I may prove that the will of God is good, acceptable and perfect (see Romans 12:2). I put off the old self with its evil practices and put on the new self (see Colossians 3:9,10). I declare myself to be a new creation in Christ (see 2 Corinthians 5:17).

By faith, I choose to be filled with the Spirit (see Ephesians 5:18) so that I can be guided into all truth (see John 16:13). I choose to walk by the Spirit so that I will not carry out the desires of the flesh (see Galatians 5:16).

I renounce all selfish goals and choose the ultimate goal of love (see 1 Timothy 1:5). I choose to obey the two greatest commandments: to love the Lord my God with all my heart, soul, mind and strength and to love my neighbor as myself (see Matthew 22:37-39).

I believe that the Lord Jesus has all authority in heaven and on earth (see Matthew 28:18) and that He is the head over all rule and authority. I am complete in Him (see Colossians 2:10). I believe that Satan and his demons are subject to me in Christ since I am a member of Christ's Body (see Ephesians 1:19-23). Therefore, I obey the command to submit to God and resist the devil (see James 4:7), and I command Satan in the name of Jesus Christ to leave my presence.

STEP 3

Bitterness vs. Forgiveness

We need to forgive others so Satan cannot take advantage of us (see 2 Corinthians 2:10,11). We are commanded to get rid of all bitterness in our lives and forgive others as we have been forgiven (see Ephesians 4:31,32). Ask God to bring to your mind the people you need to forgive by praying the following prayer aloud:

> Dear Heavenly Father,
> I thank You for the riches of Your kindness, forbearance and patience toward me, knowing that Your kindness has led me to repentance (see Romans 2:4). I confess that I have not shown that same kindness and patience toward those who have hurt me. Instead, I have held on to my anger, bitterness and resentment toward them. Please bring to my mind all the people I need to forgive in order that I may do so now. In Jesus' name, amen.

On a separate sheet of paper, list the names of people who come to your mind. At this point don't question whether you need to forgive them or not. If a name comes to mind, just write it down.

Often we hold things against ourselves as well, punishing ourselves for wrong choices we've made in the past. Write "myself" at the bottom of your list so you can forgive yourself. Forgiving yourself is accepting the truth that God has already forgiven you in Christ. If God forgives you, you *can* forgive yourself!

Also write "thoughts against God" at the bottom of your list. Obviously, God has never done anything wrong so we don't have to forgive Him. Sometimes, however, we harbor angry thoughts against Him because He did not do what we wanted Him to do. Those feelings of anger or resentment against God can become a wall between us and Him so we must let them go.

Before you begin working through the process of forgiving those on your list, take a few minutes to review what forgiveness is and what it is not.

Forgiveness is not forgetting. People who want to forget all that was done to them will find they cannot do it. Don't put off forgiving those who have hurt you, hoping the pain will one day go away. Once you choose to forgive someone, *then* Christ can come and begin to heal you of your hurts. But the healing cannot begin until you first forgive.

Forgiveness is a choice, a decision of your will. Since God requires you to forgive, it is something you can do. Sometimes it is very hard to forgive someone because we naturally want revenge for the things we have suffered. Forgiveness seems to go against our sense of what is right and fair. So we hold on to our anger, punishing people over and over again in our minds for the pain they've caused us. But we are told by God never to take our own revenge (see Romans 12:19). Let God deal with the person. Let him or her off your hook because as long as you refuse to forgive someone, you are still hooked to them. You are still chained to your past, bound up in your bitterness.

By forgiving, you let the other person off your hook, but they are not off God's hook. You must trust that God will deal with the person justly and fairly, something you simply cannot do. You might say, "But you don't know how much this person hurt me!" You're right. We don't, but Jesus does; and

He tells you to forgive. And don't you see? Until you let go of your anger and hatred, the person is still hurting you. You can't turn back the clock and change the past, but you can be free from it. You *can* stop the pain, but there is only one way to do it—forgive.

You forgive others for your sake so you can be free. Forgiveness is mainly a matter of obedience to God. God wants you to be free; there is no other way.

Forgiveness is agreeing to live with the consequences of another person's sin, but you are going to live with those consequences anyway whether you like it or not. The only choice you have is whether you will do so in the *bondage of bitterness* or in the *freedom of forgiveness*. But no one truly forgives without accepting and suffering the pain of another person's sin. That can seem unfair and you may wonder where the justice is in it, but justice is found at the Cross, which makes forgiveness legally and morally right. Jesus took the *eternal* consequences of sin upon Himself. God "made Him who knew no sin to be sin on our behalf, that we might become the righteousness of God in Him" (2 Corinthians 5:21, *NASB*). We, however, often suffer the temporary consequences of other people's sins. That is simply a harsh reality of life all of us have to face.

Do not wait for the other person to ask for your forgiveness before forgiving him or her. They may never do so. Remember, Jesus did not wait for those who were crucifying Him to apologize before He forgave them. Even while they mocked and jeered at Him, He prayed, "Father, forgive them; for they do not know what they are doing" (Luke 23:34, *NASB*).

How do you forgive from your heart? You allow God to bring to the surface the painful emotions you feel toward those who have hurt you. If your forgiveness doesn't touch the emotional core of your life, it will be incomplete. Too often we're afraid of the pain so we bury our emotions deep down inside us. Let God bring them to the surface so He can begin to heal those damaged emotions.

Forgiveness is choosing not to hold someone's sin against him or her anymore. It is common for bitter people to bring up past issues with those who have hurt them. They want them to feel bad. But we must let go of the past and choose to reject any thought of revenge. This doesn't mean you must continue to put up with the future sins of others. God does not tolerate sin and neither should you. Don't allow yourself to be continually abused by others. Take a stand against sin while continuing to exercise grace and forgiveness toward those who hurt you. You may need help in setting wise limits and boundaries to protect yourself from further abuse.

Don't wait to forgive until you feel like forgiving. You will never get there. Make the hard choice to forgive even if you don't feel like it. Once you choose to forgive, Satan will have lost his power over you in that area and God's healing touch will be free to move. **Freedom is what you will gain right now, not necessarily an immediate change in feelings.**

Now, you are ready to begin. Starting with the first person on your list, make the choice to forgive him or her for every painful memory that comes to your mind. Focus on that individual until you are sure you have dealt with all the remembered pain. Then work your way down the list in the same way.

As you begin forgiving people, God may bring to your mind painful memories you've totally forgotten. Let Him do this even if it hurts. God wants you to be free; forgiving these people is the only way. Don't try to excuse the offender's behavior, even if it is someone you are really close to.

Don't say "Lord, please help me to forgive." He is already helping you and will be with you all the way through the process. Don't say "Lord, I want to forgive…" because that bypasses the hard choice you have to make. Say instead, "Lord, I *choose* to forgive…"

For every painful memory you have for each person on your list, pray aloud:

> Lord,
> I choose to forgive _____ (name the person) _____ for _____ (say what they did to hurt you) _____ even though it made me feel _____ (share the painful feelings) _____.

After you have forgiven each person for all the offenses that come to your mind and after you have honestly expressed how you felt, conclude your forgiveness of that person by praying aloud:

> Lord,
> I choose not to hold any of these things against _____ (name) _____ any longer. I thank You for setting me free from the bondage of my bitterness toward _____ (name) _____. I now ask You to bless _____ (name) _____. In Jesus' name, I pray. Amen.

STEP 4
Rebellion vs. Submission

We live in a rebellious age. Many people only obey laws and authorities when it is convenient for them. There is a general lack of respect for those in government, and Christians are often as guilty as the rest of society in fostering a critical, rebellious spirit. Certainly we are not expected to agree with our leaders' policies that are in violation of Scripture, but we are to "honor all men; love the brotherhood, fear God, honor the king" (1 Peter 2:17, *NASB*).

It is easy to believe the lie that those in authority over us are only robbing us of the freedom to do what we want. The truth is, however, that God has placed them there for our protection and liberty.

Rebelling against God and His authorities is a very serious sin for it gives Satan a wide open avenue to attack. Submission is the only solution. God requires more, however, than just the outward appearance of submission; He wants us to sincerely submit to those in authority from the heart. When you stand under the authority of God and those He has placed over you, you cut off this dangerous avenue of demonic attack.

The Bible makes it clear that we have two main responsibilities toward those in authority over us: to pray for them (see 1 Timothy 2:1,2) and to submit to them (see Romans 13:1-7). To commit yourself to that godly lifestyle, pray the following prayer aloud from your heart:

> **Dear Heavenly Father,**
> **You have said in the Bible that rebellion is the same thing as witchcraft and as bad as idolatry (see 1 Samuel 15:23). I know I have not obeyed You in this area and have rebelled in my heart against You and against those You have placed in authority over me. Thank You for Your forgiveness of my rebellion. By the shed blood of the Lord Jesus Christ, I pray that all ground gained by evil spirits in my life due to my rebellion would be canceled. I pray that You would show me all the ways I have been rebellious. I choose now to adopt a submissive spirit and a servant's heart. In Jesus' precious name, I pray. Amen.**

Being under authority is clearly an act of faith! By submitting, you are trusting God to work through His established lines of authority, even when they are harsh or unkind or when they tell you to do something you don't want to do.

There may be times when those over you abuse their authority and break the laws which are ordained by God for the protection of innocent people. In those cases, you will need to seek help from a *higher authority* for your protection. The laws in your state may require that such abuse be reported to the police or other governmental agency. If there is continuing abuse—physical, mental, emotional or sexual—you may need further counseling from a local agency to help you deal with that situation.

If authorities abuse their position by requiring you to break God's law or compromise your commitment to Him, then you need to obey God rather than man (see Acts 4:19,20). Be careful, though. Don't assume that an authority is violating God's Word just because they are telling you to do something you don't like!

We all need to adopt a humble, submissive spirit to one another in the fear of Christ (see Ephesians 5:21). In addition, however, God has set up specific lines of authority to protect us and to give order to our daily lives.

As you prayerfully look over the following list, allow the Lord to show you any *specific ways* in which you have been rebellious to authority. Then, using the prayer of confession that follows the list, specifically confess whatever the Lord brings to your mind.

❑ Civil government, including traffic laws, tax laws; attitude toward government officials (see Romans 13:1-7; 1 Timothy 2:1-4; 1 Peter 2:13-17)

❑ Parents, stepparents or legal guardians (see Ephesians 6:1-3)

❑ Teachers, coaches, school officials (see Romans 13:1-4)

❑ Employer—past or present (see 1 Peter 2:18-23)

❑ Husband (see 1 Peter 3:1-5) or wife (see Ephesians 5:21; 1 Peter 3:7)

Note to husbands: Take a moment and ask the Lord if your lack of love for your wife could be fostering a rebellious spirit within her. If so, confess that now as a violation of Ephesians 5:22-33.

❑ Church leaders (see Hebrews 13:17)

❑ God (see Daniel 9:5,9)

For each way in which the Spirit of God brings to your mind that you have been rebellious, use the following prayer to specifically confess that sin:

Lord,
I confess that I have been rebellious toward _____ by _____ (say what you did specifically)_____. Thank You for forgiving my rebellion. I choose now to be submissive and obedient to Your Word. In Jesus' name, I pray. Amen.

STEP 5

Pride vs. Humility

Pride kills. Pride says, "I don't need God or anyone else's help. I can handle it by myself." Oh, no you can't! We absolutely need God and we desperately need each other. The apostle Paul wisely wrote, "For it is we…who worship by the Spirit of God, who glory in Christ Jesus, and who put *no confidence in the flesh*" (Philippians 3:3, emphasis mine).

That is a good definition of humility: putting no confidence in the flesh, that is, in ourselves; but, rather, being "strong in the Lord and in his mighty power" (Ephesians 6:10). Humility, therefore, is confidence properly placed *in God*.

Proverbs 3:5-7 expresses a similar thought: "Trust in the LORD with all your heart and lean not on your own understanding; in all your ways acknowledge him and he will make your paths straight. Do not be wise in your own eyes; fear the LORD and shun evil."

James 4:6-10 and 1 Peter 5:1-10 warn us that serious spiritual problems will result when we are proud. Use the following prayer to express your commitment to living humbly before God:

> **Dear Heavenly Father,**
>
> **You have said that pride goes before destruction and an arrogant spirit before a fall (see Proverbs 16:18). I confess that I have been thinking mainly of myself and not of others. I have not denied myself, picked up my cross daily and followed You (see Matthew 16:24). As a result, I have given ground to the devil in my life. I have sinned by believing I could be happy and successful on my own. I confess that I have placed my will before Yours and have centered my life around myself instead of You.**
>
> **I repent of my pride and selfishness and pray that all ground gained in my members by the enemies of the Lord Jesus Christ would be canceled. I choose to rely on the Holy Spirit's power and guidance so I will do nothing from selfishness or empty conceit, but with humility of mind I will regard others as more important than myself (see Philippians 2:3). And I choose to make You, Lord, the most important of all in my life (see Matthew 6:33).**
>
> **Please show me now all the specific ways in which I have lived my life in pride. Enable me through love to serve others and in honor to prefer others (see Romans 12:10). I ask all of this in the gentle and humble name of Jesus, my Lord. Amen.**

Having made that commitment to God in prayer, now allow Him to show you any specific ways in which you have lived in a proud manner. The following list may help you.

As the Lord brings to your mind areas of pride, use the prayer following the list to guide you in your confession.

❑ Having a stronger desire to do my will than God's will
❑ Leaning too much on my own understanding and experience rather than seeking God's guidance through prayer and His Word
❑ Relying on my own strengths and abilities rather than depending on the power of the Holy Spirit
❑ Being more concerned about controlling others than in developing self-control
❑ Often being too busy doing "important" things to take time to do little things for others
❑ Having a tendency to think that I have no needs
❑ Finding it hard to admit when I am wrong

❑ Being more concerned about pleasing people than pleasing God
❑ Being concerned about getting the credit I feel I deserve
❑ Thinking I am more humble, spiritual, religious or devoted than others
❑ Being driven to obtain recognition by attaining degrees, titles or positions
❑ Often feeling that my needs are more important than another's needs
❑ Considering myself better than others because of my academic, artistic, or athletic abilities or accomplishments
❑ Other ways I have thought more highly of myself than I should: _____
_____

For each of the above areas that has been true in your life, pray aloud:

> Lord,
>   I agree I have been proud in _____. Thank You for forgiving me for my pride. I choose to humble myself before You and others. I choose to place all my confidence in You and none in my flesh. In Jesus' name, amen.

Pride is the original sin of Lucifer. It sets one person or group against another and divides. Satan's strategy is always to divide and conquer, but God has given us a ministry of reconciliation (see 2 Corinthians 5:19).

Consider for a moment the work of Christ in breaking down the long-standing barrier of racial prejudice between Jew and Gentile:

> For he himself [Christ] is our peace, who has made the two one and has destroyed the barrier, the dividing wall of hostility, by abolishing in his flesh the law with its commandments and regulations. His purpose was to create in himself one new man out of the two, thus making peace, and in this one body to reconcile both of them to God through the cross, by which he put to death their hostility. He came and preached peace to you who were far away and peace to those who were near. For through him we both have access to the Father by one Spirit (Ephesians 2:14-18).

Many times we deny that there is prejudice or bigotry in our hearts, yet "nothing in all creation is hidden from God's sight. Everything is uncovered and laid bare before the eyes of him to whom we must give account" (Hebrews 4:13). The following is a prayer, asking God to shine His light upon your heart and reveal any area of prideful prejudice:

> Dear Heavenly Father,
>   I know that You love all people equally and that You do not show favoritism but You accept men from every nation who fear You and do what is right (see Acts 10:34,35). You do not judge people based on skin color, race, ethnic background, gender, denominational preference or any other worldly matter (see 2 Corinthians 5:16). I confess that I have too often prejudged others or regarded myself as superior because of these things. I have not always been a minister of reconciliation but have been a proud agent of division through my attitudes, words and deeds. I repent of all hateful bigotry and prideful prejudice and I ask You, Lord, to now reveal to my mind all the specific ways in which this form of pride has corrupted my heart and mind. In Jesus' name, amen.

For each area of racial or ethnic prejudice, gender superiority or denominational bigotry that the Lord brings to mind, pray the following prayer aloud from your heart:

I confess and renounce the prideful sin of prejudice against _____ (name the group) _____. **I thank You for Your forgiveness, Lord, and ask now that You would change my heart and make me a loving agent of reconciliation with _____ (name the group) _____. In Jesus' name, amen.**

STEP 6

Bondage vs. Freedom

Many times we feel trapped in a vicious cycle of sin-confess-sin-confess that never seems to end. We can become very discouraged and end up just giving up and giving in to the sins of our flesh. To find freedom we must follow James 4:7, "Submit yourselves, then, to God. Resist the devil, and he will flee from you." We submit to God by confession of sin and repentance (turning away from the sin). We resist the devil by rejecting his lies and walking in the truth.

Sin that has become a habit often requires help from a trusted brother or sister in Christ. James 5:16 says, "Confess your sins to each other and pray for each other so that you may be healed. The prayer of a righteous man is powerful and effective." Sometimes the assurance of 1 John 1:9 is enough: "If we confess our sins, he is faithful and just and will forgive us our sins and purify us from all unrighteousness."

Remember, confession is not saying "I'm sorry"; it is openly admitting "I did it." Whether you need help from other people or just the accountability of walking in the light before God, pray the following prayer aloud:

Dear Heavenly Father,
You have told me to put on the Lord Jesus Christ and not to think about how to gratify my sinful desires (see Romans 13:14). I confess that I have given in to sinful desires which wage war against my soul (see 1 Peter 2:11). I thank You that in Christ my sins are already forgiven, but I have broken Your holy law and given the devil a chance to wage war in my body (see Romans 6:12,13; James 4:1; 1 Peter 5:8). I come to You now to confess and renounce these sins of the flesh (see Proverbs 28:13; 2 Corinthians 4:2) so that I might be cleansed and set free from the bondage of sin. Please reveal to my mind now all the sins of the flesh I have committed and the ways I have grieved the Holy Spirit. In Jesus' holy name, I pray. Amen.

There are many sins of the flesh that can control us. The following list contains many of them, but a prayerful examination of Galatians 5:19-21; Ephesians 4:25-31; and Mark 7:20-23 will help you to be even more thorough. After reading these three passages, look over the following list and ask the Holy Spirit to bring to your mind the ones you need to confess. He may reveal to you others as well. For each one the Lord shows you, pray a prayer of confession from your heart. There is a sample prayer following the list.

Note: Sexual sins, divorce, eating disorders, substance abuse, abortion, suicidal tendencies and perfectionism will be dealt with later in this Step, beginning on page 63.

❑ Stealing
❑ Quarreling/fighting
❑ Jealousy/envy
❑ Complaining/criticism
❑ Lustful actions
❑ Gossip/slander
❑ Swearing
❑ Apathy/laziness
❑ Lying

❑ Hatred
❑ Anger
❑ Lustful thoughts
❑ Drunkenness
❑ Cheating
❑ Procrastination
❑ Greed/materialism
❑ Others: _____

Lord,
I confess that I have committed the sin of _____. Thank You for Your forgiveness and cleansing. I now turn away from this sin and turn to You, Lord. Strengthen me by Your Holy Spirit to obey You. In Jesus' name, amen.

It is our responsibility not to allow sin to have control over our bodies. We must not use our bodies or another person's body as an instrument of unrighteousness (see Romans 6:12,13). Sexual immorality is sin against your body, the temple of the Holy Spirit (see 1 Corinthians 6:18,19). To find freedom from sexual bondage, begin by praying the following prayer:

Lord,
I ask You to bring to my mind every sexual use of my body as an instrument of unrighteousness, so I can renounce these sins right now. In Jesus' name, I pray. Amen.

As the Lord brings to your mind every wrong sexual use of your body, whether it was done to you—rape, incest, sexual molestation—or willingly by you (including pornography, masturbation, sexual immorality), *renounce every occasion:*

Lord,
I renounce _____(name the specific use of your body)_____ with _____(name any other person involved)_____ and I ask You to break that sinful bond with _____(name)_____.

After you are finished, commit your body to the Lord by praying:

Lord,
I renounce all these uses of my body as an instrument of unrighteousness and I admit to my willful participation. I choose now to present my eyes, mouth, mind, heart, hands, feet and sexual organs to You as instruments of righteousness. I present my whole body to You as a living sacrifice, holy and acceptable, and I choose to reserve the sexual use of my body for marriage only (see Hebrews 13:4).
I reject the devil's lie that my body is not clean or that it is dirty or in any way unacceptable to You as a result of my past sexual experiences. Lord, thank You that You have totally cleansed and forgiven me and that You love and accept me just the way I am. Therefore, I choose now to accept myself and my body as clean in Your eyes. Amen.

SPECIAL PRAYERS FOR SPECIAL NEEDS

Divorce

Lord,
I confess to You any part that I played in my divorce (ask the Lord to show you specifics). Thank You for Your forgiveness, and I choose to forgive myself as well. I renounce the lie that my identity is now in being divorced. I am a child of God, and I reject the lie that says I am a second-class Christian because of the divorce. I reject the lie that says I am worthless, unlovable, and that my life is empty and meaningless. I am complete in Christ, who loves me and accepts me just as I am. Lord, I commit the healing of all hurts in my life to You as I have chosen to forgive those who have

hurt me. I also place my future into Your hands and trust You to provide the human companionship You created me to need through Your Church and, if it be Your will, through another spouse. I pray all this in the healing name of Jesus, my Savior and Lord and closest friend. Amen.

Homosexuality

Lord,

I renounce the lie that You have created me or anyone else to be homosexual and I agree that in Your Word You clearly forbid homosexual behavior. I choose to accept myself as a child of God and I thank You that You created me as a man (woman). I renounce all homosexual thoughts, urges, drives and acts, and cancel out all ways that Satan has used these things to pervert my relationships. I announce that I am free in Christ to relate to the opposite sex and my own sex in the way that You intended. In Jesus' name, amen.

Abortion

Lord,

I confess that I was not a proper guardian and keeper of the life You entrusted to me and I admit that as sin. Thank You that because of Your forgiveness, I can forgive myself. I recognize the child is in Your caring hands for all eternity. In Jesus' name, amen.

Suicidal Tendencies

Lord,

I renounce all suicidal thoughts and any attempts I've made to take my own life or in any way injure myself. I renounce the lie that life is hopeless and that I can find peace and freedom by taking my own life. Satan is a thief and comes to steal, kill and destroy. I choose life in Christ, who said He came to give me life and give it abundantly (see John 10:10). Thank You for Your forgiveness which allows me to forgive myself. I choose to believe that there is always hope in Christ. In Jesus' name, I pray. Amen.

Drivenness and Perfectionism

Lord,

I renounce the lie that my self-worth is dependent upon my ability to perform. I announce the truth that my identity and sense of worth is found in who I am as Your child. I renounce seeking the approval and acceptance of other people, and I choose to believe that I am already approved and accepted in Christ because of His death and resurrection for me. I choose to believe the truth that I have been saved, not by deeds done in righteousness, but according to Your mercy. I choose to believe that I am no longer under the curse of the law because Christ became a curse for me. I receive the free gift of life in Christ and choose to abide in Him. I renounce striving for perfection by living under the law. By Your grace, Heavenly Father, I choose from this day forward to walk by faith in the power of Your Holy Spirit according to what You have said is true. In Jesus' name, amen.

Eating Disorders or Self-Mutilation

Lord,

I renounce the lie that my value as a person is dependent upon my appearance or performance. I renounce cutting or abusing myself, vomiting, using laxatives or starving myself as a means of being in control, altering my appearance or cleansing myself of evil. I announce that only the blood of the Lord Jesus cleanses me from sin. I realize I have been bought with a price and my body, the temple of the Holy Spirit, belongs to God. Therefore, I choose to glorify God in my body. I renounce the lie that I am evil or that any part of my body is evil. Thank You that You accept me just the way I am in Christ. In Jesus' name, I pray. Amen.

Substance Abuse

Lord,

I confess that I have misused substances—alcohol, tobacco, food, prescription or street drugs—for the purpose of pleasure, to escape reality or to cope with difficult problems. I confess that I have abused my body and programmed my mind in a harmful way. I have quenched the Holy Spirit as well. Thank You for forgiving me. I renounce any satanic connection or influence in my life through my misuse of food or chemicals. I cast my anxieties onto Christ who loves me. I commit myself to yield no longer to substance abuse, but instead I choose to allow the Holy Spirit to direct and empower me. In Jesus' name, amen.

After you have confessed all known sin, pray:

Lord,

I now confess these sins to You and claim through the blood of the Lord Jesus Christ my forgiveness and cleansing. I cancel out all ground that evil spirits have gained through my willful involvement in sin. I pray this in the wonderful name of my Lord and Savior, Jesus Christ. Amen.

STEP 7

Curses vs. Blessings

The next Step to freedom is to renounce the sins of your ancestors, as well as any curses that may have been placed on you by deceived and evil people or groups.

In giving the Ten Commandments, God said, "You shall not make for yourself an idol in the form of anything in heaven above or on the earth beneath or in the waters below. You shall not bow down to them or worship them; for I, the LORD your God, am a jealous God, punishing the children for the sins of the fathers to the third and fourth generations of those who hate me, but showing love to a thousand generations of those who love me and keep my commandments" (Exodus 20:4-6).

Demonic or familiar spirits can be passed on from one generation to the next if you don't renounce the sins of your ancestors and claim your new spiritual heritage in Christ. You are not guilty for the sin of any ancestor, but because of their sin, Satan may have gained access to your family.

Some problems, of course, are hereditary or acquired from an immoral environment. But some problems are the result of generational sin. All three conditions can contribute toward causing someone to struggle with a particular sin.

Ask the Lord to show you specifically what sins are characteristic of your family by praying the following prayer. Then list those sins in the space provided below.

Dear Heavenly Father,
I ask You to reveal to my mind now all the sins of my fathers that are being passed down through family lines. I want to be free from those influences and walk in my new identity as a child of God. In Jesus' name, amen.

As the Lord brings those areas of family sin to your mind, list them. You will be specifically renouncing them later in this Step.

1. _____
2. _____
3. _____
4. _____
5. _____

6. _____
7. _____
8. _____
9. _____
10. _____

In order to walk free from the sins of your ancestors and any curses and assignments targeted against you, read the following declaration and pray the following prayer aloud. Remember, you have all the authority and protection you need in Christ to take your stand against such activity.

DECLARATION

I here and now reject and disown all the sins of my ancestors. I specifically renounce the sins of
<u>   (list here the areas of family sin the Lord revealed to you)   </u>. As one who has now
been delivered from the domain of darkness into the kingdom of God's Son, I cancel out all
demonic working that has been passed down to me from my family. As one who has been crucified and raised with Jesus Christ and who sits with Him in heavenly places, I renounce all satanic assignments that are directed toward me and my ministry. I cancel out every curse that Satan
and his workers have put on me. I announce to Satan and all his forces that Christ became a curse
for me when He died for my sins on the cross (see Galatians 3:13). I reject any and every way in
which Satan may claim ownership of me. I belong to the Lord Jesus Christ who purchased me with
His own blood. I reject all blood sacrifices whereby Satan may claim ownership of me. I declare
myself to be fully and eternally signed over and committed to the Lord Jesus Christ. By the
authority I have in Christ, I now command every familiar spirit and every enemy of the Lord Jesus
that is influencing me to leave my presence. I commit myself to my heavenly Father to do His will
from this day forward.

PRAYER

Dear Heavenly Father,
    I come to You as Your child, bought out of slavery to sin by the blood of the Lord Jesus Christ.
You are the Lord of the universe and the Lord of my life. I submit my body to You as an instrument of righteousness, a living and holy sacrifice that I may glorify You in my body. I now ask You
to fill me with the Holy Spirit. I commit myself to the renewing of my mind in order to prove that
Your will is good, acceptable and perfect for me. All this I pray in the name and authority of the
risen Lord Jesus Christ. Amen.

Even after finding freedom in Christ by going through these seven steps, you may still be attacked by demonic influences trying to regain control of your mind hours, days or even weeks later. But you don't have to let
them. As you continue to walk in humble submission to God, you can resist the devil and he *will* flee from
you (see James 4:7).

The devil is attracted to sin like flies are attracted to garbage. Get rid of the garbage and the flies will depart
for smellier places. In the same way, walk in the truth, confessing all sin and forgiving those who hurt you, and
the devil will have no place in your life to set up shop.

Realize that one victory does not mean the battles are over. Freedom must be maintained. After completing
these steps to freedom, one happy lady asked, "Will I always be like this?" I told her she would stay free as
long as she remained in right relationship with God. "Even if you slip and fall," I encouraged, "you know how
to get right with God again."

One victim of horrible atrocities shared this illustration: "It's like being forced to play a game with an ugly
stranger in my own home. I kept losing and wanted to quit but the ugly stranger wouldn't let me. Finally, I
called the police (a higher authority) and they came and escorted the stranger out. He knocked on the door
trying to regain entry, but this time I recognized his voice and didn't let him in."

What a beautiful picture of gaining and keeping your freedom in Christ! We call upon Jesus, the ultimate
authority, and He escorts the enemy of our souls out of our lives.

Maintaining Your Freedom

Your freedom must be maintained. We cannot emphasize that enough. You have won a very important battle in an ongoing war. Freedom will continue to be yours as long as you keep choosing the truth and standing firm in the strength of the Lord.

If you become aware of lies you have believed, renounce them and choose the truth. If new, painful memories surface, forgive those who hurt you. If the Lord shows you other areas of sin in your life, confess those promptly. This tool can serve as a constant guide for you in dealing with the things God points out to you. Some people have found it helpful to walk through the Steps to Freedom in Christ again. As you do, read the instructions carefully.

For your encouragement and growth, read *Victory over the Darkness* (or the youth version *Stomping Out the Darkness*), *The Bondage Breaker* (adult or youth version), *Walking in the Light* (or the youth version *Know Light, No Fear*) and *Living Free in Christ*.

To maintain your freedom in Christ, we strongly suggest the following as well:

1. Be involved in a loving, caring church fellowship where you can be open and honest with others and where God's truth is taught with grace.

2. Read and meditate on the Bible daily. Memorize key verses from the Steps to Freedom in Christ. You may want to read the Statement of Truth (in Step Two on pages 52-53) aloud daily and study the verses in it.

3. Learn to take every thought captive to the obedience of Christ. Assume responsibility for your thought life. Don't let your mind become passive. Reject all lies, choose to focus on the truth and stand firm in your true identity as a child of God in Christ.

4. Don't drift back to old patterns of thinking, feeling and acting. This can happen very easily if you become spiritually and mentally lazy. If you are struggling with walking in the truth, share your battles openly with a trusted friend who will pray for you and encourage you to stand firm.

5. Don't expect other people to fight your battles for you, however. They can help you, but they can't think, pray, read the Bible or choose the truth for you.

6. Commit yourself to daily prayer. Prayer demonstrates a life of trusting in and depending on God. You can pray the following prayers often and with confidence. Let the words come from your heart as well as your lips and feel free to change them to make *our* prayers *your* prayers.

DAILY PRAYER AND DECLARATION

Dear Heavenly Father,

I praise You and honor You as my Lord. You are in control of all things. I thank You that You are always with me and will never leave me nor forsake me. You are the only all-powerful and only wise God. You are kind and loving in all Your ways. I love You and thank You that I am united with Christ and spiritually alive in Him. I choose not to love the world or the things in the world, and I crucify the flesh and all its passions.

Thank You for the life I now have in Christ. I ask You to fill me with the Holy Spirit so I may say no to sin and yes to You. I declare my total dependence upon You and I take my stand against Satan and all his lying ways. I choose to believe the truth of God's Word despite what my feelings may say. I refuse to be discouraged because You are the God of all hope. Nothing is too difficult for You. I am confident that You will supply all my needs as I seek to live according to Your Word. I thank You that I can be content and live a responsible life through Christ who strengthens me.

I now take my stand against Satan and command him and all his evil spirits to depart from me. I choose to put on the full armor of God so I may be able to stand firm against all the devil's schemes. I submit my body as a living and holy sacrifice to God and I choose to renew my mind by the living Word of God. By so doing I will be able to prove that the will of God is good, acceptable and perfect for me. In the name of my Lord and Savior, Jesus Christ, amen.

BEDTIME PRAYER

Thank You, Lord, that You have brought me into Your family and have blessed me with every spiritual blessing in the heavenly places in Christ Jesus. Thank You for this time of renewal and refreshment through sleep. I accept it as one of Your blessings for Your children and I trust You to guard my mind and my body during my sleep.

As I have thought about You and Your truth during the day, I choose to let those good thoughts continue in my mind while I am asleep. I commit myself to You for Your protection against every attempt of Satan and his demons to attack me during sleep. Guard my mind from nightmares. I renounce all fear and cast every anxiety upon You, Lord. I commit myself to You as my rock, my fortress and my strong tower. May Your peace be upon this place of rest now. In the strong name of the Lord Jesus Christ, I pray. Amen.

CLEANSING HOME/APARTMENT/ROOM
After removing and destroying all objects of false worship, pray aloud in every room if necessary:

Heavenly Father,
I acknowledge that You are the Lord of heaven and earth. In Your sovereign power and love, You have given me all things richly to enjoy. Thank You for this place to live. I claim my home as a place of spiritual safety for me (and my family) and protection from all the attacks of the enemy. As a child of God, raised up and seated with Christ in the heavenly places, I command every evil spirit claiming ground in this place, based on the activities of past or present occupants including me, to leave and never return. I renounce all curses and spells directed against this place. I ask You, Heavenly Father, to post Your holy, warring angels around this place to guard it from any and all attempts of the enemy to enter and disturb Your purposes for me (and my family). I thank You, Lord, for doing this in the name of the Lord Jesus Christ, amen.

LIVING IN A NON-CHRISTIAN ENVIRONMENT
After removing and destroying all objects of false worship from your possession, pray aloud in the place where you live:

Thank You, Heavenly Father, for a place to live and to be renewed by sleep. I ask You to set aside my room (my portion of this room) as a place of spiritual safety for me. I renounce any allegiance given to false gods or spirits by other occupants. I renounce any claim to this room (space) by

Satan based on the activities of past or present occupants, including me. On the basis of my position as a child of God and joint heir with Christ who has all authority in heaven and on earth, I command all evil spirits to leave this place and never return. I ask You, Heavenly Father, to station Your holy, warring angels to protect me while I live here. In Jesus' mighty name, I pray. Amen.

Continue to walk in the truth that your identity and sense of worth comes through who you are in Christ. Renew your mind with the truth that your *acceptance, security* and *significance* are in Christ alone.

We recommend that you meditate on the following truths daily, perhaps reading the entire list aloud, morning and evening, for the next few weeks. Think about what you are reading and let your heart rejoice in the truth.

In Christ

I renounce the lie that I am rejected, unloved, dirty or shameful
because IN CHRIST I am completely accepted. God says…

John 1:12	I am God's child.
John 15:15	I am Christ's friend.
Romans 5:1	I have been justified.
1 Corinthians 6:17	I am united with the Lord and I am one spirit with Him.
1 Corinthians 6:19,20	I have been bought with a price. I belong to God.
1 Corinthians 12:27	I am a member of Christ's Body.
Ephesians 1:1	I am a saint, a holy one.
Ephesians 1:5	I have been adopted as God's child.
Ephesians 2:18	I have direct access to God through the Holy Spirit.
Colossians 1:14	I have been redeemed and forgiven of all my sins.
Colossians 2:10	I am complete in Christ.

I renounce the lie that I am guilty, unprotected, alone or abandoned
because IN CHRIST I am totally secure. God says…

Romans 8:1,2	I am free forever from condemnation.
Romans 8:28	I am assured that all things work together for good.
Romans 8:31-34	I am free from any condemning charges against me.
Romans 8:35-39	I cannot be separated from the love of God.
2 Corinthians 1:21,22	I have been established, anointed and sealed by God.
Philippians 1:6	I am confident that the good work God has begun in me will be perfected.
Philippians 3:20	I am a citizen of heaven.
Colossians 3:3	I am hidden with Christ in God.
2 Timothy 1:7	I have not been given a spirit of fear, but of power, love and a sound mind.
Hebrews 4:16	I can find grace and mercy to help in time of need.
1 John 5:18	I am born of God and the evil one cannot touch me.

I renounce the lie that I am worthless, inadequate, helpless or hopeless
because IN CHRIST I am deeply significant. God says…

Matthew 5:13,14	I am the salt of the earth and the light of the world.
John 15:1,5	I am a branch of the true vine, Jesus, a channel of His life.
John 15:16	I have been chosen and appointed by God to bear fruit.
Acts 1:8	I am a personal, Spirit-empowered witness of Christ.
1 Corinthians 3:16	I am a temple of God.
2 Corinthians 5:17-21	I am a minister of reconciliation for God.
2 Corinthians 6:1	I am God's coworker.
Ephesians 2:6	I am seated with Christ in the heavenly realm.
Ephesians 2:10	I am God's workmanship, created for good works.
Ephesians 3:12	I may approach God with freedom and confidence.
Philippians 4:13	I can do all things through Christ who strengthens me!

I am not the great "I Am" of Exodus 3:14; John 8:24,28,58,
"but by the grace of God I am what I am" (1 Corinthians 15:10).

Seeking the Forgiveness of Others

"Therefore, if you are offering your gift at the altar and there remember that your brother has something against you, leave your gift there in front of the altar. First go and be reconciled to your brother; then come and offer your gift. Settle matters quickly with your adversary who is taking you to court. Do it while you are still with him on the way, or he may hand you over to the judge, and the judge may hand you over to the officer, and you may be thrown into prison. I tell you the truth, you will not get out until you have paid the last penny." Matthew 5:23-26

Verse 24

 STOP: "Leave your gift there in front of the altar"

 GO: "First go"

 YIELD: "And be reconciled to your brother"

 U-TURN: "Then come and offer your gift."

THE MOTIVATION FOR SEEKING FORGIVENESS

Matthew 5:23-26 is the key passage on seeking forgiveness. Several points in these verses bear emphasizing:

The worshiper, coming before God to offer a gift, remembers that someone has something against him. The Holy Spirit is the One who brings to his mind the wrong he has done.

Only the actions that have hurt other people need to be confessed to them. If you have had jealous, lustful or angry thoughts toward others which they don't know about, these are to be confessed to God alone.

An exception to this principle occurs when restitution needs to be made. If you stole or broke something, damaged someone's reputation, etc., you need to go to that person and make it right even if he or she is unaware of what you did.

THE PROCESS OF SEEKING FORGIVENESS

1. Write out what you did wrong and why you did it.

2. Make sure you have already forgiven that person for whatever he or she may have done to you.

3. Think through exactly how you will ask him or her to forgive you. Be sure to:

    a. Label your action as "wrong."

    b. Be specific and admit what you did.

    c. Make no defenses or excuses.

    d. Do not blame the other, and do not expect or demand that he or she ask you for your forgiveness.

    e. Your confession should lead to the direct question: "Will you forgive me?"

4. Seek the right place and the right time to approach the offended person.

5. Ask for forgiveness in person with anyone with whom you can talk face-to-face with the following exception: DO NOT go alone when your safety is in danger.

6. Except where no other means of communication is possible, DO NOT write a letter.

    a. A letter can be very easily misread or misunderstood.

b. A letter can be read by the wrong people, those having nothing to do with the offense or the confession.

c. A letter can be kept when it should have been destroyed.

7. Once you sincerely seek forgiveness, you are free, whether the other person forgives you or not (see Romans 12:18).

8. After forgiveness, fellowship with God in worship (see Matthew 5:24).

Additional resources to be used with the Steps for young adults:
See the bibliography for complete information on each resource.

Books:

Victory over the Darkness and *Study Guide*

Living Free in Christ

Daily in Christ

Breaking Through to Spiritual Maturity

The Bondage Breaker and *Study Guide*

Spiritual Warfare

Know Light, No Fear

Leading Teens to Freedom in Christ

Audio/Visual Series:

"Free in Christ"

"Resolving Personal Conflicts"

"Resolving Spiritual Conflicts"

The only way to solve personal and spiritual problems is through our belief in the finished work of Jesus Christ. He alone can meet our deepest needs of life—acceptance, identity, security and significance.

Rather than being another counseling technique, these Steps are meant to be an encounter with God. They are a tool to help you submit to God and resist the devil so you can live a fruitful life by recognizing who you are in Christ.

Many Christians will be able to work through these Steps on their own, but even this experience would be greatly enhanced if you first read *Stomping Out the Darkness* and *The Bondage Breaker Youth Edition*. This will help you understand the reality of the spiritual world and your relationship to it, something with which our western world is often unfamiliar.

Others will need assistance in working through these Steps because of the battle that is going on for their minds. The process of taking others through the Steps to Freedom in Christ is explained in the book *Leading Teens to Freedom in Christ*. Another person can support you in prayer as you work through the issues of applying the wisdom of James 5:16: "Therefore confess your sins to each other, and pray for each other so that you may be healed. The prayer of a righteous man is powerful and effective."

Spiritual freedom is meant for every Christian, young or old. Being "free in Christ" is to have the desire and power to worship God and do His will. It is to know God's truth, believe God's truth and live according to God's truth. It is to walk with God in the power of the Holy Spirit and to experience a life of love, joy and peace. It is not a life of perfection, but progress! All these qualities may not be yours now, but they are meant for everyone who is in Christ.

If you have received Christ as your Savior, He has already set you free through His victory over sin and death on the cross. However, experiencing our freedom in Christ through repentance and faith and maintaining our life of freedom in Christ are two different issues. Establishing people free in Christ makes it possible for them to walk by faith according to what God says is true and live by the power of the Holy Spirit and not carry out the desires of the sinful nature (see Galatians 5:16). But if freedom is not a constant reality for you, it may be because you do not understand how Christ can help you deal with the pain of your past or the problems of your present life. It is your responsibility as one who knows Christ to do whatever is needed to maintain a right relationship with God and others. Your eternal life is not at stake; you are safe and secure in Christ. But your daily victory is at stake if you fail to understand who you are in Christ and live according to that truth.

We've got great news for you! You are not a helpless victim caught between two nearly equal but opposite heavenly superpowers, God and Satan. Only God is all-powerful, always-present and all-knowing. Sometimes, however, the presence and power of sin and evil in our lives can seem more real to us than the presence and power of God. But that is part of Satan's tricky lie. Satan is a deceiver, and he wants you to think he is stronger than he really is. But he is also a defeated enemy and you are, in Christ, the victor. Understanding who God is and who you are in Christ are the two most important factors in determining your daily victory over sin and Satan. The greatest causes of spiritual defeat are false beliefs about God, not understanding who you are as a child of God and making Satan out to be as powerful and present as God is.

The battle is for your mind. You may experience nagging thoughts like, *This isn't going to work* or *God doesn't love me*. These thoughts are lies, implanted in your mind by deceiving spirits. If you believe them, you will really struggle as you work through these Steps. These opposing thoughts can control you only if you believe them.

If you are working through these Steps by yourself, don't pay attention to any lying or threatening thoughts in your mind. If you're working through the Steps with a youth pastor, pastor or counselor (which we strongly recommend), then share any opposing thought with that person. Whenever you uncover a lie and choose to believe the truth, the power of Satan is broken.

You must cooperate with the person who is trying to help you. Do this by sharing what is going on inside your mind. Also, if you experience any physical discomfort (e.g., headache, nausea, tightness in the throat, etc.), don't be alarmed. Just tell the person you are with so he/she can pray for you.

As believers in Christ, we can pray with authority to stop any interference by Satan. Here is a prayer and declaration to get you started. All prayers and declarations throughout the Steps should be read aloud.

Prayer:

Dear Heavenly Father,

We know that You are always here and present in our lives. You are the only all-knowing, all-powerful, ever-present God. We desperately need You, because without Jesus we can do nothing. We believe the Bible because it tells us what is really true. We refuse to believe the lies of Satan. We stand in the truth that all authority in heaven and on earth has been given to the resurrected Christ. Because we are in Christ, we share His authority in order to make followers of Jesus and set captives free. We ask You to protect our thoughts and minds and lead us into all truth. We choose to submit to the Holy Spirit. Please reveal to our minds everything You want to deal with today. We ask for and trust in Your wisdom. We pray for Your complete protection over us. In Jesus' name, amen.

Declaration:

In the name and the authority of the Lord Jesus Christ, we command Satan and all evil spirits to let go of _____(name)_____ in order that _____(name)_____ can be free to know and choose to do the will of God. As children of God, seated with Christ in the heavenlies, we agree that every enemy of the Lord Jesus Christ be bound to silence. We say to Satan and all of his evil workers that you cannot inflict any pain or in any way stop or hinder God's will from being done today in _____(name's)_____ life.

Here are seven steps to help you be free from your past. You will cover the areas where Satan most often takes advantage of us and where strongholds have been built. Christ purchased your victory when He shed His blood for you on the cross. You will experience your freedom when you make the choice to believe, confess, forgive, renounce and forsake. No one can do that for you. The battle for your mind can only be won as you *personally* choose truth.

As you go through these Steps to Freedom in Christ, remember that Satan cannot read your mind; thus he won't obey your thoughts. Only God knows what you are thinking. As you go through each Step, it is important that you submit to God inwardly and resist the devil by reading *aloud* each prayer—verbally renouncing, forgiving, confessing, etc.

You are going to be taking a thorough look at your life in order to get radically right with God. If it turns out that you have another kind of problem that is negatively affecting your life and is not covered in these Steps, you will have lost nothing. If you are open and honest during this time, you will greatly benefit anyway by becoming right with God and close to Him again.

May the Lord greatly touch your life during this time. He will give you the strength to make it through. It is essential that you work through *all* seven Steps, so don't allow yourself to become discouraged and give up. Remember, the freedom that Christ purchased for all believers on the cross is meant for *you*!

Note: If you are taking someone through the Steps to Freedom, refer to the supplement section 1: "Preparation for Taking Someone Through the Steps to Freedom" at the end of the youth Steps on pages 100-102. Use the checklist to go over the events of his or her life so that you understand the areas that might need to be dealt with. If a Confidential Personal Inventory (see appendix pp. 225-235) has been completed, you may want to review it at this time.

STEP 1

Counterfeit vs. Real

The first step toward experiencing your freedom in Christ is to renounce—to reject and turn your back on all past, present and future involvement with—any participation in satanic-inspired occult practices, things done in secret or non-Christian religions. You must renounce any activity or group that denies Jesus Christ, offers direction through any source other than the absolute authority of the written Word of God, or requires secret initiations, ceremonies, promises, pacts or covenants. Begin with the following prayer:

Dear Heavenly Father,
I ask You to guard my heart and my mind and to reveal to me anything that I have done or that anyone has done to me which is spiritually wrong. Reveal to my mind any and all involvement I have knowingly or unknowingly had with cult or occult practices, and/or false teachers. I ask this in Jesus' name. Amen.

Even if you took part in something as a game or as a joke, you need to renounce it. Satan will try to take advantage of anything he can in our lives. Even if you just stood by and watched others do it, you need to renounce it. Even if you did it just once and had no idea it was evil, still you need to renounce it. You want to remove any and every possible foothold of Satan in your life.

NON-CHRISTIAN SPIRITUAL EXPERIENCES CHECKLIST

(Please check all those that apply to you.)

- ❑ Out-of-body experience (astral projection)
- ❑ Bloody Mary and other occult games
- ❑ Table or body lifting (Light-as-a-Feather)
- ❑ Magic Eight Ball
- ❑ Ouija board
- ❑ Using spells or curses
- ❑ Chants/mantras
- ❑ Mental control of others
- ❑ Automatic writing
- ❑ Spirit guides
- ❑ Fortune-telling/tarot cards
- ❑ Palm reading/tea leaves
- ❑ Astrology/horoscopes
- ❑ Hypnosis
- ❑ Seances
- ❑ Black or white magic
- ❑ Dungeons and Dragons or other fantasy role-playing games such as Magic
- ❑ Video or computer games involving occult powers or cruel violence
- ❑ Blood pacts or cutting yourself on purpose
- ❑ Objects of worship/good luck charms
- ❑ Superstitions
- ❑ Sexual spirits
- ❑ New Age medicine (use of crystals)
- ❑ Idolizing rock stars, actors/actresses, sports heroes, etc.

- ❑ Masons
- ❑ Christian Science
- ❑ Science of the Mind
- ❑ Science of Creative Intelligence
- ❑ The Way International
- ❑ Unification Church (Moonies)
- ❑ The Forum (EST)
- ❑ Church of the Living Word
- ❑ Children of God (Children of Love)
- ❑ Mormonism
- ❑ Jehovah's Witnesses
- ❑ Scientology
- ❑ Unitarianism
- ❑ Roy Masters
- ❑ Silva Mind Control
- ❑ Transcendental Meditation (TM)
- ❑ Yoga
- ❑ Hare Krishna
- ❑ Hinduism
- ❑ Bahaism
- ❑ New Age
- ❑ Islam
- ❑ Muslim/Black Muslim
- ❑ Martial arts involving Eastern mysticism, meditation or devotion to sensei
- ❑ Buddhism, including Zen
- ❑ Rosicrucianism
- ❑ Native American spirit worship
- ❑ Other_____

NOTE: This is not a complete list. If you have any doubts about an activity not included here, renounce your involvement in it. If it has come to mind here, trust that the Lord wants you to renounce it.

List below those things that especially glorified Satan, caused fear or nightmares, or were gruesomely violent.

Anti-Christian Movies   **Anti-Christian Music**

Anti-Christian TV Shows or Video Games   **Anti-Christian Books, Magazines and Comics**

1. Have you ever heard, seen or felt an evil spiritual presence in your room or somewhere else?

2. Do you or have you had an imaginary friend, spirit guide or angel offering you guidance and companionship?

3. Have you ever heard voices in your head or had repeating negative, nagging thoughts such as *I'm dumb, I'm ugly, Nobody loves me, I can't do anything right*, etc. as if a conversation were going on in your head? Explain.

4. Have you ever consulted a medium, spiritist or channeler?

5. What other spiritual experiences have you had that would be considered out of the ordinary—know something supernaturally, special spiritual gifts, contact with aliens, etc.?

6. Have you ever been involved in satanic worship of any kind or attended a concert at which Satan was the focus?

7. Have you ever made a vow or pact?

Once you have completed the above checklist, confess and renounce each item you were involved in by praying aloud the following prayer, repeating the prayer separately for each item on your list:

Lord,
    I confess that I have participated in _____. I renounce any and all influence and involvement with _____ and thank you that in Christ I am forgiven.

Note to parent or counselor: If the individual you are leading through the Steps to Freedom has ever been involved in any satanic ritual or heavy occult activity (or you suspect it because of blocked memories, severe and recurring nightmares or severe sexual bondage), guide that person through the renunciations and affirmations found in the supplement section 2 at the end of the youth Steps on page 103.

STEP 2

Deception vs. Truth

God's Word is true, and we need to accept the truth deep in our hearts (see Psalm 51:6). What God says is true whether we feel it is true or not!

Jesus is the truth (see John 14:6), the Holy Spirit is the Spirit of truth (see John 16:13), and the Word of God is truth (see John 17:17). We ought to speak the truth in love (see Ephesians 4:15). The believer in Christ has no business deceiving others either by lying, exaggerating, telling little lies or stretching the truth. Satan is the father of lies (see John 8:44) and he seeks to keep people in bondage through deception (see Revelation 12:9; 2 Timothy 2:26), but it is the truth in Jesus that sets us free (see John 8:32-36).

We will find real joy and freedom when we stop living a lie and walk openly in the truth. King David wrote, after confessing his sin, "Blessed is the man...in whose spirit is no deceit" (Psalm 32:2).

How can we find the strength to walk in the light (see 1 John 1:7-9)? When we are sure that God loves and accepts us, we can be free to own up to our sin, face reality and not run or hide from painful circumstances.

Start this step by praying the following prayer aloud. Don't let any opposing thoughts such as, *This is a waste of time* or *I wish I could believe this stuff but I just can't* keep you from praying and choosing the truth. Belief is a choice. If you choose to believe what you feel, then Satan, the father of lies, will keep you in bondage. You must choose to believe what God says, regardless of what your feelings might say. Even if you have a hard time doing so, pray the following prayer:

Dear Heavenly Father,

I know You want me to face the truth, and that I must be honest with You. I know that choosing to believe the truth will set me free. I have been deceived by Satan and I have deceived myself. I thought I could hide from You, but You see everything and still love me. I pray in the name of the Lord Jesus Christ, asking You to rebuke all of Satan's demons that are deceiving me. By faith I have received You into my life and am now seated with Christ in the heavenlies (see Ephesians 2:6). I acknowledge that I have the responsibility to submit to You and the authority to resist the devil and when I do, he will flee from me (see James 4:7).

Since You accept me just as I am in Christ, I can be free to face my sin. I ask for the Holy Spirit to guide me into all truth. I ask You to "Search me, O God, and know my heart; test me and know my anxious thoughts. See if there is any offensive way in me, and lead me in the way everlasting" (Psalm 139:23,24). In the name of Jesus, I pray. Amen.

There are many ways in which Satan, the god of this world (see 2 Corinthians 4:4), seeks to deceive us. Just as he did with Eve, the devil tries to convince us to rely on ourselves and to try to get our needs met through the world around us, rather than trusting in our Father in heaven. Place a check beside each type of deception that applies to you:

Ways You Can Be Deceived by the World

❏ Believing that accumulating money and possessions will bring happiness (see Matthew 13:22; 1 Timothy 6:10)
❏ Believing that eating food and drinking alcohol without restraint will make you happy (see Proverbs 20:1; 23:19-21)
❏ Believing that a sexy, attractive body and personality will get you what you want or need (see Proverbs 31:10; 1 Peter 3:3,4)
❏ Believing that gratifying sexual lust will bring true fulfillment (see Ephesians 4:22; 1 Peter 2:11)

❑ Believing that you can sin and get away with it and not have it affect your heart and character (see Hebrews 3:12,13)

❑ Believing that your needs cannot be totally taken care of by God (see 2 Corinthians 11:2-4,13-15)

❑ Believing that you are important and strong, you can do whatever you want and no one can touch you (see Obadiah 3; 1 Peter 5:5; Proverbs 16:18)

Use the following prayer of confession for each item that you have believed. Pray through each item separately.

> Lord,
> I confess that I have been deceived by _____. I thank You for Your forgiveness and I commit myself to believing only Your truth. Amen.

It is important to know that in addition to being deceived by the world, false teachers and deceiving spirits, you can also fool yourself. Now that you are alive in Christ, forgiven and totally accepted, you don't need to live a lie or defend yourself like you used to. Christ is now your truth and defense. Check each of the following statements that apply to your life.

Ways You Can Deceive Yourself

❑ Hearing God's Word but not always doing it (see James 1:22; 4:7)

❑ Saying you have no sin (see 1 John 1:8)

❑ Thinking you are something you're not (see Galatians 6:3)

❑ Thinking you are wise in the things of the world (see 1 Corinthians 3:18,19)

❑ Thinking you can be a good Christian and still hurt others by what you say (see James 1:22)

❑ Thinking your secret sin—such as pornography, voyeurism, hatred, etc.—will only hurt you and will not hurt others (see Exodus 20:4,5)

Use the following prayer of confession for each item above that you have believed. Pray through each item separately.

> Lord,
> I confess that I have deceived myself by _____. I thank You for Your forgiveness and commit myself to believing Your truth.

Wrong Ways of Defending Yourself

❑ Refusing to face the bad things that have happened to you (denial of reality)

❑ Escaping from the real world through daydreaming, TV, movies, computer or video games, music, etc. (fantasy)

❑ Withdrawing from people to avoid rejection (emotional insulation)

❑ Reverting (going back) to a less threatening time of life (regression)

❑ Taking out frustrations on others (displaced anger)

❑ Blaming others for your problems (projection)

❑ Making excuses for poor behavior (rationalization)

Use the following prayer of confession for each item above that you have participated in. Pray through each item separately.

Lord,

    I confess that I have defended myself wrongly by _____. I thank You for Your forgiveness and commit myself to trusting in You to defend and protect me.

If you are not experiencing that close relationship with your heavenly Father, it may be because of lies that you have believed about Him.

> **Note:** For more information on "The Truth About Our Heavenly Father" and "Dealing with Fears" see the supplement sections 3 and 4 at the end of the youth Steps on pages 104-106.

Choosing the truth may be difficult if you have been living a lie and have been deceived for some time. The Christian needs only one defense, Jesus. Knowing that you are completely forgiven and accepted as God's child sets you free to face reality and declare your total dependence upon Him.

Faith is the biblical response to the truth, and believing the truth is a choice we can all make. If you say, "I want to believe God, but I just can't," you are being deceived. Of course you can believe God because what God says is always true.

Faith is something you decide to do, whether or not you feel like doing it. Believing the truth doesn't make it true, however. **It's true; therefore, we believe it.**

The New Age movement twists the truth by saying that we create reality through what we believe. We can't create reality with our minds. We face reality with our minds. Simply "having faith" is not the key issue here. It's what or who you believe in that makes the difference. You see, everybody believes in something and everybody lives according to what he or she believes. The question is: Is the object of your faith trustworthy? If what you believe is not true, then how you live will not be right.

For centuries, Christians have known that it is important to tell others what they believe. Read aloud the following Statements of Truth, thinking about the words as you read them. Read it every day for several weeks. This will help you renew your mind and replace any lies you have believed with the truth.

STATEMENTS OF TRUTH

I believe there is only one true and living God (see Exodus 20:2,3) who is the Father, Son and Holy Spirit. He is worthy of all honor, praise and glory. I believe that He made all things and holds all things together (see Colossians 1:16,17).

I recognize Jesus Christ as the Messiah, the Word who became flesh and lived with us (see John 1:1,14). I believe He came to destroy the works of Satan (see 1 John 3:8), that He disarmed the rulers and authorities and made a public display of them, having triumphed over them (see Colossians 2:15).

I believe that God showed His love for me by having Jesus die for me, even though I was sinful (see Romans 5:8). I believe that God rescued me from the dark power of Satan and brought me into the kingdom of His Son, who forgives my sins and sets me free (see Colossians 1:13,14).

I believe I am spiritually strong because Jesus is my strength. I have authority to stand against Satan because I am God's child (see 1 John 3:1-3). I believe that I was saved by the grace of God through faith, that it was a gift and not the result of any works of mine (see Ephesians 2:8,9).

I choose to be strong in the Lord and in the strength of His might (see Ephesians 6:10). I put no confidence in the flesh (see Philippians 3:3) because my weapons of spiritual battle are not of the flesh but are powerful through God for the tearing down of Satan's strongholds (see 2 Corinthians 10:4). I put on the whole armor of God (see Ephesians 6:10-20), and I resolve to stand firm in my faith and resist the evil one (see 1 Peter 5:8,9).

I believe that apart from Christ I can do nothing (see John 15:5), yet I can do all things through Him who strengthens me (see Philippians 4:13). Therefore, I choose to rely totally on Christ. I choose to abide in Christ in order to bear much fruit and glorify the Lord (see John 15:8). I announce to Satan that Jesus is my Lord (see 1 Corinthians 12:3), and I reject any counterfeit gifts or works of Satan in my life.

I believe that the truth will set me free (see John 8:32). I stand against Satan's lies by taking every thought captive in obedience to Christ (see 2 Corinthians 10:5). I believe that the Bible is the only reliable guide for my life (see 2 Timothy 3:15,16). I choose to speak the truth in love (see Ephesians 4:15).

I choose to present my body as an instrument of righteousness, a living and holy sacrifice, and to renew my mind with God's Word (see Romans 6:13; 12:1,2). I put off the old self with its evil practices and put on the new self (see Colossians 3:9,10). I am a new creation in Christ (see 2 Corinthians 5:17).

I trust my Heavenly Father to direct my life and give me power to live by the Holy Spirit (see Ephesians 5:18), so that He can guide me into all truth (see John 16:13). I believe He will give me strength to live above sin and not carry out the desires of my flesh. I crucify the flesh, choose to be led by the Holy Spirit and obey Him (see Galatians 5:16,24).

I renounce all selfish goals and choose the greatest goal of love (see 1 Timothy 1:5). I choose to obey the two greatest commandments: to love the Lord my God with all my heart, soul, and mind and to love my neighbor as myself (see Matthew 22:37-39).

I believe that Jesus has all authority in heaven and on earth (see Matthew 28:18) and that He rules over everything (see Colossians 2:10). I believe that Satan and his demons have been defeated by Christ and are subject to me since I am a member of Christ's Body (see Ephesians 1:19,20; 2:6). Therefore, I obey the command to submit to God and to resist the devil (see James 4:7) and I command Satan, by the authority of the Lord Jesus Christ, to leave my presence.

STEP 3

Bitterness vs. Forgiveness

When you fail to forgive those who hurt you, you become a wide-open target for Satan. God commands us to forgive others as we have been forgiven (see Ephesians 4:32). You need to obey this command so that Satan can't take advantage of you (see 2 Corinthians 2:10,11). Christians are to forgive others and show them mercy because our heavenly Father has shown mercy to us (see Luke 6:36). Ask God to bring to your mind the names of those people you need to forgive by praying the following prayer aloud. Remember to let this prayer come from your heart as well as your mouth!

Dear Heavenly Father,
I thank You for Your great kindness and patience which has led me to turn from my sins (see Romans 2:4). I know I have not always been completely kind, patient and loving toward those who have hurt me. I have had bad thoughts and feelings toward them. I ask You to bring to my mind all the people I need to forgive (see Matthew 18:35). I ask You to bring to the surface all my painful memories so I can choose to forgive these people from my heart. I pray this in the precious name of Jesus who has forgiven me and who will heal me from my hurts. Amen.

On a sheet of paper, make a list of the people who come to your mind. At this point, don't question whether you need to forgive a certain person or not. If a name comes to your mind, write it down.

Finally, write "myself" at the bottom of the list. Forgiving yourself means accepting God's cleansing and forgiveness. Also write "thoughts against God." We sometimes harbor angry thoughts toward God. We can expect or even demand that He act in a certain way in our lives, and when He doesn't do what we want in the way we want, we can get angry. Those feelings can become a wall between us and God, and even though we don't actually need to forgive Him because He is perfect, we do need to let those feelings go.

Forgiveness is not forgetting. People who want to be able to forget all their pain before they get around to forgiving others usually find they cannot. God commands us to forgive now. Confusion sometimes arises because Scripture says that God will remember our sins no more (see Hebrews 10:17). But God knows everything and can't forget as if He had no memory of our sin. His promise is that He will never use our past against us (see Psalm 103:10). The key issue is this: We may not be able to forget our past, but we can be free from it by forgiving others. When we bring up the past and use it against others, we are showing that we have not yet forgiven them (see Mark 11:25).

Forgiveness is a choice, a decision of the will. Since God requires us to forgive, it is something we can do. Forgiveness seems hard because it pulls against our sense of what is right and fair. We naturally want revenge for the things we have suffered. But we are told by God never to take our own revenge (see Romans 12:19). You might be thinking *Why should I let them off the hook?* And that is exactly the problem! As long as you do not forgive, you are still hooked to those who hurt you! You are still chained to your past. **By forgiving, you let them off your hook, but they are not off God's hook.** We must trust Him to deal with the other person justly, fairly and mercifully—something we cannot do.

You say, "But you don't know how much this person hurt me." But until you let go of your hate and anger, they will continue to be able to hurt you. You finally stop the pain by forgiving them. **You forgive for your sake, so that you can be free. Forgiveness is mainly an issue of obedience between you and God. God wants you to be free; this is the only way.**

Forgiveness is agreeing to live with the consequences of another person's sin. Forgiveness costs you something. You choose to pay the price for the evil you forgive. **But you will live with the consequences whether you want to or not. Your only choice is whether you will do so in the bondage of bitterness or in the freedom of forgiveness.** Of course, Jesus took the eternal consequences of all sin upon Himself. God "made him who had no sin to be sin for us, so that in him we might become the righteousness of God" (2 Corinthians 5:21). We need, however, to accept the temporary consequences of what was done to us. But no one truly forgives without suffering the pain of another's sin. That can seem unfair and we wonder, where is the justice? It is found at the Cross, which makes forgiveness legally and morally right. As those who crucified Jesus mocked and jeered, Jesus prayed, "Father, forgive them, for they do not know what they are doing" (Luke 23:34).

How do you forgive from your heart? You allow God to bring to the surface the mental agony, emotional pain and feelings of hurt towards those who hurt you. If your forgiveness does not reach down to the emotional core of your life, it will be incomplete. Too often we try to bury the pain inside us, making it hard to get in touch with how we really feel. Though we may not know how to or even want to bring our feelings to the surface, God does. Let God bring the pain to the surface so that He can deal with it. This is where God's gentle healing process begins.

Forgiveness is the decision not to use their offenses against them. It is not unusual for us to remember a past, hurtful event and find the anger and hate we felt returning. It is tempting to bring up the issue with the one who hurt us in order to make that person feel bad. But we must choose to take that thought of revenge captive to the obedience of Christ and choose to maintain forgiveness. This doesn't mean that you must continue to put up with the future sins of others. God does not tolerate sin and neither should you. Nor should you put yourself in the position of being continually abused and hurt by the sins of others. You need to take a stand against sin while continuing to forgive those who hurt you.

Don't wait to forgive until you feel like forgiving. You will never get there. Your emotions will begin to heal once you have obeyed God's command to forgive. Satan will have lost his power over you in that area, and God's healing touch will take over. **For now, it is freedom that will be gained, not necessarily a feeling.**

As you pray, God may bring to mind painful memories that you had totally forgotten. Let Him do this, even if it hurts. God wants you to be free; forgiving these people is the only way. Don't try to excuse the offender's behavior, even if it is someone close to you.

Remember, forgiveness is dealing with your own pain and leaving the other person to deal with God. Good feelings will follow in time. Freeing yourself from the past is the critical issue right now.

Don't say, "Lord, please help me to forgive." He is already helping you and will be with you all the way through the process. Don't say, "Lord, I want to forgive" because that bypasses the hard choice we have to make. Say, "Lord, I forgive." As you move down your list, focus on each individual until you are sure you have dealt with all the remembered pain, everything the person did that hurt you, and how it made you feel: rejected, unloved, unworthy, dirty, etc.

It's time to begin. For each person on your list, pray aloud:

Lord,
I forgive _____(name the person)_____ for _____(say what they did to hurt you; be specific)_____, even though it made me feel _____(share the painful memories or feelings)_____.

Once you have dealt with every offense that has come to your mind and you have honestly expressed how that person hurt you, then conclude by praying:

Lord,
I choose not to hold any of these things against _____(name)_____ any longer. I thank You for setting me free from the bondage of my bitterness toward him/her. I choose now to ask You to bless _____(name)_____. In Jesus' name, amen.

STEP 4

Rebellion vs. Submission

We live in rebellious times. Often young people today don't respect people who God has placed in authority over them. You may have a problem living in submission to authority. You can easily be deceived into thinking that those in authority over you are robbing you of your freedom. In reality, however, God has placed them there for your protection.

Rebelling against God and His authorities is serious business. It gives Satan an opportunity to attack you. Submission is the only solution. God requires more of you, however, than just the outward appearance of submission. He wants you to sincerely submit to your authorities (especially parents) from the heart. Your commanding general, the Lord Jesus Christ, is telling you to "get into ranks and follow Me!" He promises that He will not lead you into temptation, but will deliver you from evil (see Matthew 6:13).

The Bible makes it clear that we have two main responsibilities toward those in authority over us: to pray for them and to submit to them. Pray the following prayer aloud from your heart.

> **Dear Heavenly Father,**
> **You have said in the Bible that rebellion is the same thing as witchcraft, and being self-willed is like serving false gods (see 1 Samuel 15:23). I know that I have disobeyed and rebelled in my heart against You and those You have placed in authority over me. I thank You for Your forgiveness of my rebellion. By the shed blood of the Lord Jesus Christ, I pray that all doors that I opened to evil spirits through my rebellion would now be closed. I pray that You will show me all the ways I have been rebellious. I now choose to adopt a submissive spirit and servant's heart. In Jesus' precious name, I pray. Amen.**

Rebellion will often be expressed through an uncooperative attitude and a critical spirit. The following *actions* are some possibilities of rebellion. Check those that apply to the different authorities in your life.

❑ Refusing to obey or follow legitimate instructions
❑ Ignoring instructions or requirements or adjusting them to suit myself
❑ Believing it is my right to criticize those in authority over me
❑ Making critical statements about authority figures
❑ Rejecting the advice of others who have experience and wisdom
❑ Finding fault easily with a person, group or organization, particularly those in authority
❑ Reading a negative bias into things that others say or do
❑ Passing along negative information to others who are not part of the problem or solution
❑ Withdrawing from communications with others (often shown by short, clipped responses or silence)
❑ Speaking disrespectfully to another person or about another person
❑ Having to have the last words in a conversation

> **Lord,**
> **I agree with You that I have been rebellious by** _____. **Thank you for forgiving me for my rebellion.**

We are all told to submit to one another as equals in Christ (see Ephesians 5:21). In addition, however, God uses specific lines of authority to protect us and give order to our daily lives. Being under authority is an act of faith! By submitting, we are trusting God to work through His lines of authority. Place a check beside any of the following to which you have been rebellious:

❑ Civil government, including traffic laws, drinking laws, etc. (see Romans 13:1-7; 1 Peter 2:13-17)
❑ Parents, stepparents or legal guardians (see Ephesians 6:1-3)
❑ Teachers, coaches and school officials (see Romans 13:1-4)
❑ Your boss (see 1 Peter 2:18-23)
❑ Husband (see 1 Peter 3:1-5) or wife (see Ephesians 5:21; 1 Peter 3:7). **Note to husbands:** Take a moment and ask the Lord if your lack of love for your wife could be fostering a rebellious spirit within her. If so, confess that now as a violation of Ephesians 5:22,23.
❑ Church leaders: pastor, youth pastor, Sunday School teacher (see Hebrews 13:17)
❑ God (see Daniel 9:5,9)

Use the following prayer to ask the Lord to forgive you for those times you have been rebellious in attitude or actions:

> **Lord,**
> **I agree with You that I have been rebellious toward** _____(authority)_____ **by** _____(action)_____. **Thank You for forgiving my rebellion. I choose to be submissive and to treat others with kindness and respect. In Jesus' name, amen.**

At times parents, teachers, employers and other authority figures may abuse their authority and break the laws which are ordained by God for the protection of innocent people. In those cases, you need to seek help from a *higher authority* for your protection. The laws in your state may require you to report such abuse to the police or other protective agencies. If there is continuing abuse—physical, mental, emotional or sexual—at home or anywhere else, counseling may be needed to change the situation. If someone abuses their authority by asking you to break God's law or compromise yourself, you need to obey God rather than man (see Acts 4:19,20).

STEP 5

Pride vs. Humility

Pride is a killer. Pride says, "I can do it! I can get myself out of this mess without God or anyone else's help." Oh no, we can't! We absolutely need God and we desperately need each other. Paul wrote, "For it is we…who worship by the Spirit of God, who glory in Christ Jesus, and who put no confidence in the flesh" (Philippians 3:3).

Humility is confidence properly placed in God. We are to be "strong in the Lord and in his mighty power" (Ephesians 6:10). James 4:6-10 and 1 Peter 5:1-10 tell us that spiritual problems will follow when we are proud. Use the following prayer to express your commitment to live humbly before God:

> **Dear Heavenly Father,**
>
> You have said that pride goes before destruction and an arrogant spirit before a fall (see Proverbs 16:18). I confess that I have been thinking mainly of myself and not of others. I have not denied myself, picked up my cross daily and followed You (see Matthew 16:24). As a result, I have given ground to the enemy in my life. I have believed that I could be successful by living according to my own power and resources.
>
> I now confess that I have sinned against You by placing my will before Yours and by centering my life around myself instead of You. I renounce my pride and my selfishness and close any doors I've opened in my life or physical body to the enemies of the Lord Jesus Christ. I choose to rely on the Holy Spirit's power and guidance so that I can do Your will.
>
> I give my heart to You and stand against all of Satan's attacks. I ask You to show me how to live for others. I now choose to make others more important than me and to make You the most important Person of all in my life (see Romans 12:10; Matthew 6:33). Please show me specifically now the ways in which I have lived pridefully. I ask this in the name of my Lord Jesus Christ. Amen.

Having made that commitment in prayer, now allow God to show you any specific areas of your life where you have been prideful, such as:

- ❑ I have a stronger desire to do my will than God's will.
- ❑ I rely on my own strengths and abilities rather than on God's.
- ❑ I too often think my ideas are better than other people's ideas.
- ❑ I want to control how others act rather than develop self-control.
- ❑ I sometimes consider myself more important than others.
- ❑ I have a tendency to think I don't need other people.
- ❑ I find it difficult to admit when I am wrong.
- ❑ I am more likely to be a people-pleaser than a God-pleaser.
- ❑ I am overly concerned about getting credit for doing good things.
- ❑ I often think I am more humble than others.
- ❑ I often think I am smarter than my parents.
- ❑ I often feel my needs are more important than other people's needs.
- ❑ I consider myself better than others because of my academic, artistic or athletic abilities and accomplishments.
- ❑ Other _____

For each of the above areas that has been true in your life, pray aloud:

> Lord,
>   I agree I have been prideful in the area of _____. Thank You for forgiving me for this pridefulness. I choose to humble myself and place all my confidence in You. Amen.

STEP 6

Bondage vs. Freedom

The next Step to Freedom deals with the sins that have become habits in your life. If you have been caught in the vicious cycle of sin-confess-sin-confess, realize that the road to victory is sin-confess-*resist* (see James 4:7). Habitual sin often requires help from a trusted brother or sister in Christ. James 5:16 says, "Confess your sins to each other and pray for each other so that you may be healed. The prayer of a righteous man is powerful and effective." Seek out a stronger Christian who will lift you up in prayer and hold you accountable in your areas of weakness.

Sometimes the assurance of 1 John 1:9 is sufficient: "If we confess our sins, he is faithful and just and will forgive us our sins and purify us from all unrighteousness."

Remember, confession is not saying "I'm sorry"; it's openly admitting "I did it." Whether you need the help of others or just the accountability to God, pray the following prayer aloud:

> **Dear Heavenly Father,**
> **You have told us to put on the Lord Jesus Christ and not to think about how to gratify sinful desires (see Romans 13:14). I agree that I have given in to sinful desires which wage war against my soul (1 Peter 2:11).**
> **I thank You that in Christ my sins are forgiven, but I have broken Your holy law and given the devil an opportunity to wage war in my body (see Romans 6:12,13; James 4:1; 1 Peter 5:8). I come before Your presence now to admit these sins and to seek Your cleansing (see 1 John 1:9), that I may be freed from the bondage of sin. I now ask You to reveal to my mind the ways that I have broken Your moral law and grieved the Holy Spirit. In Jesus' precious name, I pray. Amen.**

There are many habitual sins that can control us. The following list contains some of the more common sins of the flesh. Look through the following list and ask the Holy Spirit to reveal to your mind which ones from the past or the present you need to confess. He may bring to mind others that are not here. For each one God reveals, pray the following prayer of confession from the heart.

> **Note:** Sexual sins, eating disorders, substance abuse, abortion, suicidal tendencies and perfectionism can be dealt with in the supplement section 5: "Special Prayers for Specific Needs" at the end of the youth Steps on pages 107-108.

❑ Stealing/shoplifting
❑ Lying
❑ Fighting
❑ Quarreling/arguing
❑ Hatred
❑ Jealousy/envy
❑ Anger
❑ Complaining/criticism
❑ Depression/hopelessness

❑ Impure thoughts
❑ Eagerness for lustful pleasure
❑ Cheating
❑ Gossip/slander
❑ Procrastination—putting things off
❑ Swearing
❑ Greed/materialism
❑ Apathy/laziness
❑ Other _____

Lord,
I admit that I have committed the sin of _____. I thank You for
Your forgiveness and cleansing. I turn away from this sin and turn to You, Lord. Strengthen me
by Your Holy Spirit to obey You. In Jesus' name, amen.

It is our responsibility to take control over sin in our bodies. We must not use our bodies or someone else's as
an instrument of unrighteousness (see Romans 6:12,13). If you are or have been struggling with sexual sins
such as pornography, masturbation, heavy petting, heavy kissing, oral sex, same-sex relationships, voyeurism,
phone sex, computer/internet sex or sexual intercourse, pray as follows:

Lord,
I ask You to reveal to my mind every sexual use of my body as an instrument of unrighteousness. In Jesus' precious name, I pray. Amen.

As the Lord brings to your mind every sexual use of your body, whether it was done to you (i.e., rape, incest
or any other form of sexual abuse) or willingly by you, *renounce every occasion*:

Lord,
I renounce _____ (name the specific misuse of your body) _____ with _____ (name
the person involved)_____ and I ask You to break that sinful bond with
_____ (name)_____.

After you have completed this exercise, commit your body to the Lord by praying aloud from your heart:

Lord,
I renounce all these uses of my body as an instrument of unrighteousness and ask you to break
all bondages Satan has brought into my life through my involvement. I admit my participation.
Lord, I choose to present my eyes, my mouth, my mind, my hands and feet, my whole body to You
as instruments of righteousness. I now present my body to You as a living sacrifice, holy and
acceptable to You, and I choose to reserve the sexual use of my body for marriage only (see
Hebrews 13:4).
I reject the lie of Satan that my body is not clean or that it is dirty or in any way unacceptable
to You as a result of my past sexual experiences. Lord, I thank You that You have totally cleansed
and forgiven me and that You love me just as I am. Therefore, I can accept myself and my body as
cleansed in Your eyes. In Jesus' name, amen.

STEP 7

Curses vs. Blessings

The last step to freedom is to renounce the sins of your ancestors and any curses which may have been placed on you. In giving the Ten Commandments, God said, "You shall not make for yourself an idol in the form of anything in heaven above or on the earth beneath or in the waters below. You shall not bow down to them or worship them; for I, the LORD your God, am a jealous God, punishing the children for the sins of the fathers to the third and fourth generation of those who hate me" (Exodus 20:4,5).

Demonic or familiar spirits can be passed on from one generation to the next if you don't renounce the sins of your ancestors and claim your new spiritual heritage in Christ. *You are not guilty for the sin of any ancestor,* but because of their sins, Satan may have gained access to your family.

Some problems, of course, are hereditary or acquired from an immoral environment. But other problems can be the result of generational sin. All three conditions can contribute toward causing someone to struggle with a particular sin.

Ask the Lord to show you specifically what sins are characteristic of your family by praying the following prayer. Then list those sins in the space provided below.

Dear Heavenly Father,
I ask You to reveal to my mind all the sins of my ancestors that are being passed down through family lines. I want to be free from those influences and walk in my new identity as a child of God. Amen.

As the Lord brings those areas of family sins to your mind, list them below.
You will be specifically renouncing them later in this step.

1. _____   3. _____
2. _____   4. _____

In addition, deceived and evil people may try to curse you, or satanic groups may try to target you. You have all the authority and protection you need in Christ to stand against such curses. In order to walk free from the sins of your ancestors and any demonic influences, read the following declaration and pray the following prayer aloud. Let the words come from your heart as you remember the authority you have in Christ Jesus.

DECLARATION

I here and now reject and disown all the sins of my ancestors. I specifically renounce the sins of _____ (list here the areas of family sin the Lord revealed to you) _____. As one who has been delivered from the domain of darkness and placed into the kingdom of God's Son, I cancel out all demonic working that was passed down to me from my family. As one who is crucified and raised with Jesus Christ and who sits with Him in heavenly places, I renounce all satanic assignments that are directed toward me and my ministry. I cancel out every curse that Satan and his workers have put on me. I announce to Satan and all his forces that Christ became a curse for me (see Galatians 3:13) when He died for my sins on the cross. I reject any and every way in which Satan may claim ownership of me.

I belong to the Lord Jesus Christ who purchased me with His own blood. I reject all the blood sacrifices whereby Satan may claim ownership of me. I declare myself to be eternally and completely signed over and committed to the Lord Jesus Christ. By the authority that I have in Jesus Christ, I now command every familiar spirit and every enemy of the Lord Jesus Christ that is influencing me to leave my presence. I commit myself to my Heavenly Father to do His will from this day forward.

PRAYER

Dear Heavenly Father,

I come to You as Your child, purchased by the blood of the Lord Jesus Christ. You are the Lord of the universe and the Lord of my life. I submit my body to You as an instrument of righteousness, a living sacrifice, that I may glorify You in my body. I ask You to fill me with Your Holy Spirit to lead and empower me to know and do Your will. I commit myself to the renewing of my mind in order to prove that Your will is good, perfect and acceptable for me. All this I do in the name and authority of the Lord Jesus Christ. Amen.

Maintaining Your Freedom

Now that you have gone through these seven steps, you may find demonic influences attempting to gain control of your mind again days or even months later. One person shared that she heard a spirit say to her mind, "I'm back" two days after she had been set free. "No, you're not!" she proclaimed aloud. The attack stopped immediately.

The devil is attracted to sin like flies are attracted to garbage. Get rid of the garbage and the flies will depart for smellier places. In the same way, walk in the truth, confessing all sin and forgiving those who hurt you, and the devil will have no place in your life to set up shop.

Realize that one victory does not mean the battles are over. After completing the steps, one happy girl asked, "Will I always be like this?" I told her that she would stay free as long as she remained in right relationship with God. "Even if you slip and fall," I encouraged, "you know how to get right with God again."

One victim of incredible abuse shared this illustration: "It's like being forced to play a game with an ugly stranger in my own home. I kept losing and wanted to quit, but the ugly stranger wouldn't let me. Finally I called the police, a higher authority, and they came and escorted the stranger out. He knocked on the door trying to regain entry, but this time I recognized his voice and didn't let him in."

What a beautiful illustration of gaining freedom in Christ. We call upon Jesus, the final and most powerful authority, and He escorts the powers of darkness out of our lives.

Freedom must be maintained. We cannot emphasize that point enough. You have won a very important battle in an ongoing war. Freedom will remain yours as long as you keep choosing truth and standing firm in the strength of the Lord. If new memories should surface, if you become aware of lies you have believed or other non-Christian experiences you have had, renounce them and choose the truth. If you realize that there are some other people you need to forgive, Step Three will remind you of what to do. Most people have found it helpful to walk through the Steps to Freedom in Christ again. As you do, read the instructions carefully.

We recommend that you read the book *Stomping Out the Darkness* to strengthen your understanding of your identity in Christ. *The Bondage Breaker Youth Edition* will help you overcome spiritual problems. If you struggle with sexual bondage or desire to learn more about friendships and dating, we recommend *Purity Under Pressure*. To maintain your freedom, we strongly suggest the following as well:

- Get involved in a loving church youth group or Bible study where you can be open and honest with other believers your age.

- Study your Bible daily. There are many great youth Bibles around for you to use. Begin to get into God's Word and memorize key verses. Remember it is the *truth that sets you free and it is the truth that keeps you free!* You may want to say the Statements of Truth (on pp. 85-86) aloud daily and study the verses. In addition, the youth devotionals *Extreme Faith, Reality Check, Awesome God* and *Ultimate Love* have been developed especially for you.

- Learn to take every thought captive to the obedience of Christ. Assume responsibility for your thought life. Don't let your mind go passive. Reject all lies, choose to focus on the truth and stand firm in your identity in Christ.

- Don't drift away! It is very easy to become lazy in your thoughts and slip back into old habits or patterns of thinking. Share your struggles openly with a trusted friend who will pray for you.

- Don't expect others to fight your battles for you. They can't and they won't. Others can encourage you, but they can't think, pray, read the Bible or choose the truth for you.

• Commit yourself to daily prayer. Prayer is dependence upon God. You can pray often and with confidence the suggested prayers listed in the supplement section 6: "Prayers" at the end of the youth Steps on pages 109-110.

Additional resources to be used with Youth Steps:
See the bibliography for complete information on each resource.

Books:

Stomping Out the Darkness

The Bondage Breaker Youth Edition

Busting Free!

Know Light, No Fear

To My Dear Slimeball

Purity Under Pressure

Extreme Faith

Reality Check

Awesome God

Ultimate Love

The Common Made Holy Youth Edition

Leading Teens to Freedom in Christ

Audio/Visual Series:

"Busting Free!"

In Christ

I Am Accepted

John 1:12	I am a child of God.
John 15:15	I am Jesus' chosen friend.
Romans 5:1	I am holy and acceptable to God (justified).
1 Corinthians 3:16	I am united to the Lord and am one spirit with Him.
1 Corinthians 6:19,20	I have been bought with a price. I belong to God.
1 Corinthians 12:27	I am a part of Christ's Body, part of His family.
Ephesians 1:1	I am a saint, a holy one.
Ephesians 1:5	I have been adopted as God's child.
Colossians 1:14	I have been bought back (redeemed) and forgiven of all my sins.
Colossians 2:10	I am complete in Christ.

I Am Secure

Romans 8:1,2	I am free forever from punishment.
Romans 8:28	I am sure all things work together for good.
Romans 8:31-34	I am free from any condemning charges against me.
Romans 8:35-39	I cannot be separated from the love of God.
Colossians 3:3	I am hidden with Christ in God.
Philippians 1:6	I am sure that the good work that God has started in me will be finished.
Ephesians 2:19	I am a citizen of heaven with the rest of God's family.
Hebrews 4:16	I can find grace and mercy in times of need.
1 John 5:18	I am born of God and the evil one cannot touch me.

I Am Significant

Matthew 5:13,14	I am salt and light for everyone around me.
John 15:1,5	I am part of the true vine, joined to Christ and able to produce lots of fruit.
John 15:16	I am handpicked by Jesus to bear fruit.
Acts 1:8	I am a Spirit-empowered witness of Christ.
1 Corinthians 3:16; 6:19	I am a temple where the Holy Spirit lives.
2 Corinthians 5:17-21	I am at peace with God and He has given me the work of making peace between Himself and other people.
2 Corinthians 6:1	I am God's coworker.
Ephesians 2:6	I am seated with Christ in heaven.
Ephesians 2:10	I am God's building project, His handiwork, created to do His work.
Philippians 4:13	I am able to do all things through Christ who gives me strength!

Supplements to the Youth Steps

SECTION 1

Preparation for Taking Someone Through the Steps to Freedom

Before you start these Steps to Freedom, go over the events of your life so that you understand the areas that might need to be dealt with. If you have the Confidential Personal Inventory (see appendix pp. 225-235), it would be helpful to complete that now.

Family History

❑ Religious background of parents and grandparents

❑ Your home life from childhood to the present

❑ Any history of physical or emotional problems in the family

❑ Adoption, foster care, guardians

Personal History

Spiritual Journey

❑ Do you know if you are saved?

   If yes, how do you know you are saved? When did it happen?

Eating Habits

❑ Do you make yourself vomit, take laxatives, or starve yourself to lose weight?

❑ Do you binge or eat uncontrollably?

Free Time

   How many hours of TV do you watch per day?

   What are your favorite TV shows?

How much time do you spend playing video/computer games each day?

How much time do you spend listening to music each day?

What kind of music do you listen to?

How much time do you spend reading each day?

What do you spend most of your time reading?

❑ Do you smoke?   ❑ Chew tobacco?   ❑ Drink alcohol?

❑ Do you use street drugs? If so, what kind?

❑ Do you use prescription drugs? What for?

❑ Have you ever run away from home?

❑ Do you have trouble sleeping too little or too much?

❑ Do you have frequent or recurring nightmares?

❑ Were you ever raped or abused sexually, physically, verbally or emotionally?

❑ Do you suffer from distracting thoughts while in church, prayer or Bible study?

Physical Life
Check all those that apply:

❑ Frequent headaches/migraines
❑ Constant tiredness
❑ Dizziness
❑ Stomach problems

❑ Memory problems
❑ Fainting spells
❑ Allergies

Thought Life
Check all those that apply:

❑ Daydreaming/fantasy
❑ Thoughts of inferiority
❑ Thoughts of inadequacy
❑ Perfectionism
❑ Lust

❑ Insecurity
❑ Worry
❑ Thoughts of self-hatred
❑ Doubts about salvation or God's love
❑ Thoughts of suicide

Emotional Life

Check all those that apply:

- ❏ Feelings of frustration
- ❏ Anger
- ❏ Anxiety
- ❏ Depression
- ❏ Guilt
- ❏ Loneliness
- ❏ Worthlessness
- ❏ Bitterness

- ❏ Fear of death
- ❏ Fear of losing your mind
- ❏ Fear of confusion
- ❏ Fear of failure
- ❏ Fear of going to hell
- ❏ Fear of the dark
- ❏ Fear of parents divorcing
- ❏ Other fears: _____

SECTION 2

Satanic Ritual Abuse Renunciations

If you have been involved in any satanic rituals or heavy occult activity, you need to say aloud the following special renunciations and affirmations.

Read across the page, renouncing the first item in the column under "Kingdom of Darkness" and then affirming the first truth in the column under "Kingdom of Light." Continue down the entire list in that manner.

Kingdom of Darkness	Kingdom of Light
I renounce ever signing my name over to Satan or having my name signed over to Satan..	I announce that my name is now written in the Lamb's Book of Life.
I renounce any ceremony where I might have been married to Satan.	I announce that I am the Bride of Christ.
I renounce any and all covenants, agreements or promises that I made with Satan..	I announce that I have made a new covenant with Christ.
I renounce all satanic assignments for my life, including duties, marriage and children.	I announce and commit myself to know and do only the will of God and I accept only His guidance for my life.
I renounce all spirit guides assigned to me.	I announce and accept only the leading of the Holy Spirit.
I renounce ever giving of my blood in the service of Satan.	I trust only in the shed blood of my Lord Jesus Christ.
I renounce ever eating of flesh or drinking of blood in satanic worship.	By faith I take Holy Communion which represents the body and the blood of the Lord Jesus.
I renounce all guardians and satanic parents that were assigned to me.	I announce that God is my heavenly Father and the Holy Spirit is my Guardian by whom I am sealed.
I renounce any baptism whereby I am identified with Satan.	I announce that I have been baptized into Christ Jesus and my identity is now in Him.
I renounce every sacrifice made on my behalf by which Satan may claim ownership of me.	I announce that only the sacrifice of Christ has any claim on me. I belong to Him. I have been purchased by the blood of the Lamb.

All satanic rituals, covenants, promises, and assignments must be specifically renounced as the Lord brings them to your mind. Some people who have been subjected to Satanic Ritual Abuse (SRA) develop multiple personalities (alters) in order to cope with their pain. In this case, you need someone who understands spiritual conflicts to help you maintain control and not be deceived into false memories. You can continue to walk through these Steps to Freedom in Christ in order to resolve all that you are aware of. Only Jesus can bind up the brokenhearted, set captives free and make us whole.

SECTION 3
The Truth About Our Heavenly Father

Sometimes we are greatly hindered from walking by faith in our Father God because of lies that we have believed about Him. We are to have a healthy fear of God—awe of His holiness, power and presence—but we are not to be afraid of Him. Romans 8:15 says, "For you did not receive a spirit that makes you a slave again to fear, but you have received the Spirit of sonship. And by him we cry, 'Abba, Father.'" The following exercise will help break the chains of those lies and enable you to begin to experience that intimate "Abba Father" relationship with Him. Work your way down this list, one by one, left to right. Begin each one with the statement at the top of that list. Read through the list aloud.

I renounce the lie that my heavenly Father is …	I choose to accept the truth that my heavenly Father is…
Distant and disinterested.	Intimate and involved (see Psalm 139:1-18).
Insensitive and uncaring.	Kind and compassionate (see Psalm 103:8-14).
Stern and demanding.	Accepting and filled with joy and love (see Romans 15:7; Zephaniah 3:17).
Passive and cold.	Warm and affectionate (see Isaiah 40:11; Hosea 11:3,4).
Absent or too busy for me.	Always pleased with me and eager to spend time with me (see Hebrews 13:5; Jeremiah 31:20; Ezekiel 34:11-16).
Never satisfied with what I do, impatient or angry.	Patient, slow to anger, and pleased with me in Christ (see Exodus 34:6; 2 Peter 3:9).
Mean, cruel or abusive.	Loving, gentle and protective of me (see Jeremiah 31:3; Isaiah 42:3; Psalm 18:2).
Trying to take all the fun out of life for me.	Trustworthy and wants to give me a full life. His will is good, perfect and acceptable (see Lamentations 3:22,23; John 10:10; Romans 12:1,2).
Controlling or manipulative.	Full of grace and mercy, and gives me freedom to fail (see Hebrews 4:15,16; Luke 15:11-16).
Condemning or unforgiving.	Tenderhearted and forgiving; His heart and arms are always open to me (see Psalm 130:1-4; Luke 15:17-24).
Nit-picking, nagging or perfectionistic.	Smiling as He thinks of me and proud of me as His growing child (see Romans 8:28-29; Hebrews 12:5-11; 2 Corinthians 7:4).

If you are struggling with walking by faith it might be because of the fears that plague your life. To experience freedom from the bondage of fear, go through the following prayers and renunciations.

SECTION 4

Dealing with Fears

A central part of walking in the truth and rejecting deception is dealing with the fears that plague our lives. First Peter 5:8 says that our enemy, the devil, prowls around like a roaring lion, seeking people to devour. Just as a lion's roar strikes terror into the hearts of those who hear it, so Satan uses fear to try to paralyze Christians. His intimidation tactics are designed to rob us of faith in God and drive us to try to get our needs met through the world or the flesh.

Fear weakens us, causes us to be self-centered and clouds our minds so that all we can think about is the thing that frightens us. But fear can only control us if we let it.

God, however, does not want us to be mastered by anything, including fear (see 1 Corinthians 6:12). Jesus Christ is to be our only Master (see 2 Timothy 2:21; John 13:13). In order to begin to experience freedom from the bondage of fear and to be able to walk by faith in God, pray the following prayer from your heart.

> **Dear Heavenly Father,**
> **I confess to You that I have listened to the devil's roar and have allowed fear to master me. I have not always walked by faith in You but instead have focused on my feelings and circumstances (see 2 Corinthians 4:16-18; 5:7). I thank You for forgiving me for my unbelief.**
> **Right now I renounce the spirit of fear and affirm the truth that You have not given me a spirit of fear but of power, love and a sound mind (see 2 Timothy 1:7). Lord, please reveal to my mind now all the fears that have been controlling me so that I can renounce them and be free to walk by faith in You. I thank You for the freedom You give me to walk by faith and not by fear. In Jesus' powerful name, I pray. Amen.**

The following list may help you to recognize some of the fears that the devil has used to keep you from walking by faith. Check the ones that apply to your life. Write down any others that the Spirit of God brings to your mind. Then, one by one, renounce those fears aloud, using the suggested renunciation that follows the list.

- ❑ Fear of death
- ❑ Fear of Satan
- ❑ Fear of failure
- ❑ Fear of rejection by people
- ❑ Fear of disapproval
- ❑ Fear of financial problems
- ❑ Fear of never getting married
- ❑ Fear of becoming homosexual
- ❑ Fear of the death of a loved one
- ❑ Fear of going crazy
- ❑ Fear of being a hopeless case
- ❑ Fear of losing my salvation
- ❑ Fear of having committed the unpardonable sin
- ❑ Fear of not being loved by God
- ❑ Fear of embarrassment
- ❑ Fear of being victimized
- ❑ Fear of marriage
- ❑ Fear of divorce
- ❑ Fear of pain

- ❑ Fear of never being able to love or be loved by anyone
- ❑ Other specific fears that come to mind now _____
_____

I renounce the _____ (name of the fear) _____ because God has not given me a spirit of fear. I choose to live by faith in the God who has promised to protect me and meet all my needs as I walk by faith in Him (see Psalm 27:1; Matthew 6:33,34).

After you have finished renouncing all the specific fears that you have allowed to control you, pray the following prayer from your heart:

Dear Heavenly Father,
I thank You that You are trustworthy. I choose to believe You, even when my feelings and circumstances tell me to fear. You have told me not to fear, for You are with me; not to anxiously look about me for You are my God. You will strengthen me, help me and surely uphold me with Your righteous right hand (see Isaiah 41:10). I pray this with faith in the name of Jesus, my Master. Amen.

SECTION 5

Special Prayers for Specific Needs

If you have struggled with or are currently struggling with homosexuality, suicidal tendencies, eating disorders or cutting yourself, substance abuse, drivenness and perfectionism, or have had an abortion or not assumed your responsibilities for an unborn child; pray the appropriate special prayers for specific needs.

ABORTION

Note to men: Just as mothers are called to be responsible for the life that God has entrusted to them, so too, the father shares in this responsibility. If you have failed to fulfill your role as a father, pray the following prayer:

> Lord,
>
> I confess that I was not a proper guardian and keeper of the life You entrusted to me and I admit that as sin. I choose to accept Your forgiveness, and I now commit that child to You for Your care for all eternity. In Jesus' name, amen.

DRIVENNESS AND PERFECTIONISM

> Lord,
>
> I renounce the lie that my self-worth is dependent on my ability to perform. I announce the truth that my identity and sense of worth is found in who I am as Your child. I renounce seeking the approval and acceptance of other people and I choose to believe that I am already approved and accepted in Christ because of His death and resurrection for me. I choose to believe the truth that I have been saved, not by deeds that I have done, but according to Your mercy. I choose to believe that I am no longer under the curse of the law because Jesus became a curse for me. I receive the free gift of life in Christ and choose to abide in Him. I renounce striving for perfection by living under the law. By Your grace, Heavenly Father, I choose from this day forward to walk by faith according to what You said is true by the power of the Holy Spirit. In Jesus' name, amen.

EATING DISORDERS OR CUTTING YOURSELF IN A DESTRUCTIVE WAY

> Lord,
>
> I renounce the lie that my value as a person is dependent upon my physical beauty, my weight or size. I renounce cutting myself, vomiting, using laxatives or starving myself as a means of cleansing myself of evil or altering my appearance. I announce that only the blood of the Lord Jesus Christ cleanses me from sin.
>
> I accept the reality that there may be sin present in me due to the lies I have believed and the wrongful use of my body, but I renounce the lie that I am evil or that any part of my body is evil. My body is the temple of the Holy Spirit and I belong to God. I am totally accepted by God in Christ just as I am. In Jesus' name, amen.

HOMOSEXUALITY

Lord,

I renounce the lie that You have created me or anyone else to be homosexual, and declare that You created me a man (or a woman). I renounce all homosexual thoughts, urges or drives, as well as any bondage of Satan that have perverted my relationships with others. I announce that I am free to relate to the opposite sex and my own sex in the way that You intended. In Jesus' name, amen.

SUBSTANCE ABUSE

Lord,

I confess that I have misused substances—alcohol, tobacco, food, prescription or street drugs—for the purpose of pleasure, to escape reality or to cope with difficult problems. I confess that I have abused my body and programmed my mind in a harmful way. I have not allowed Your Holy Spirit to guide me. I ask Your forgiveness, and I reject any satanic connection or influence in my life because of my misuse of drugs or food. I cast my cares onto Christ who loves me, and I commit myself to no longer give in to substance abuse, but instead to allow the Holy Spirit to lead and empower me. In Jesus' name, amen.

SUICIDAL TENDENCIES

Lord,

I renounce suicidal thoughts and any attempts I may have made to take my own life or in any way injure myself. I renounce the lie that life is hopeless and that I can find peace and freedom by taking my own life. Satan is a thief, and he comes to steal, kill and destroy. I choose life in Christ who said He came to give me life and to give it to the full. I choose to accept Your forgiveness and to believe that there is always hope in Christ. In Jesus' name, amen.

After you have confessed all known sin, say:

I now confess these sins to You and claim through the blood of the Lord Jesus Christ my forgiveness and cleansing. I cancel all ground that evil spirits have gained through my willful involvement in sin. I ask this in the wonderful name of my Lord and Savior, Jesus Christ. Amen.

Prayers

DAILY PRAYER

Dear Heavenly Father,

I honor You as my Lord. I know that You are always present with me. You are the only all-powerful and all-wise God. You are kind and loving in all Your ways. I love You and I thank You that I am united with Christ and spiritually alive in Him. I choose not to love the world, and I crucify the flesh and all its passions.

I thank You for the life that I now have in Christ, and I ask You to fill me and guide me with Your Holy Spirit so I may live my life free from sin. I declare my dependence upon You and I take my stand against Satan and all his lying ways. I choose to believe the truth and I refuse to be discouraged. You are the God of all hope and I am confident that You will meet my needs as I seek to live according to Your Word. I express with confidence that I can live a responsible life through Christ who strengthens me.

I now take my stand against Satan and command him and all his evil spirits to depart from me. I put on the whole armor of God. I submit my body as a living sacrifice and renew my mind by the living Word of God in order that I may prove that the will of God is good, acceptable and perfect. I ask these things in the powerful and precious name of my Lord and Savior, Jesus Christ. Amen.

BEDTIME PRAYER

Thank You, Lord, that You have brought me into Your family and have blessed me with every spiritual blessing in the heavenly realms in Christ. Thank You, too, for providing this time of renewal through sleep. I accept it as part of Your perfect plan for Your children and I trust You to guard my mind and my body during sleep. As I have thought about You and Your truth during the day, I choose to let those thoughts continue in my mind while I am asleep. I commit myself to You for Your protection from every attempt of Satan or his demons to attack me during the night. I commit myself to You as my rock, my fortress and my resting place. I pray in the strong name of the Lord Jesus Christ. Amen.

CLEANSING HOME/APARTMENT/ROOM

After destroying all articles of false worship—crystals, good-luck charms, occult objects, games, etc.—from your room, pray aloud in your sleeping area:

Thank You, Heavenly Father, for a place to live and be renewed by sleep. I ask You to set aside my room (or portion of room) as a place of safety for me. I renounce any worship given to false gods or spirits by other occupants, and I renounce any claim to this room (space) by Satan based on what people have done here or what I have done in the past.

On the basis of my position as a child of God and a joint heir with Christ who has all the authority in heaven and on earth, I command all evil spirits to leave this place and never to return. I ask

You, Heavenly Father, to appoint guardian angels to protect me while I live here. I pray this in the name of the Lord Jesus Christ. Amen.

Continue to seek your identity and sense of worth through who you are in Christ. Renew your mind with the truth that your *acceptance*, *security* and *significance* are in Christ alone. Meditate on the following list of who you are "In Christ" daily, reading the entire list aloud, morning and evening, over the next few weeks.

Steps to Setting Your Child Free

Ages 9–12

PRELIMINARY INSTRUCTIONS FOR PARENTS, PASTORS OR COUNSELORS

Whenever I travel by air, I hear the flight attendants dutifully point out the safety features of the aircraft and the proper use of the oxygen masks should they lose cabin pressure. They always tell the parents to place their own oxygen masks on before attempting to help their children. Panic-stricken parents gasping for air are in no position to help their children. Although the air is thin, the children are in no immediate danger. They can wait until the parents have safely resolved their own issues.

The same is true for helping our children. They need us to be strong and confident in the Lord. We cannot impart what we don't possess. If the parents are not living free in Christ, they will have a difficult, if not impossible, time leading their children to freedom. Pastors, counselors, teachers and parents must be totally dependent upon the Lord in order to be effective in helping children. Jesus is the wonderful Counselor and only He can grant repentance and set captives free.

Have you been patient when wronged by your child? Have you been kind or harsh? Have you corrected your child's opposition with gentleness? Have you known the truth well enough to teach him or her what to do when he or she is under spiritual attack? You may need to start by asking your child to forgive you for the times you have not disciplined him or her in

love or understood the true nature of his or her problem.

At the risk of sounding redundant, let me say again that the parent, pastor, teacher or counselor working with the child must be *sure* of his or her own identity and freedom in Christ *before* trying to help someone else. Understand also, that helping your children find spiritual freedom in Christ by resolving their personal and spiritual conflicts through genuine repentance does *not* produce instant spiritual maturity in them. All other aspects of growth and normal development are still in process. Be careful to use terms a child can understand. The wording of the following prayers and doctrinal statements have been modified from the adult *Steps to Freedom in Christ* in order to meet younger children's needs.

The theological basis and practical aspects for this approach to counseling is given in my book *Helping Others Find Freedom in Christ*. The youth edition is entitled *Leading Teens to Freedom in Christ* which I coauthored with Rich Miller. The youth edition provides hands-on help for parents as does my parenting book *Spiritual Protection for Your Children* (the book from which these Steps are taken).

Children must be told that *they* are not the problem but that they *have* a problem for which they

must assume their own responsibility. If our attitude is "What's wrong with you, anyway?" they will probably become defensive. We asked one young boy if he had thoughts in his head telling him what to do. He said he did, and we asked what the thoughts were saying. "I'm no good!" he replied. The frustrated parents of this adopted child had all but thrown in the towel trying to control his *behavior* and had not thought to ask about his *beliefs*. The thoughts he was struggling with were *I am hopeless and incorrigible*.

The goal is to help children resolve their personal and spiritual conflicts *in Christ* and find the peace of God that passes all understanding. For the rest of his or her life the child needs to know that he or she must be responsible for what he or she thinks and does. For this discipleship counseling process to work you must have the child's cooperation to share any mental opposition or thoughts he or she is having that are in direct opposition to what you are attempting to do.

The power of Satan is in the lie. As soon as the lie is exposed, the power is broken. The control center is the mind. If Satan can get the child to believe a lie, he can control that child's life. Thoughts such as, *This isn't going to work* or *God doesn't love me*, etc. can interfere only if the child believes the lies.

We often tell people it doesn't make any difference if the thoughts are coming from a loud speaker on the wall, the devil, or inside their own heads—in any case, the child should not pay attention to them.

There are two reasons that most people, including our children, don't share what is going on inside. First, if they even remotely suspect we won't receive the information appropriately, they won't share it. Patronizing responses such as, "You're just having a bad day" or "It will go away" or "You have an overactive imagination" or judgmental statements such as "You need to see a shrink!" keep people from revealing what they are really thinking. This last response is feared the most. People often fear they are going crazy; therefore, anything we do to suggest that possibility will only drive them away. Many adults fear they are going crazy and are frightened by the prospect of being drugged. We have assured many people that nothing they could share would surprise us. The thoughts keeping them in fear or bondage are often threatening or vulgar. Once they know we understand that the voices are not their own thoughts and that they can be stopped, they freely share what is going on inside.

Second, they may be threatened by the voices. Usually the threats are that they will be harmed when they get home or back in their bedrooms. The threat can be directed toward others such as their parents or siblings. Children often believe they have to obey the voices to save someone else. All of these threats are for intimidation to cause them not to share what is really going on inside. Demons are like cockroach-es. They come out and lurk in darkness. They fear being exposed. When we turn on the light of Christ, they scurry for the shadows.

When children share openly and choose the truth, they find their freedom in Christ. The battle isn't at home or in their rooms; it's in their minds. If they resolve their problems in our church offices or in the kitchen, they will also be resolved in their bedrooms. One person called hours later and said with a great deal of delight, "They're not here [in her home] either!" They never were there. She found her freedom in Christ in her heart and mind.

Children will be set free by what *they* do, not by what *we* do. Remember that Satan is under no obligation to obey our thoughts. Children must exercise their faith and pray these prayers aloud, thus assuming personal responsibility which then helps resolve the issues standing between themselves and God. Mental interference is common during the early stages of the Steps to Setting Your Child Free, but we can gain enough control by exercising our authority in Christ in prayer, assisting the person to stay focused on Christ and do what is needed to get right with God.

Even though some people struggle through the Steps, a valuable lesson is learned in the process. They begin to learn the nature of the spiritual battle and how to have victory whenever they are under attack. If we try to cast out a demon for them, they will believe it is always necessary to call us when they are under future attacks. *They* need to learn how to call upon the Lord. He is the Savior. Parents, pastors, teachers or counselors are only the facilitators in the process, not the Deliverer. Children under attack will always benefit by praying themselves. Again, it is not what we do that sets them free; it is what they choose to renounce, confess, forgive, believe etc.

It is important to watch children closely throughout the Steps, especially their eyes. If they start to mentally drift, ask them what they are thinking or hearing. In some cases they may be seeing something. The moment they share it, the lie is exposed and its power is broken. If they experience a lot of interference, slow down or you may lose control in the process. We sometimes instruct children to take a brief break, to get up and walk around the room to refocus their minds, and to ensure them of their volitional control which they must choose to exercise.

Children commonly experience headaches or feel as though they are becoming sick. Some will say they are going to throw up. Usually the physical symptoms lessen or stop when they share them. If not, pray again against Satan's harassment. If they say they have to leave, let them go—they will be back within minutes. Never try to physically restrain them. In the midst of a battle they will feel violated if anyone touches them. Remember, the weapons of our warfare are not of the flesh (see 2 Corinthians 10:3-5). Prayer is our weapon against such attacks.

Trust is an essential prerequisite. If children trust us, they will believe what we say. Trust must be preceded by our assurance that they are fully accepted, significant and secure. The more we explain and reassure them, the more they will believe and trust us. They have a greater chance of finding freedom from all of the lies they have believed when they feel safe.

Don't get into a shouting match. Authority does not increase with volume. If you as the facilitator find yourself shouting, you are probably responding in the flesh. God does everything decently and in order. It is important that you follow along as the child reads to make sure words are not being misread or left out that might change the meaning.

Please note the concluding comments and special renunciations which are found at the end of the Steps. They give additional help and explanation for difficult cases and for the important aftercare issues for all children.

Steps to Setting Your Child Free

Ages 9–12

> **Note:** Information in boxes or parentheses is instructive material for the parent or counselor and should not be read to the child.

Parents/counselors share:

Jesus wants you to be free! Free from your past, free from the problems you have right now and free from any fear you may have of the future. If you have received Jesus as your Savior, He has already won your battles for you through His death on the cross. If you haven't been living free in Christ, maybe you just haven't understood what Jesus has done for you.

Here's the good news! You may be young, but you don't have to live with sin and evil in your life! Satan wants you to think he is stronger than he really is. He really is a defeated foe, far below the feet of Jesus. You are in Christ, the winner! In Christ you are fully loved, accepted, secure and significant.

Satan doesn't want you to find your freedom in Christ, so be sure to tell me how you are feeling and what you are thinking as we go along. If you get any bad thoughts or feel sick in any way, please tell me. It's usually the enemy trying to distract you. If we stop and pray, we can tell him to go away. I can pray with you at any time. We're going to start now. I'm going to read this prayer aloud with you.

> **Dear Heavenly Father,**
>
> Thank You for Your presence in this room and in our lives. You are everywhere, all-powerful, and know all things. We need You and know that we can do nothing without You. We believe the Bible because it tells us what is really true. We refuse to believe the lies of Satan. We ask You to rebuke Satan and place a hedge of protection around this room so we can do Your will. Because we are children of God, we take authority over Satan and command Satan not to bother _____(name)_____ so _____(name)_____ can know and choose to do the will of God. In the name and authority of the Lord Jesus Christ, we command Satan and all his forces to be bound and silenced so they cannot inflict any pain or in any way prevent God's will from being accomplished in _____(name's)_____ life. We ask the Holy Spirit to fill us and direct us into all truth. In Jesus' name, we pray. Amen.

STEP 1

Saying No to Things That Are Spiritually Wrong

Now we are ready to start. We're going to go through seven Steps to help you be free in Christ. Remember, you can only win your battles when you *personally* choose to believe, pray and confess. Confession is simply agreeing with God. Satan cannot read your mind (see Job 1:11; 2:5; compare with 1:20-22; 2:10); only God can do that (see 1 Samuel 16:7; Psalms 44:21; 139:1-6; Jeremiah 11:20; 17:10; Romans 8:27). Therefore, you must read each prayer *aloud*. This tells Satan you really mean what you say and that you want to follow Jesus.

You and the Lord are about to take a close-up look at your life to help you have a great relationship with God. It is important to go through all seven Steps, so don't get discouraged and give up. Remember, the FREEDOM Christ purchased on the cross for all believers is meant for *you*! The first step is to say no or renounce—turn your back and walk away from—anything you have done that is spiritually wrong or against Christianity or God. Satan tries to use past experiences to draw us away from God and to control the way we think and behave. You need to be honest about these experiences with God so Satan will not be able to use his lies against you anymore. Begin by reading the following prayer aloud:

> **Dear Heavenly Father,**
> **I ask You to help me remember anything I have done that is spiritually wrong. If someone has done something to me that is wrong, please help me to remember it. I want to be free in Christ and able to do Your will. I ask this in Jesus' name. Amen.**

Even if you did something as a game or a joke, you need to turn your back on it. Satan will try to take advantage of us through the wrong things that we have done. Even if you were just watching others do it, you need to turn your back on it. Even if you had no idea it was evil, you need to turn your back on it and honor only the Lord Jesus.

Put a check mark by anything you have been involved in. Also, write down anything else that comes to mind that is not listed.

❑ Out-of-body experience
❑ Bloody Mary
❑ Magic Eight Ball
❑ Automatic writing in a trance
❑ Fortune-telling/tarot cards
❑ Palm reading
❑ Hypnosis
❑ Black or white magic
❑ Dungeons & Dragons or similar games
❑ Video/computer games implying occult powers or violence
❑ Movies or TV shows that are anti-Christian
❑ Martial arts
❑ Light-as-a-Feather
❑ Other experiences _____

❑ Ouija board
❑ Table lifting
❑ Putting spells or curses on people
❑ Spirit guides
❑ The Magic card game
❑ Astrology/horoscopes
❑ Seances
❑ Meditation
❑ Blood pacts
❑ Music that is anti-Christian
❑ Books, magazines, comics that are anti-Christian
❑ Non-Christian religions (the spiritual beliefs of)
❑ Belief in special powers from Care Bears, Trolls, Power Rangers, etc.

Parents/counselors ask:

1. Have you ever heard or seen a spiritual being in your room?

2. Have you had an imaginary friend that talks to you?

3. Do you hear voices in your head that tell you what to do?

4. Have you ever made a promise to the devil?

5. What other non-Christian experiences have you had?

6. Have you ever been involved in the worship of Satan or attended a concert where they sang about Satan?

7. Are you afraid to go to bed at night because of nightmares?

Now that you have completed the checklist, pray the following prayer for each experience:

> **Dear Heavenly Father,**
>   I confess that I have been involved in _____. Thank You for Your forgiveness. I renounce—turn my back on— _____.
> In Jesus' name, amen.

Note to parents, pastors or counselors: If the child has been subjected to satanic rituals, sexual abuse, or has any eating disorders, please go to Special Renunciations at the end of these Steps, beginning on page 129.

STEP 2

Choosing Truth and Rejecting Lies

God's Word is true, and we need to accept that truth deep in our hearts (see Psalm 51:6). King David wrote, "Blessed is the man...in whose spirit is no deceit" (Psalm 32:2). Start this important Step by praying the following prayer aloud:

Dear Heavenly Father,

I know You want only the truth from me, and I must be honest with You. I have been fooled by the father of lies, and I have fooled myself. I thought I could hide from You, but You see everything and still love me. I pray in the name of the Lord Jesus Christ, and ask You, Heavenly Father, to rebuke all of Satan's demons by Your power. Because I have asked Jesus into my life, I am now Your child; therefore, I command all evil spirits to leave me alone. I ask the Holy Spirit to lead me into all truth. I ask You to look into my heart and over my life. Show me if there is anything in me that I am trying to hide, because I want to be free. In Jesus' name, I pray. Amen.

Parents share:

I just want to remind you how much I love you and how thankful I am that God has given you to me as my child. I want our relationship to be honest, and I want us to be able to trust each other as we go through these Steps. Speaking the truth in love is important because we are members of one Body (see Ephesians 4:15,25). We can walk in the light so we can have fellowship and friendship with each other (see 1 John 1:5-9). Only the truth can set us free, and we should speak that truth to each other in love.

Read aloud the following statements of faith and truth from the Bible:

I believe there is only one true God who is the Father, Son and Holy Spirit. I believe He made all things and holds all things together.

I believe Jesus Christ is the Son of God who defeated Satan and all his demons.

I believe God loves me so much He had His own Son go to the cross and die to pay for all my sins. Jesus rose again and delivered me from Satan because He loves me, not because of how good or bad I act.

I believe I am spiritually strong because Jesus is my strength. I have the authority to stand against Satan because I am God's child. In order to stay strong, I am going to obey God and believe His Word. I put on the armor of God so I can stay strong in the Lord.

I believe I cannot win spiritual battles without Jesus, so I choose to stay close to Him. I also resist the devil and command him in Jesus' name to leave me alone.

I believe the truth will set me free. If Satan tries to put bad thoughts into my mind, I will not pay any attention to them. I will not listen to Satan's lies and I will not do what he wants me to do. I believe the Bible is true and I choose to believe it. I choose to love others and always speak the truth in love.

I choose to use my body to do only good things. I will not let Satan into my life by using my body in wrong ways. I believe what God wants me to do is always the best thing for me, and I choose to do it.

I ask my Heavenly Father to fill me with His Holy Spirit, guide me into all truth and make it possible for me to live a good Christian life. I love the Lord my God with all my heart, soul and mind.

Some very important decisions for truth have just been made that will have a lasting impact.

Parents or counselor: This is a good time to share with each other how you are feeling and what you are thinking.

STEP 3

Forgiving Others

God commands us to forgive others as Jesus has forgiven us (see Ephesians 4:32). When you do not forgive those who have hurt you, you become a target for Satan. You need to obey the Lord's command so Satan can't take advantage of you (see 2 Corinthians 2:11). Ask God to bring to your mind the names of the people you need to forgive by praying the following prayer aloud:

> **Dear Heavenly Father,**
> **I thank You for Your kindness, patience and love for me. I know at times I have not been very loving and patient toward others, especially those I don't like. I have been thinking bad thoughts about other people and holding onto bad feelings. I ask You to bring to my mind those people I need to forgive. I ask this in the wonderful name of Jesus who will heal me from my hurts. Amen.**

On a sheet of paper, list the names of everyone you have bad feelings toward. The Lord will bring them to your mind. It's okay to put Mom and Dad on your list if you need to forgive them for something. Forgiving people who have hurt you is God's way of setting you free from painful past experiences. Unless we forgive, the past will continue to cause us pain and have a hold on us. Take ample time to finish the list of names.

Now that you have finished your list, let's think about the meaning of real forgiveness.

Parents/counselor: Read aloud the statements in dark print.

Forgiveness is not forgetting. You may not be able to forget your past, but you can be free from it by forgiving others. Once you forgive someone, you don't need to bring up the past and use it against them ever again.

Forgiveness is a choice. Forgiveness seems difficult because we all naturally want revenge for the things done to us, but God tells us never to take our own revenge (see Romans 12:19).

Forgiveness is like removing a painful fishhook. Forgiving is like removing sharp fishhooks others have put in us. It is a painful process, but when we forgive people, we are no longer hooked to them. As long as those fishhooks are still in us, we are still bound to those people.

When I let someone off my hook, they are not off God's hook. We must trust Jesus to deal with the other person justly, fairly and mercifully. That is something we cannot do. "It is mine to avenge; I will repay," says the Lord (Deuteronomy 32:35).

Forgiveness means we accept that we can't change what happened. If someone steals your bike or calls you a name, you can't change that. You can be mad for a long time, or you can forgive them and let God deal with them. People do bad things and we can't always stop them, but we can choose not to let what they did control us.

God wants you to forgive *from your heart.* To do this, you need to be very honest and admit the hurt and the hate. Go through your list of names one at a time. Focus on each person until all the pain is out. Then go on to the next person.

Pray the following prayer aloud for each name:

Lord,
I forgive _____(name the person)_____ for _____(say what they did to hurt you)_____. It made me feel _____(say how you felt)_____. In Jesus' name, amen.

STEP 4

Saying No to Rebellion

We live in rebellious times. Some children don't respect people in positions of authority. The Bible teaches us that God has placed these people in authority over us: parents, teachers, church leaders, police officers, God, etc. It's easy to think that those in authority over us are robbing us of our freedom. Actually, God has placed them there for our protection so we can enjoy our freedom. God assures us that living under authority is for our good.

Rebelling against God and His authorities is serious business. Rebellion comes from Satan and it gives Satan an opportunity to attack us. Obedience to God is the only answer. He wants us to submit to those in authority over us.

However, God never tells us to do something wrong or to obey someone telling us to do something wrong. If any of these people are telling you to do something bad, ask for help from someone you trust. If, however, these people are telling you to do something that is not morally wrong—even if you don't like it—you are to obey. The following is a list of different authority figures. If you have disobeyed anyone in the list below, put a check by them and pray the following prayer aloud:

❑ Parents
❑ School teachers
❑ Sunday School teachers
❑ God

❑ Grandparents
❑ Police officers
❑ Church leaders
❑ Others _____

Dear Heavenly Father,
    You have said in the Bible that rebellion is the same thing as witchcraft, and disobedience is like honoring other gods. I know I have disobeyed and rebelled in my heart against You and _____(name of others)_____**. Thank You for Your forgiveness of my rebellion. By the shed blood of the Lord Jesus Christ I resist all evil spirits who took advantage of my rebellion. I now choose to be obedient and submissive to those in authority over me. In Jesus' precious name, I pray. Amen.**

STEP 5

Rejecting Pride and Choosing Humility

Pride says, "I am better than everyone else." It also says, "I can do this all by myself, without God or anyone else!" Oh no, we can't! We absolutely need God, and we desperately need each other. Paul wrote, "Do nothing out of selfish ambition or vain conceit, but in humility consider others better than yourselves" (Philippians 2:3). He also said we are to be "strong in the Lord and in the strength of His might" (Ephesians 6:10, *NASB*). We will have spiritual problems when we are proud (see James 4:6-10; 1 Peter 5:1-10). Pride is what caused Satan to be cast out of heaven. The following is a list of some of the ways we are prideful. If any of them are true of you, place a check mark next to them, then pray the following prayer to promise you will live humbly before God:

❑ I don't need God or anybody else to help me!

❑ I never do anything wrong!

❑ I'm better than others!

Dear Heavenly Father,

I confess that I often think only of myself. Sometimes I think I am better than others. Sometimes I have believed I am the only one who cares about me so I have had to take care of myself. Lord, I have turned away from You and not let You love me. I am tired of living for myself and by myself. I turn my back on the selfish life and ask that You fill me with Your Holy Spirit so I can do Your will. By giving my heart to You, I stand against all the ways Satan would attack me. I ask You to show me how to live for others. I now choose to make others more important than myself and make You the most important of all. I ask this in the name of Jesus Christ. Amen.

STEP 6

Putting Off Sin and Putting On Freedom

The next Step to Freedom deals with sins that have become habits in our lives. Many sins can control us. The Bible says, "Let us put aside the deeds of darkness and put on the armor of light. Rather, clothe yourselves with the Lord Jesus Christ, and do not think about how to gratify the desires of the sinful nature" (Romans 13:12,14). Pray the following prayer aloud:

Dear Heavenly Father,
  I agree with You that I have done some bad things. I ask You to help me know all the things I have done that are wrong so that you will set me free.

The following list contains some common sins. Put a check by the sins you have committed and then pray the following prayer for each sin:

❑ Stealing/shoplifting
❑ Fighting
❑ Envying
❑ Complaining
❑ Cheating
❑ Greed
❑ Vandalism—damaging someone else's property
❑ Other _____

❑ Lying
❑ Jealousy
❑ Outbursts of anger
❑ Desire for sexual pleasures
❑ Swearing/cussing
❑ Laziness

Lord,
  I have committed the sin of _____. Thank You for Your forgiveness and cleansing. I turn away from this sin and turn to You, Lord. In Jesus' name, amen.

God has completely forgiven you of those sins. Don't ever let Satan put you down or make you think you are still guilty of them. Whenever sin creeps back into your life, remember 1 John 1:9: "If we confess our sins, He is faithful and righteous to forgive us our sins and to cleanse us from all unrighteousness" (*NASB*). Jesus will always answer this prayer!

Finish by praying the following prayer:

Lord,
  I thank You for forgiving me for all my sins. I ask You to fill me with Your Holy Spirit so I will not keep sinning. I now command Satan to leave, and I choose to live the right kind of life so I can be free. In Jesus' name, I pray. Amen.

Note to parent, pastor or counselor: If the child has been subjected to sexual sins, satanic ritual abuse or eating disorders, please refer to Special Renunciations at the end of these Steps on pages 126-129.

STEP 7

Sins of the Fathers

The last Step to Freedom is to renounce—turn your back on—the sins of your parents and grandparents. The Bible says God brings "the punishment for the fathers' sins into the laps of their children after them" (Jeremiah 32:18). You are not guilty for the sins of other family members but because of their sins, Satan may have gained a foothold in your family. To be free from this evil influence, pray the following prayer aloud:

> Dear Heavenly Father,
>   I come to You as Your child, bought by the blood of the Lord Jesus Christ. I turn my back on all the sins that have been committed in my family. I have been set free from the power of darkness and I am now in the kingdom of Jesus. Jesus has broken all ties and workings of Satan passed on to me from my ancestors. I am spiritually alive in Christ and united with Him. Because I am owned by Jesus, I reject any and all ways Satan may claim ownership of me. I announce to all the forces of evil that I am forever and completely committed and signed over to the Lord Jesus Christ. I now command every evil spirit and every enemy of the Lord Jesus Christ to leave my presence forever. I now ask You, Heavenly Father, to fill me with Your Holy Spirit. I present my body to You so people will know You live in me. All this I do in the name of the Lord Jesus Christ. Amen.

Staying Free and Close to Jesus

Becoming free and staying free in Christ are two different issues. The battle for your mind will continue. As you live your life you will still be tempted to do wrong things. Consider the following suggestions to stay free in Christ:

1. Make sure you have the right kind of friends.
2. Always think and speak the truth in love.
3. Read your Bible daily.
4. Honor your mother and your father.
5. Obey all those who have authority over you.
6. Don't let problems build up. Share your struggles with someone you can trust.
7. Don't try to live the Christian life by yourself.
8. Always call upon God when you think you are under attack.
9. If something tries to scare you, tell it to leave in the name of Jesus.
10. Enjoy the wonderful life God has given you and all He has created. Remember, Christ will meet all your needs according to His riches in glory.

Read the "In Christ" statements on the following page aloud with the child.

In Christ

I Am Accepted

John 1:12	I am God's child.
John 15:15	I am Christ's friend.
Romans 5:1	I have been justified (made right in God's eyes).
1 Corinthians 6:17	I am united with the Lord and one with Him in spirit.
1 Corinthians 6:20	I have been bought with a price. I belong to God.
1 Corinthians 12:27	I am a member of Christ's Body.
Ephesians 1:1	I am a saint.
Ephesians 1:5	I have been adopted (chosen) as God's child.
Ephesians 2:18	I can go right to God through the Holy Spirit.
Colossians 1:14	I have been redeemed (bought by God) and forgiven of all my sins.
Colossians 2:10	I am complete in Christ.

I Am Secure

Romans 8:1,2	I am free from punishment.
Romans 8:28	I am sure that all things work together for good.
Romans 8:33,34	I am free from any condemning charges against me.
Romans 8:35-39	I cannot be separated from the love of God.
2 Corinthians 1:21,22	I have been established, anointed and sealed by God.
Colossians 3:3	I am hidden with Christ in God.
Philippians 1:6	I am sure that the good work that God has begun in me will be perfected.
Philippians 3:20	I am a citizen of heaven.
2 Timothy 1:7	I have not been given a spirit of fear but of power, love and a sound mind.
Hebrews 4:16	I can find grace and mercy in time of need.
1 John 5:18	I am born of God and the evil one cannot touch me.

I Am Significant

Matthew 5:13,14	I am the salt and light of the earth.
John 15:1,5	I am a branch of the true vine, joined to Christ.
John 15:16	I have been chosen and appointed to bear fruit.
Acts 1:8	I am Christ's personal witness.
1 Corinthians 3:16	I am God's temple.
2 Corinthians 5:17-21	I am a minister of peace (bringing others to God).
2 Corinthians 6:1	I am God's coworker.
Ephesians 2:6	I am seated with Christ heaven.
Ephesians 2:10	I am God's workmanship.
Ephesians 3:12	I may approach God with freedom and confidence.
Philippians 4:13	I can do all things through Christ who strengthens me.

Note 1: Binding Satan does not ensure total release for the victim. If this were true, all the New Testament would have to say is bind Satan throughout the world and cast him to some faraway planet. The Lord will cast him into the abyss in the final days but until then he roars around. We do, however, have all the authority in Christ we need to do His will, live a righteous life and fulfill the ministry to which God has called us. Binding Satan is an agreement with Scripture, an acknowledgment of God's sovereignty and an announcement to the enemy of our authority in Christ.

Note 2: Our children will be genetically predisposed to certain strengths and weaknesses. The environment they were raised in will also affect them for good and evil. Could there also be an unrighteous inheritance? We think the answer is yes. Look at the words of Jeremiah 32:17,18: "Ah Lord God! Behold, Thou hast made the heavens and the earth by Thy great power and by Thine outstretched arm! Nothing is too difficult for Thee, who showest lovingkindness to thousands, but repayest the iniquity of fathers into the bosom of their children after them, O great and mighty God. The Lord of hosts is His name" *(NASB)*.

In our experience, sins passed on from one generation to another are the second most common ground Satan has for gaining access to our children. In little children that is about all it can be because they haven't yet had the opportunity to become involved in sex and drugs, etc.

Special Renunciations

SPECIAL RENUNCIATIONS FOR SEXUAL SINS

A child who has unfortunately been subjected—voluntarily or involuntarily—to sexual sins will need to renounce them and his or her participation. It is important to explain to the child that renouncing any unwilling participation does not mean he or she was at fault. However, the child needs to understand that even forced participation needs to be renounced because Satan has brought bondage into the child's life through that involvement (see Romans 6:12,13). The child also needs to understand that any threats made by his or her perpetrator should not stop him or her from walking in the light and renouncing these acts.

Caution: Children are highly susceptible to adult suggestions and often have creative imaginations. Do not ask leading questions. Some children are clever enough to tell us what they think we want to hear and lead us down a wrong path. They might also fabricate a story to abdicate themselves from their own responsibilities. If children are paying attention to deceiving spirits, those voices could be giving them false memories. False memories usually come from dreams, hypnosis or counterfeit "words of knowledge" given to them by others. Never use such "evidence" against another person unless you have some external, hard evidence to substantiate the accusations. Such accusations should not even be made against an elder in the church unless two or three witnesses can substantiate the accusations.

It is our responsibility not to allow sin to reign in our mortal bodies by not using our bodies as instruments of unrighteousness (see Romans 6:12,13). If the child has struggled with sexual sins or has been subjected involuntarily to sexual acts, have the child read or repeat the following prayer:

Dear Heavenly Father,
    I ask You to help me remember every sexual use of my body. In Jesus' precious name, I pray. Amen.

As the Lord brings to the child's mind every sexual misuse of his or her body, whether it was done unwillingly—rape, incest or other sexual abuse—or willingly, have the child read or repeat the following renunciation for each occasion:

> Dear Heavenly Father,
>   I renounce _____ (name the specific sexual participation) _____ with _____ (name the person) _____ and ask You to break that bond. In Jesus' name, I pray. Amen.

Now have the child read or repeat the following prayer:

> **Dear Heavenly Father,**
>   **I turn my back on all these uses of my body. I ask You to break all bondage Satan has brought into my life through these involvements. I confess my participation. I now present my body to You as a living sacrifice, holy and acceptable to You. I reserve the sexual use of my body only for marriage. I renounce Satan's lie that my body is not clean or that it is dirty or unacceptable because of my sexual experiences. Lord, I thank You that You have totally cleansed and forgiven me, that You love and accept me no matter what. Therefore, I accept myself and my body as clean. In Jesus' name, I pray. Amen.**

SPECIAL RENUNCIATIONS FOR SATANIC RITUAL ABUSE

A child who has had the horrible experience of being involuntarily subjected to satanic rituals will need to renounce his or her forced participation. Sarah was an 11-year-old girl who had been raised the first five years of her life in a coven. Sarah's mother had given her life to Christ several months before she came for counseling. Sarah had also prayed to receive Christ, but they were still being harassed and oppressed. They were experiencing nightmares, dreams of snakes, banging noises, etc.

We took Sarah through the spiritual inventory in Step One. She renounced all the practices of the coven to which she had been subjected. She had three spirit guides. After renouncing them by name, the voices stopped! Forgiveness was a big step for her (Step Three) because many people had deeply hurt her. After we finished, we asked her how she felt. She replied, "Like I'm sitting in the lap of God!"

There are specific activities satanists use in all their rituals. When we encounter people who recall satanic ritual involvement, we have them repeat the renunciations that follow.

Remember the same caution as mentioned previously: Children are highly susceptible to adult suggestions and often have creative imaginations. Do not ask leading questions. Some children are clever enough to tell us what we want to hear and lead us down a wrong path. They could also be fabricating a story to abdicate themselves from their own responsibility. If children are paying attention to deceiving spirits, those voices could be giving them false memories. False memories usually come from dreams, hypnosis or counterfeit "words of knowledge" others have given them. Never use such "evidence" against another person unless you have some external, hard evidence to substantiate the accusations. Such accusations should not even be made against an elder in the church unless there are two or three witnesses.

Notice in the following list that satanic rituals often counterfeit Christian acts of worship. Have the child read across the page, left to right, renouncing the first item in the column under "Kingdom of Darkness," then affirming the first truth in the column under "Kingdom of Light." Continue through the list to the end.

Kingdom of Darkness	Kingdom of Light
I renounce ever signing my name over to Satan or having my name signed over to Satan.	I announce that my name is now written in the Lamb's Book of Life.
I renounce any ceremony where I may have been married to Satan.	I announce that I am the Bride of Christ.
I renounce any and all covenants or agreements with Satan.	I announce that I have a new covenant with Christ.
I renounce any sacrifices that were made for me where Satan would claim ownership of me.	I announce that I belong to God because of the sacrifice of Jesus on the cross for me.
I renounce ever giving of my blood in satanic ritual.	I trust only in the shed blood of Jesus for my salvation.
I renounce ever eating of flesh or drinking of blood for satanic worship.	By faith, I take communion which represents Jesus' body and blood which was given for me.
I renounce all guardians and surrogate parents that were assigned to me by satanists.	I announce that God is my heavenly Father and the Holy Spirit is my guardian.
I renounce every sacrifice made on my behalf by satanists whereby they may claim ownership of me.	I announce that Christ is my sacrifice and I belong to Him because I have been bought and purchased by the blood of the Lamb.
I renounce any ceremony where I was assigned to be a high priest(ess) for satanic service, and I renounce Satan's lie that he owns me	I announce that in Christ I am a chosen race, a royal priesthood, a holy nation, a person for God's own possession. I belong to Him.

SPECIAL RENUNCIATIONS FOR EATING DISORDERS

People with eating disorders are often driven by compulsive thoughts to eliminate things from their bodies by defecating, vomiting or cutting themselves. Many falsely believe they are purging themselves of evil. It is not uncommon to see cuts on the arms of those struggling with anorexia. Many cut themselves in secretive ways. One young lady would meticulously cut herself under her pants in the groin area so others wouldn't see. Suicidal thoughts are a given for these people.

Another young lady had starved herself down to 78 pounds. By the time I had a chance to talk with her, she was taking 75 laxatives a day. I asked her about her thought life—if she had ever shared fully what was going on inside her mind. She hadn't, of course, and was intimidated by thoughts threatening her that worse things would happen when she got home if she ever did.

I suggested, "This isn't about food, is it?"

"No, but everybody thinks it is," she responded.

Every attempt to control her behavior had only resulted in the problem getting worse. She had no idea who she was in Christ and no understanding about the nature of the spiritual battle going on for her mind. Years of counseling and hospitalizations ended when she finally understood. She responded in tears after finding her freedom in Christ, saying, "I can't believe all the lies I have been believing and listening to."

Typically, those with eating disorders are physically attractive. From the time they were very little, they have received strokes for their looks. Their self-concepts are based on appearance. They become so body-conscious that their minds are fertile ground for the enemy. Instead of buffeting their bodies and making them their slaves (see 1 Corinthians 9:27), they have become enslaved to their bodies. Many have been sexually abused. They also think their bodies are evil or something evil exists in them that they have to get rid of. The evil is spiritual, not physical. These people need to first establish their identities in Christ, and then begin developing their character to obtain a legitimate sense of worth. Have them renounce and then announce as follows:

Kingdom of Darkness	Kingdom of Light
I renounce as lies from Satan, cutting myself to clean myself of evil.	I announce that only the blood of Jesus can cleanse me (see Hebrews 9:14).
I renounce throwing up to clean myself of evil and reject the lie that I am fat or that my self-worth is found in my physical appearance.	I announce that all food created by God is good, and nothing is to be rejected by those who know the truth (see 1 Timothy 4:1-5).
I renounce taking laxatives to clean myself of evil by going to the bathroom.	I announce that it is not what enters into the mouth that defiles me, but what comes from the heart (see Matthew 15:10-20).

Additional resources to be used with the Steps for children:
See the bibliography for complete information on each resource.
Books:

Spiritual Protection for Your Children

The Seduction of Our Children

Audio/Visual Series:

"The Seduction of Our Children"

Steps to Setting Your Child Free

Ages 0—8

PRELIMINARY INSTRUCTIONS FOR PARENTS, PASTORS OR COUNSELORS

Younger children in this age group can't read the Steps, so the parent, pastor, teacher or counselor must share with them what they must do. The best thing going for us in this process is their childlike faith. Children at this age seldom question what a responsible adult shares with them. They have not yet learned to be defensive about the thoughts they are thinking.

You cannot overemphasize the love of God and His powerful presence in their lives. Children can accept the fact that God is in them and bigger than Satan. And we need to understand that children in the Lord have the same authority we do as adults. Therefore, they can resist the devil.

If the child has not yet trusted in Christ as his/her Savior, this might be a good opportunity for you to lead that child to Christ, then proceed through the Steps. If the child does not choose to trust in Christ at this time, refer to chapter 20, "Praying for Your Child" in the book *Spiritual Protection for Your Children*. These steps are adapted from this book. For further explanation of this process see *Helping Others Find Freedom in Christ*, or the youth edition, *Leading Teens to Freedom in Christ*.

Take seriously the fearful comments of children. If they complain of horrible nightmares or see frightening things in their rooms, encourage them to share all their experiences. Listen without judgment. If we make light of their experiences, they will conclude that we don't care or understand. In either case, they may never share again, which is the worst thing that can happen.

Many children have imaginary "friends" they play with. This can be harmless *unless* the imaginary friend is talking back. Then it is no longer imaginary. New Age proponents are actually encouraging children to have spirit friends or spirit guides.

A child's trust and dependence on spirit friends is incredibly dangerous and will result in spiritual bondage. Problems like this must be identified as soon as possible. Satan disguises himself as an angel of light, so young children probably won't see the danger. They might even be reluctant to give it up. As harmless as it may initially appear, only oppression and tragedy will follow as the relationship progresses.

Young children don't understand the term "renounce," so we have them say *no* to Satan and *yes* to Jesus. For instance, if they have been sexually molested, have them say, "I say no to the way _____(name)_____ touched me and I give my body to Jesus." As much as possible, we have the child assume his or her responsibility.

The following is a modified version of the Steps to Freedom to accommodate children ages five to eight. They are followed by instructions for helping children under the age of five. If the child can read, have him/her do so as he/she prays and works through the prayers. If he/she cannot read, then have him/her repeat the prayers after you.

You may discover that your child has dabbled in some of these things, or your child may in the future mention them to you in casual conversation. Helping ourselves and our children find and maintain our freedom in Christ is not simply a one-time event, but a matter of watching for and capturing teachable moments when our children are ready and willing to listen.

As Deuteronomy 6:4-7 says:

Hear, O Israel: The Lord our God, the Lord is one. Love the Lord your God with all your heart and with all your soul and with all your strength. These commandments that I give you today are to be upon your hearts. Impress them on your children. Talk about them when you sit at home and when you walk along the road, when you lie down and when you get up.

Steps to Setting Your Child Free

Ages 5–8

> **Note:** Information enclosed in boxes or parentheses is instructive material for the parent or counselor and should not be read to the child.

Parents/counselors share:

Jesus wants you to be free—free from any sins and free from any fears. If you have received Jesus as your Savior, He has already won your battles for you on the cross. Here's the good news for you: You don't have to live with sin and evil in your life! Satan wants you to think he is stronger than he really is, but he has been *defeated* by Jesus. Be happy you have Jesus, the Winner, with you all the time!

Satan doesn't really want you to be free in Christ so be sure to tell me how you are feeling and what you are thinking as you go along. I can pray with you whenever you need to.

We're going to start now. I'm going to pray this prayer aloud:

> Dear Heavenly Father,
>
> We thank You for Your presence in this room and in our lives. You are everywhere, all-powerful, and You know all things. We need You and know that we can do nothing without You. We believe the Bible because it tells us what is really true. We refuse to believe the lies of Satan. We ask You to silence and bind Satan and place a hedge of protection around this room so we can do Your will. We are children of God so we take our authority in Christ over Satan and command him not to bother _____(name)_____ , so _____(name)_____ can know and choose to do the will of God. In the name of Jesus and His authority, we command Satan and all his forces to be bound and silenced so they cannot inflict any pain or in any way prevent God's will from being accomplished in _____(name's)_____ life. We ask the Holy Spirit to fill us and direct us into all truth. In Jesus' wonderful name, we pray. Amen.

STEP 1

Saying No to Things That Are Spiritually Wrong

Now we are ready to start. We're going to proceed through seven Steps to help you live free in Christ. God can hear your prayers whether you pray aloud or not. Always remember that Satan cannot read your mind so it is important that you express your belief in Jesus and the Bible by saying each prayer aloud. I'll help you with each prayer.

The first step is to say no to anything you have done that is spiritually wrong. Read or repeat this prayer after me:

> **Dear Heavenly Father,**
> **Please help me remember anything I have done or been a part of that is spiritually wrong. If someone has done something to me that is wrong, would You also help me remember that? I ask this in Jesus' name. Amen.**

The Bible teaches that God is good and that He has an evil enemy, Satan, who fights against Him. God is so much stronger that Satan never wins. Satan is a liar and tries to trick us so he can get us to listen to him and obey him, rather than the one true loving God.

It is wrong to listen to or obey any spirit other than God. God always wants the best for us and He will protect us from all evil spirits.

Parents or Counselors: At this point, talk with the child about any experiences he or she has had with things that are spiritually wrong. The following list is for you to use as a resource so you can be aware of things to which children are exposed. This is only a partial list. If some of these things come up in the course of your conversation, be sure the child says no to each involvement (see the prayer at the end of the list). Be sensitive to the extent of their involvement without creating in them a curiosity or desire to become more involved in wrong behaviors. Put a check mark by anything the child mentions, even if he or she only watched someone else do it or had no idea it was evil.

❑ Video or computer games that suggest occult powers or cruel violence
❑ Inappropriate books, magazines or comics
❑ Inappropriate movies or TV shows
❑ Music that is anti-Christian
❑ Dungeons & Dragons (or similar games)
❑ Magic card game
❑ Out-of-body experiences
❑ Bloody Mary game
❑ Table lifting
❑ Ouija board
❑ Magic Eight Ball
❑ Putting curses or spells on people
❑ Blood pacts
❑ Fortune-telling, tarot cards, palm reading
❑ Astrology/horoscopes
❑ Hypnosis

❑ Seances
❑ White or black magic
❑ Martial arts (any false beliefs that they may teach)
❑ Meditation
❑ Writing in a trance
❑ Non-Christian religions
❑ Other _____

Have the child read or repeat the following prayer for each experience:

> **Dear Heavenly Father,**
>   I confess that I have taken part in _____. Thank You for forgiveness in Jesus. I say *no* to _____ and I say *yes* to God. In Jesus' name, amen.

Parent or counselor: Again, be sensitive to the child's involvement as you ask the following questions:

1. Have you ever been afraid of something you heard or saw in your room?

2. Have you had an imaginary friend that talks to you?

3. Do you hear voices in your head that tell you what to do? Have you done what they told you to do?

4. Have you ever made a promise to the devil?

5. Has anyone ever told you to close your eyes and imagine you are going to a different place or told you to do something wrong?

6. Have you had any other experiences that would hurt your relationship with God?

7. Are you afraid to go to bed at night because of nightmares?

Now have the child read or repeat the following prayer:

> **Dear Heavenly Father,**
>   I confess that I have been involved in _____. Thank You for Your forgiveness. I say *no* to _____ and I say *yes* to God.

Parent or Counselor: If the child has been subjected to satanic rituals, sexual molestation or has any eating disorders, please refer to Special Renunciations at the end of the Steps for children *ages 9–12* (pp. 126-129).

STEP 2

Choosing Truth and Rejecting Lies

The Bible is true, and we need to accept that truth deep in our hearts (see Psalm 51:6). King David wrote, "Blessed is the man...in whose spirit is no deceit" (Psalm 32:2). Start this important step by reading or repeating the following prayer aloud:

> Dear Heavenly Father,
>   I know that You want me to tell the truth. You know everything about me and You still love me. Because I have asked Jesus into my life, I am now Your child. I command all evil spirits to leave me alone. Show me if there is anything I am trying to hide, because I want to be free. I choose to believe the truth about who You are and who I am as Your child. In Jesus' name, I pray. Amen.

For parents only to read to their children:

I just want to remind you how much I love you and how thankful I am that God has given you to me as my son/daughter. I want us to trust each other as we go through these steps. Speaking the truth in love is important because in Christ we are in God's family together (see Ephesians 4:15,25).

Have the child read or repeat the following statements of faith aloud:

1. I believe there is only one true God who is the Father, Son and Holy Spirit.
2. I believe Jesus is the Son of God who defeated Satan and all his demons.
3. I believe God loves me so much that He had His own Son die on the cross to save me from all my sins.
4. I have the authority to stand against Satan's lies because I am God's child. I put on the armor of God so I can be strong in the Lord.
5. I believe the truth will set me free.
6. I choose to use my body to do only good things.
7. I ask God to fill me with His Holy Spirit. I love God with all my heart, soul and mind.

STEP 3

Forgiving Others

God tells us to forgive others just like He has forgiven us (see Ephesians 4:32). Ask God to bring to your mind the names of the people who have hurt you and who you need to forgive by praying the following prayer aloud:

Dear Heavenly Father,
Bring to my mind the people I need to forgive. I know Jesus will heal me from my hurts. In Jesus' name, I pray. Amen.

(Parents/counselor share): I'll help you make a list of all the people you need to forgive. Remember that forgiving people who have hurt you is God's way of setting *you* free from painful past experiences. (Take time to make a list.)

Now that you have finished your list, you can forgive the people as Jesus has forgiven you. Pray about each person until all the pain is gone. Then go on to the next person. Read or repeat the following prayer aloud for each name:

Lord,
I forgive _____ (name the person) _____ for _____ (say what they did to hurt you) _____. It made me feel _____ (say how you felt) _____. Amen.

STEP 4

Saying No to Rebellion

Many children today don't respect people who tell them what to do. God is the One who has placed these people in authority over us—parents, teachers, church leaders, police officers, government leaders, etc. God has placed them there for our protection. God assures us that living under authority is for our good.

Ignoring or fighting against God and the people He puts over us is wrong. It gives Satan an opportunity to deceive us. Obedience to God and His ways is the only answer. He wants you to obey your parents, grandparents, teachers, church leaders, police officers, etc. If any of these people are asking you to do something that is wrong, you need to tell someone else that you trust. Have you ever disobeyed your parents, grandparents, teachers, church leaders, or police officers? Read or repeat the following prayer aloud:

Dear Heavenly Father,

The Bible teaches that rebellion is as wrong as witchcraft, and disobedience is like honoring false gods. I know I have disobeyed and rebelled in my heart against You. I have also disobeyed _____(name of person)_____. I confess and say no to my disobedience and rebellion. By the shed blood of Jesus, I resist all evil spirits who took advantage of my rebellion and disobedience. I now choose to be obedient to those in authority over me. In Jesus' precious name, I pray. Amen.

STEP 5

Rejecting Pride and Choosing Humility

Pride says, "I am better than everyone else." It also says, "I can do this all by myself, without God or anyone else!" Oh no, we can't! We absolutely need God, and we desperately need each other. Paul wrote, "Do nothing out of selfish ambition or vain conceit, but in humility consider others better than yourselves" (Philippians 2:3). He also said we are to be "strong in the Lord and in his mighty power" (Ephesians 6:10). We will always have spiritual problems when we are proud (see James 4:6-10; 1 Peter 5:1-10). Read or repeat the following prayer to promise that you will live humbly before God:

Dear Heavenly Father,
  I have often thought only of myself. Sometimes I think I am better than others. Please forgive me for my pride. I need You and I need other people to help me live right. I now choose to make others more important than myself and to make You the most important of all. I ask this in the name of Jesus Christ. Amen.

STEP 6

Putting Off Sin and Putting On Freedom

The next Step to Freedom deals with sins and wrong things that have become habits in our lives. Many sins can control us. The Bible says, "Let us put aside the deeds of darkness and put on the armor of light. Rather, clothe yourselves with the Lord Jesus Christ, and do not think about how to gratify the desires of the sinful nature" (Romans 13:12,14). Read or repeat the following prayer aloud:

Dear Heavenly Father,
    I agree with You that I have done some bad things. I ask You to help me know all the things I have done that are wrong and choose those things that are right. In Jesus' name, amen.

Parents/counselor share:

The following list contains some of the more common sins. I will read a list of them—if you have done these things in your life, tell me so we can talk to the Lord about them. I will put a check mark by them. For each sin, you will read or repeat the prayer that follows.

- ❑ Stealing/shoplifting
- ❑ Lying
- ❑ Fighting
- ❑ Calling names
- ❑ Anger
- ❑ Bad thoughts
- ❑ Cheating
- ❑ Swearing
- ❑ Laziness
- ❑ Wishing you had what someone else has
- ❑ Other _____

    Lord,
    I have sinned by _____. Thank You for Your forgiveness and cleansing. I say no to this sin and say YES to You. In Jesus' name, I pray. Amen.

Parents/counselor share:

God has completely forgiven you of those sins. Don't ever let Satan put you down or make you think you are still guilty of them. Whenever sin creeps back into your life, remember 1 John 1:9: "If we confess our sins, he is faithful and just and will forgive us our sins and purify us from all unrighteousness." "Faithful" means that God always does what He says He will do.

Read or repeat the following prayer:

> Lord,
>   I thank You for forgiving me for all my sins. I now command Satan to leave me. I choose to live the right kind of life so that I can be free. In Jesus' name, I pray. Amen.

Note to parent or counselor: If the child has been subjected to sexual sins, satanic ritual abuse or eating disorders, please refer to Special Renunciations at the end of the Steps for children *ages 9–12* (pp. 129-132).

STEP 7

Sins of the Fathers

The last Step to Freedom is to say no to the sins of your parents and grandparents. The Bible says God brings "the punishment for the fathers' sins into the laps of their children after them" (Jeremiah 32:18). You are not guilty for the sins of any other family member, but because of their sin, Satan may have gotten a foot in the doorway of your family. Read or repeat the following prayer aloud:

> **Dear Heavenly Father,**
> I say no to all the sins of my family. Jesus has broken all the works of Satan passed on to me from my parents and grandparents. Because I am owned and loved by Jesus, I reject any ways Satan may claim ownership of me. I announce to all the forces of evil that I am forever and completely committed and signed over to the Lord Jesus Christ. I now ask You, Heavenly Father, to fill me with Your Holy Spirit. I present my body and whole life to You. In the name of Jesus, amen.

STAYING FREE AND CLOSE TO JESUS

Review the following important discipleship issues with your child:

Now that you are free in Christ, let's talk about staying free and close to Jesus.

1. Make sure you have the right kind of friends.
2. Always think and speak the truth in love.
3. Read your Bible daily (or have someone read it to you).
4. Obey your mother and your father.
5. Obey all those who have authority over you.
6. Don't let problems build up. Share your struggles with those you can trust.
7. Don't try to live the Christian life by yourself.
8. Always call upon God when you think you are under attack.
9. If something tries to scare you, tell it to leave in the name of Jesus.
10. Enjoy the wonderful life God has given you, and all He has created. Christ will meet all your needs according to His riches in glory.

Read this encouraging list aloud together (and review it often):

In Christ

I Am Accepted

John 1:12	I am God's child.
John 15:15	I am Jesus' friend.
1 Corinthians 6:20	I have been bought with a price. I belong to God.
Ephesians 1:5	I have been adopted (chosen) as God's child.
Colossians 1:14	I have been redeemed and forgiven of all my sins.

I Am Safe and Secure

Romans 8:28	I am sure that all things work together for good.
Romans 8:35	I cannot be separated from the love of God.
Philippians 3:20	I am a citizen of heaven.
2 Timothy 1:7	I have not been given a spirit of fear, but of power, love and a sound mind.
1 John 5:18	I am born of God and the evil one cannot touch me.

I Am Significant

Matthew 5:13,14	I am the salt and light of the earth.
2 Corinthians 6:1	I am God's coworker.
Ephesians 2:6	I am seated with Christ in heaven.
Ephesians 3:12	I may come to God with freedom and confidence.
Philippians 4:13	I can do all things through Christ who strengthens me.

Steps to Setting Your Child Free

Ages 0–4

Because children in this age group cannot read, parents must assume responsibility for them and exercise their authority in Christ. Children of these ages *can* understand the love and power of Jesus in their lives, however. Their childlike faith will be an encouragement to you as you pray for them, and what they learn in your prayers may lead them to put their trust in Christ someday. This is the only time we encourage you to place your hands on your children, if they will allow you to do so as you pray for them.

After I finished a conference, a pastor shared with me how he was finally able to help his young daughter. She was waking up every night terrified and complaining that something was in her room. He and his wife initially did what most parents would do. They accompanied her to the room, and after looking in the closet and under the bed, declared that nothing was there. This had been occurring for three months. The child hadn't seen any bad movies or lived long enough to commit any major sins.

During the week of the conference, the parents began to understand what was happening. Friday evening they sat down with her and explained that she had Jesus in her heart (she had trusted in Christ at an early age), and because Jesus was in her heart, she could tell whatever was in her room to leave because Jesus was bigger and stronger than it was. She didn't come into her parents' room that night and the next morning she proclaimed boldly, "It came into my room last night. I told it to get out in Jesus' name, and it left!"

A veteran missionary attending my class at seminary shared that his child had been having nighttime visitations. He and his wife personally confessed all their sins and then laid their hands on their child, commanding Satan to leave their child in the name of Jesus. The nightmares ended.

You can adapt for your child any of the prayers in the other Steps to Setting Your Child Free or other youth or adult versions of the Steps to Freedom in Christ. You can pray for your children like this:

Dear Heavenly Father,
   I bring my child, _____ (name) _____ , before You. I declare myself and my family to be under Your authority. I acknowledge my dependency upon You, for apart from Christ I can do nothing. I ask for Your protection during this time of prayer. I assume my responsibility for all that You have entrusted to me, and I now commit my life, my marriage and my family to You. I declare my child to be eternally signed over to the Lord Jesus Christ. Because I am in Christ and seated with Him in the heavenlies, I take authority over the enemy by renouncing any and all assignments Satan has on my child, _____ (name) _____. I accept only the will of God for myself and my family. I now command Satan and all his demons to stop bothering my child, _____ (name) _____ , and to leave. I ask for a hedge of protection around him/her and my home. I submit myself to You and ask You to fill me with Your Holy Spirit. I dedicate myself and my child, _____ (name) _____ , as temples of the living God. I ask this in the precious name of Jesus, our Lord and Savior. Amen.

Our children are precious gifts from God. We must do everything we can to protect them from the god of this world. We can do that by being the parents He wants us to be, by surrounding them with a Christ-centered home and by lifting them up in prayer such as the one that follows. Suggestions for praying more specifically for your children are offered in the book *Spiritual Protection for Your Children*.

PRAYING FOR YOUR CHILD

Daily Prayer

Dear Heavenly Father,

I ask that _____(name)_____ may be filled with the knowledge of Your will in all spiritual wisdom and understanding so _____(name)_____ may walk in a manner worthy of Your name. May he/she please You in all respects, bearing fruit in every good work and increasing in the knowledge of You. I pray that _____(name)_____ be strengthened with all power according to Your glorious might so he/she may be steadfast and patient. I ask, Heavenly Father, that _____(name)_____ would see Your mighty work and joyfully give thanks to You who has qualified us to share in the inheritance of the saints (see Colossians 1:9-12). I pray that _____(name)_____ will continue to grow in wisdom and stature and in favor with God and others (see Luke 2:52). In Jesus' precious name, I pray. Amen.

Additional resources to be used with the Steps for children:
See the bibliography for complete information on each resource.

Books:

Spiritual Protection for Your Children
The Seduction of Our Children

Audio/Visual Series:

"The Seduction of Our Children"

Steps to Setting Your Marriage Free

Important Note: We strongly encourage you to work through the *personal* Steps to Freedom in Christ before beginning the Steps to Setting Your Marriage Free as a couple. Becoming one in Christ and achieving marital freedom cannot be accomplished if both husband and wife have not first found their personal freedom in Christ.

We encourage you to read the book, *The Christ-Centered Marriage,* and complete the inductive study guide. (These Steps are adapted from chapter 14 of the book and study guide.) Ideally, it would be best if you both read *Victory over the Darkness* and *The Bondage Breaker* first or attend a Living Free in Christ conference. These books (or the conference) will help you resolve personal and spiritual conflicts and instruct you in how to live the Christian life by faith in the power of the Holy Spirit. The conference is available on audio or videocassette.

Share with each other your desire for the Holy Spirit to lead you into all truth. Relate to each other that you are willing to assume your responsibility for whatever God reveals to you. The conviction of the Holy Spirit will lead you to repentance *without regret* (see 2 Corinthians 7:9,10). He will reveal to your mind what is keeping you from having an intimate marriage and will enable you to resolve the conflicts that have kept you from experiencing oneness in Christ. Every Christian couple should desire the life of Christ in their marriage, thus displaying God's splendor.

You must both agree to assume your own responsibility and not attack the other person's character or family. Allow the Holy Spirit to bring understanding and conviction. This process will not work unless you both desire and agree to speak the truth in love and walk in the light. The Lord loves you and wants to see you free from your past, alive in Him, and committed to one another in a loving and intimate way.

TIPS FOR ONE SPOUSE GOING THROUGH THE MARRIAGE STEPS ALONE

If your spouse is not willing to go through these Marriage Steps, you can still gain great benefit by going through them alone. *Finding Personal Freedom in Your Marriage* is the version of the Steps designed for only one spouse. For a copy, contact Freedom in Christ Ministries (phone: 562-691-9128). When and if your husband or wife is willing to go through the marriage Steps with you, use this version designed for both spouses.

TIPS FOR GROUPS

If you are going through this process at a weekend retreat, we suggest that you set aside Friday evening to Sunday morning, and that Friday evening be spent in corporate prayer and fellowship. If any of the couples have not gone through the individual Steps to Freedom in Christ, then Friday night would be the time to do it.

The best accommodations for the retreat should provide space for both group meetings and privacy for each couple. Each Step begins with instruction by a facilitator, followed in most Steps by the group praying an opening prayer. Steps One through Six provide perforated worksheet pages for recording notes and answers and may be discarded after the retreat is over. Each couple then completes the Step together in private. Sunday School classes, discipleship groups, and small group ministries who are reading the book and using the study guide can process these Steps in their normally scheduled meetings. You could work through one Step a week or schedule a weekend retreat as mentioned above.

TIPS FOR COUPLES WORKING ALONE

If you have a relatively mature relationship with mutual trust and respect, you can work your way through these Steps without outside assistance. The theology and practicality of this process is given in the book, *The Christ-Centered Marriage.* If your relationship is experiencing extreme difficulty, we suggest that you have a responsible person whom you both trust assist you.

Note: The information needed for the following outline and diagrams may be found in the introduction to Dr. Anderson's *The Christ-Centered Marriage* book on pages 10–17 or Step One of the video seminar.

The Preeminence of Christ

"Do not suppose that I have come to bring peace to the earth. I did not come to bring peace, but a sword. For I have come to turn 'a man against his father, a daughter against her mother, a daughter-in-law against her mother-in-law—and a man's enemies will be the members of his own household.' Anyone who loves his father or mother more than me is not worthy of me; anyone who loves his son or daughter more than me is not worthy of me; and anyone who does not take his cross and follow after me is not worthy of me. Whoever finds his life will lose it, and whoever loses his life for my sake will find it" (Matthew 10:34-39).

MARRIAGE AND FAMILY DISCIPLINES

A. Marriages and families without Christ can promote a false pursuit of self-worth by focusing only on the following:

  1. Appearance

  2. Performance

  3. Status

B. The following are personal needs that only Christ can meet:

  1. Life

  2. Identity

  3. Acceptance

  4. Security

  5. Significance

C. God works primarily through committed relationships.

MARRIAGE AND FAMILY DISCIPLINES WITH CHRIST

Before you begin the process: In order to resolve conflicts, you have to address many issues that can be quite negative. Therefore, begin the Steps to Setting Your Marriage Free by encouraging each other. Answer the following questions, then share your answers with your spouse:

What three character qualities do you most appreciate about your spouse?

1.

2.

3.

What three things does your spouse do that you really appreciate?

1.

2.

3.

A PRAYER OF COMMITMENT BY HUSBAND AND WIFE

Dear Heavenly Father,

We love You and we thank You for Your grace, truth, love, power, forgiveness and blessings in Christ. We can love each other because You first loved us. We can forgive because we have been forgiven, and we can accept one another just as You have accepted us. We desire nothing more than to know and do Your will. We ask for Your divine guidance and protection during this time of seeking freedom in our marriage. We give ourselves emotionally to You and each other and ask You to free us so we can share from our hearts.

We buckle on the belt of Your truth, put on the breastplate of Your righteousness, and commit ourselves to the gospel of peace. We hold up the shield of faith and stand against the flaming arrows of the enemy. We commit ourselves to take every thought captive in obedience to You. We put on the helmet of salvation which assures us of Your forgiveness, Your life and our freedom in You. We put off the old self and put on the new self which is being renewed in Your image. We take the sword of the Spirit, the spoken Word of God, to defend ourselves against the father of lies.

We acknowledge our dependence upon You and understand that apart from Christ we can do nothing. We pray that You will grant us genuine repentance and living faith. We desire our marriage to become a beautiful picture of Your relationship with us. We ask You to fill us with your Holy Spirit, lead us into all truth, and set our marriage free in Christ. In Jesus' precious name, we pray. Amen.

STEP 1

Establish God's Priority for Marriage

Ask the Lord to reveal if you have completely left your father and mother. Remember the words of Jesus: "Anyone who loves his father or mother more than me is not worthy of me; anyone who loves his son or daughter more than me is not worthy of me" (Matthew 10:37).

This does not mean that you don't honor your father and mother, but it does mean that you can have only one Lord in your life. It means your *spiritual* heritage must take precedence over your *natural* heritage. "For this reason a man will leave his father and mother and be united to his wife, and they will become one flesh. The man and his wife were both naked, and they felt no shame" (Genesis 2:24,25).

> **Note:** The information needed for the following outline and diagram may be found in chapter 1: "God's Perfect Design" in Dr. Anderson's *The Christ-Centered Marriage* book on pages 21–37 or Step One of the video seminar.

A. Leaving
1. Physically
2. Spiritually
3. Mentally
4. Emotionally
5. Financially
B. Cleaving (see Fig. 1.1)

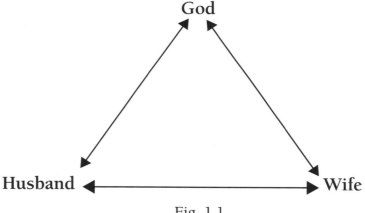

Fig. 1.1

In what ways could we be holding on to some unhealthy ties that are keeping us from committing ourselves fully to the Lord and then to each other? Ask the Lord to reveal to you the ways that you have not yet left your father and mother and have not cleaved (been faithful) only to one another.

PRAY TOGETHER

Dear Heavenly Father:
We humbly submit ourselves to You and ask for Your divine guidance. We ask that You reveal to our minds any way that we have allowed our physical heritage to be more important than our spiritual heritage. Show us anything in our lives that has taken on a greater sense of importance to us than our relationship with You. We also ask You to show us in what ways we have not honorably left our mothers and our fathers—physically, spiritually, mentally, emotionally or financially. We desire to be spiritually bonded to You in order that we may be fully bonded to each other. In Jesus' name, we pray. Amen.

As a couple, each of you should sit silently before the Lord and individually and honestly consider your relationship to God and to your own parents. Do not consider the relationship your spouse has with his/her own parents. Let the Lord be the judge, and allow your spouse to assume responsibility for his/her relationship with his/her own parents. Each one should consider the following questions:

1. Is my relationship with God the most important relationship in my life?

2. Is my relationship with my spouse the second most important relationship in my life?

3. Does the approval of relatives mean more to me than the approval of God?

4. Am I still trying to live up to the expectations of my relatives?

5. Would I be willing to sever any other relationship that would threaten my relationship with God and my spouse even if it included my physical family?

Leaving your father and mother cannot mean dishonoring them. Being disrespectful to your parents cannot lead to freedom. Consider the following questions:

1. Have you gone against your parents' counsel in getting married?

2. If so, have you prayerfully tried to reconcile your differences and receive their blessing?

3. In what ways have you been disrespectful of your parents or not shown them appreciation?

4. Write down any way that you are still bonded to your own parents or stepparents in an ungodly way:

Physically

Spiritually

Mentally

Emotionally

Financially

When you have both finished your lists, privately confess your issues to God. Then share with each other what you have learned. If it has affected your relationship with each other in a negative way, ask each other for forgiveness. If you have been unduly critical of your in-laws, you should ask your spouse to forgive you.

Conclude this Step with the following prayer together:

Dear Heavenly Father,

We thank You for revealing these important issues to us. We rededicate our lives to You and to each other. Our desire is to become one flesh and one spirit in Christ. May Your Holy Spirit bond us together in love for You and for each other. Show us how we can rightly relate to our earthly parents and other relatives. Forgive us for any way we have dishonored our parents and show us how we can honor them according to Your will. In Jesus' precious name, we pray. Amen.

A note for those who have been married previously: You may want to ask the Lord if there remains any unhealthy bonding between you and any former spouses and their families. The process would be the same as above.

STEP 2

Break Cycles of Abuse

In this Step first ask the Lord to reveal to your minds the family sins and iniquities that have been passed on to you from previous generations. Second, as a couple ask the Lord to reveal sins and wrong patterns of behavior within your own marriage. Before you begin the first part, however, realize that most Christian families are just doing the very best they can, and it would be wrong to see *only* their sins and iniquities. Take the time to encourage your spouse by sharing your answers to the following:

What habits, customs, traditions, and values have you observed in your spouse's family that you really appreciate?

Because of one man—Adam—sin entered into the world and consequently all have sinned. This transmission of sin has affected every generation and every people group of the world. The fact that there are generational cycles of abuse is a well-attested social phenomena. Here is an opportunity to find freedom in Christ by breaking the curse of ancestral sins and by making a concerted effort to stop the cycles of abuse. If we do not face these issues, we will teach what we have been taught, discipline our children the way we have been disciplined and relate to our spouses the way our parents related to each other. Scripture teaches that those who are fully trained will be like their teachers. Childhood training isn't just based on what is said, it's also based on what is modeled. Family values are more caught than taught.

When we were born physically alive but spiritually dead, we had neither the presence of God in our lives nor the knowledge of His ways. We were preprogrammed by sin to live our lives independently of God. During those formative years of our lives, we learned how to cope, survive, and succeed without God. When we came to Christ, nobody pushed the "clear" button in that marvelous computer we call the mind. That is why Paul says we must no longer be conformed to this world, but be transformed by the renewing of our minds (see Romans 12:2).

We have all developed many defense mechanisms to protect ourselves. Denial, projection, blaming and many other self-protective behaviors are no longer necessary now that we are in Christ. We are accepted for who we are and that gives us the freedom to be real and honest. Jesus is our defense. We can walk in the light and speak the truth in love. We can't fix our past, but we can be free from it by the grace of God. Just trying not to be like our parents or other role models in our lives is still letting those people determine who we are and what we are doing. Thank God for the good lessons learned, but let the Lord renew your mind and free you from your past.

Strongholds have been erected in our minds primarily from the environment in which we were raised and the traumatic experiences in our past. Those strongholds will affect our temperaments and the way we relate to our spouses and children. They will remain unless we renew our minds according to the Word of God. They result in patterns of behavior that we have learned over time.

> **Ah, Sovereign LORD, you have made the heavens and the earth by your great power and outstretched arm. Nothing is too hard for you. You show love to thousands but bring the punishment for the fathers' sins into the laps of their children after them (Jeremiah 32:17,18).**

Note: The information needed for the following outline and diagrams may be found in chapter 7: "Resolving Conflicts" in Dr. Anderson's *The Christ-Centered Marriage* book on pages 132–139 or Step Two of the video seminar.

IDENTIFYING GENERATIONAL SINS

A. Generational sins (see Exodus 20:5; Isaiah 65:6,7; Jeremiah 32:18)

1. Conflict styles

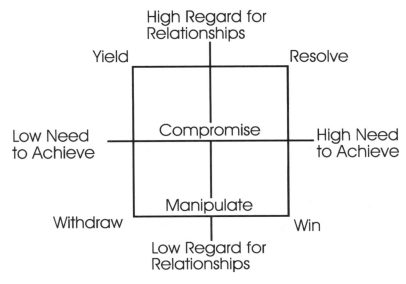

2. Communication styles

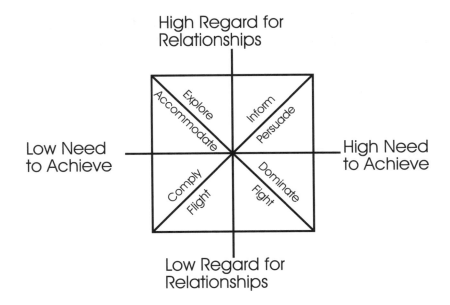

B.   Generational spiritual oppression (see Hosea 4:12,13)

C.   Generational confession (see Leviticus 26:39-42; Nehemiah 9:2,3; Psalm 106:6; Jeremiah 14:19-21)

D.   Marital/corporate sins

   1.   Breaking spiritual bondage

   2.   Renewing the mind

Pray together the following prayer:

> **Dear Heavenly Father,**
>   You are the only perfect parent that we have. We thank You for our natural parents who brought us into this world. We acknowledge that they were not perfect, nor were our families and the communities where we grew up. We ask that You reveal to our minds the dysfunctional patterns and family sins of our ancestors that have been going on for generations. Reveal to us the strongholds in our minds that have kept us from fully honoring You and embracing the truth. Give us the grace to face the truth and not to be defensive. Only You can meet our deepest needs of acceptance, security, significance and a sense of belonging. We thank You that You have made us new creations in Christ. We desire to be free from our past so we can be all that You want us to be. In Jesus' name, we pray. Amen.

As a couple, allow the Lord to reveal any and all family sins of your ancestors. Each spouse should consider his/her own upbringing and family heritage. Individually and honestly answer the following questions:

1.   What sins seemed to be repeated over and over again in your family, such as lying, criticizing, drinking, compulsive gambling, cheating, pride, bitterness, adultery, divorce, incest, sexual abuse, etc.?

2.   How did your family deal with conflict?

   How do you now deal with it?

3. How did each member of your family communicate?

   Can you speak the truth in love?

4. How did your parents discipline their children?

   How do you discipline your children?

5. Where did your parents get their significance?

   Security?

   Acceptance?

   Where do you get your significance, security and acceptance?

6. Did your parents exhibit the spiritual fruit of self-control or were they controllers or enablers?

Which are you?

7. What was their religious preference?

What non-Christian beliefs—cultic or occultic—or idols did they embrace? (An idol can be anything that has greater prominence in their lives than Christ.)

8. What lies did they believe?

How has this affected you?

9. What other ancestral sins has God revealed to your mind?

After you have individually made a list, share what you have learned with each other. Remember there is no condemnation for those who are in Christ Jesus (see Romans 8:1), and we are to accept one another as Christ has accepted us (see Romans 15:7). Mutual sharing allows both to understand and accept each other.

We are not responsible for our parents' sins but because our parents sinned, we have been taught, trained and disciplined in ways that may not be healthy. Denial and cover-up will only perpetuate the sins of our ancestors and affect us and our children. It is our responsibility to face these issues and stop the cycle of abuse so it is not passed on to the next generation. The Lord instructs us to confess our iniquity and the iniquity of our forefathers (see Leviticus 26:40).

Each spouse should now pray individually and aloud in the presence of the other the following prayer for every family sin of your ancestors that you have written down.

Dear Heavenly Father,
I confess _____(name every sin)_____ as sinful and displeasing to You. Thank You for Your forgiveness. I now turn from those sins, reject them and ask You to break their hold on our marriage. In Jesus' name, amen.

CURRENT PATTERNS IN YOUR MARRIAGE

We are to confess not only the family sins of our ancestors but also our own sins. Individual and personal sins are dealt with in the personal Steps to Freedom in Christ. However, marriages also have corporate sins that must be confessed and forsaken. Corporate sins are patterns of behavior in a marriage that are displeasing to God and contrary to His revealed will. They do not differ from individual sins in nature. Sin is still sin whether practiced by an individual or in a marriage. A pattern of sinfulness within a marriage, however, calls for husband and wife together to deal with it. Examples of corporate sins within marriage might be:

1. Engaging together in sinful activities that displease God or damage others;

2. Taking part together in non-Christian religious rituals or any cult or occult ceremonies or practices;

3. Agreeing together on any sin: covering up for each other, lying, theft, adultery, divorce, cheating on taxes, drunkenness, child abuse, etc.;

4. Withholding tithes and offerings from God;

5. Falling into patterns of gossip, slander, filthy language or other sins of the tongue in *conversations with each other*;

6. Tolerating sinful behavior in our children, especially while they live under our roof, such as foul language, sex outside of marriage, gambling, alcohol, drugs, or anything that contradicts God's written Word;

7. Reading or viewing pornographic material or anything produced by psychics, mediums, occult practitioners, cults or false religions.

As a couple, pray the following prayer together:

> **Dear Heavenly Father,**
> **As we seek You, bring to our minds all the corporate sins that we have committed in our marriage and family. Remind us of the sins of our ancestors and their families. Open our eyes to any tendency to repeat the same dysfunctional patterns. Give us discernment to identify and renounce corporate sins in our marriage that we have tolerated or have not dealt with adequately. Then grant us grace that we may confess them, renounce them, turn away from them, and commit ourselves never to return to them. In Jesus' cleansing name, we pray. Amen.**

Begin to identify your marriage's corporate sins. Usually this Step starts slowly but gradually gains momentum. Be patient and work for general agreement. When husband and wife reach a consensus on those items that they agree are corporate marriage sins, write them down on a separate sheet of paper.

In the presence of each other, confess all that the Lord has revealed to you. Then ask each other's forgiveness for the ways that your involvement in these sins has hurt the other and damaged your marriage. Once you have completed this Step, destroy the paper on which you have written these sins.

When you both are finished, make the following declaration:

We confess and renounce our own corporate sins and all those sins of our ancestors. We declare by the grace of God that we are new creations in Christ. We commit ourselves and our marriage to the Lord Jesus Christ. We take our place in Christ and by His authority we command Satan to flee from us, our marriage and our family. We belong to God, and we are a part of His family and under His protection. We put on the armor of God and commit ourselves to stand firm in our relationship to our heavenly Father.

Satan's grip from generational sins and cycles of abuse can be broken instantly. However, it will take time to renew our minds and overcome patterns of the flesh. An experienced pastor or committed Christian counselor can often help in this process.

We must accept one another and build up one another. Growth in character will also take time, and we must be patient with each other. Unconditional love and acceptance frees individuals so they can accept themselves and grow in the grace of the Lord.

Conclude this Step with the following prayer:

Dear Heavenly Father:

Thank You for Your unconditional love and acceptance. We give ourselves and each other to You. Enable us by Your grace to accept each other as You have accepted us and to be merciful as You have been merciful. Show us how we can build up one another, encourage one another and forgive one another. We acknowledge that we have not attained the full stature of Christ, but we desire to be like You in our marriage and in all we do.

We face up to our own corporate sins, as well as the family sins of our ancestors. We honestly confess our participation in them and agree that this behavior is unacceptable to You. We disown them and repudiate them. In Jesus' name, we break all the influence of their dysfunctional patterns upon us and our marriage. We cancel out all advantages, schemes and other works of the devil that have been passed from our ancestors to us and to our marriage. We break any foothold or stronghold built from the enemy's influence, and we give our hearts to You for the renewing of our minds.

We invite the Holy Spirit to apply the shed blood of the Lord Jesus on Calvary's cross to our corporate sins and to our ancestral sins. Through God's grace, by faith, we claim the work of Christ in His death and resurrection as our ransom from sin, release from guilt and removal of shame. In Jesus' precious name, we pray. Amen.

STEP 3

Balance Rights and Responsibilities

In this Step ask the Lord to reveal to your minds any ways that you have not related to each other in a godly way. You are responsible for your own character and to meet the needs of your spouse.

> **Note:** The information needed for the following diagram may be found in chapter 4: "Conforming to His Image" in Dr. Anderson's *The Christ-Centered Marriage* book on pages 75-78 or in Step Three of the video seminar.

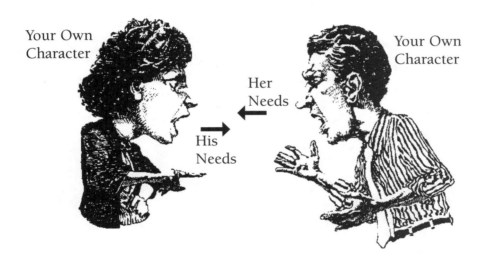

Your Own Character

Her Needs

His Needs

Your Own Character

Scripture teaches that we are to be submissive to one another's needs, which include loving, accepting and respecting one another. Pray together the following prayer, asking the Lord to reveal any ways that self-centered living and demanding your own rights have kept you from assuming your responsibilities to love and accept one another.

Pray the following together:

Dear Heavenly Father,
   We thank You for Your full and complete love and acceptance. Thank You that the unselfish sacrifice of Christ's death on the cross and His resurrection have met our greatest need for forgiveness and life. We ask You to reveal to our minds any ways that we have been selfish in our relationship with each other. Show us how we have not loved each other, accepted each other, respected each other or submitted to the needs of each other in the fear of Christ. Show us how we have been angry, jealous, insecure, manipulative or controlling. In Jesus' name, we pray. Amen.

As a couple, sit silently before the Lord and allow Him to reveal any and all ways that you have not in word or deed:

1. Loved your spouse as you should have (see Ephesians 5:22; Titus 2:4,5).

2. Accepted your spouse as you should have (see Romans 15:7).

3. Respected your spouse as you should have (see Ephesians 5:33).

4. Submitted to your spouse as you should have (see Ephesians 5:21).

5. Appreciated your spouse as you should have (see 1 Peter 3:1-9).

6. Trusted God to bring conviction and self-control in your spouse (see John 16:8; Galatians 5:22,23).

When you have finished completing the above, confess aloud what the Lord has shown you and ask your spouse's forgiveness for not being what God called you to be. Do not overlook the times and ways that you have communicated rejection, disrespect or shown lack of appreciation.

7. Now share with each other your personal needs that you feel are not being met.
   (**Caution:** Do not attack the other person's character or suggest what your spouse should or shouldn't do. That is his or her responsibility.)

8. Share with each other the times and the ways that your spouse has shown love, acceptance, respect and appreciation to you.

Conclude this Step with the following prayer of commitment:

Dear Heavenly Father,
We have fallen short of Your glory and have not lived up to our responsibilities. We have been selfish and self-centered. Thank You for Your forgiveness. We commit ourselves to an increasing pattern of love, acceptance, and respect for each other. We will submit to each other's needs in reverence to Christ. Restore to us our first love. In Jesus' name, we pray. Amen.

STEP 4

Break Sexual Bondage

> **Note:** Before you begin Step Four, *individual* freedom from sexual bondage must be achieved. You should have already dealt with your individual issues in "Step Six: Bondage vs. Freedom" in the personal Steps to Freedom in Christ. If you have not dealt with them, "Step Six: Bondage vs. Freedom" is provided on pages 29-32. As mentioned in the introduction, everyone is strongly encouraged to work through the Steps to Freedom in Christ for individuals for the complete process.

Sexual Purity

For this is the will of God, your sanctification; that is, that you abstain from sexual immorality; that each of you know how to possess his own vessel in sanctification and honor, not in lustful passion, like the Gentiles who do not know God (1 Thessalonians 4:3-5, *NASB*).

Sexual Need

The husband should fulfill his marital duty to his wife, and likewise the wife to her husband. The wife's body does not belong to her alone but also to her husband. In the same way, the husband's body does not belong to him alone but also to his wife. Do not deprive each other except by mutual consent and for a time, so that you may devote yourselves to prayer (1 Corinthians 7:3-5).

Sexual Honor

Marriage should be honored by all, and the marriage bed kept pure, for God will judge the adulterer and all the sexually immoral (Hebrews 13:4).

Sexual Lust

"But I tell you that anyone who looks at a woman lustfully has already committed adultery with her in his heart" (Matthew 5:28).

A spouse cannot resolve his/her partner's problem with lust; only Christ can break that bondage. It may be necessary to read *A Way of Escape* if either or both have been struggling with sexual bondage. However, you can and should meet one another's sexual needs.

Pray the following together:

Dear Heavenly Father,
We know that You desire for us to be free from sexual bondage and to be responsive and respectful of each other's needs. Free us from our lust and may our sexual union be one of honest love and respect for each other. We now ask You to reveal to our minds any way that we have

sexually violated our marital commitment to each other. Give us the grace to speak the truth in love and the desire to be intimately bonded together sexually. If we have not been honest about our sexual needs and desires, show us how to be honest and to express our desires to our mate. Give us the freedom to communicate in such a way that we may fully express our love for each other. In Jesus' precious name, we pray. Amen.

As a couple, sit silently before the Lord and allow Him to guide you. Ask Him to cover these next few minutes with grace. Sex is a very intimate expression of love and can be a tremendous cause for guilt and insecurity when experienced outside the will of God.

1. In what ways have you not been honest about your sexual relationship together?

2. What have you been doing together that you now think to be wrong?

3. How have your consciences been violated? Or have either of you violated the conscience of the other?

These questions need to be answered honestly and forgiveness of each other sought. The best way to find out if you have violated the other person's conscience is to ask!

Complete this Step with the following prayer:

Dear Heavenly Father,
We stand naked before You. You know the thoughts and intentions of our hearts. We desire to be sexually free before You and with each other. We acknowledge that we have sinned. Thank You for Your forgiveness and cleansing. We now give our bodies to You and to each other. Fill us with Your Holy Spirit and bond us together in love. May our sexual relationship be holy in Your sight and an expression of our love to each other. In Jesus' name, we pray. Amen.

Then declare:

In the name and authority of the Lord Jesus Christ, we command Satan to leave our presence. We present our bodies to the Lord Jesus Christ and reserve the sexual use of our bodies for each other only. We renounce the lie of Satan that sex is dirty or that our bodies are dirty. We stand naked and unashamed before God and each other.

STEP 5

Release Old Hurts

Forgiveness is what sets us free from our past. It is routinely necessary in any marriage because we don't live with perfect people. Resentment and bitterness will tear us apart. Forgiveness is the first step in reconciliation which is essential for bonding together. We also need to forgive others so that Satan cannot take advantage of us (see 2 Corinthians 2:10,11). We are to be merciful just as our heavenly Father is merciful (see Luke 6:36). We are to forgive as we have been forgiven (see Ephesians 4:31,32).

   As a couple, start this Step by making a time line, beginning with the day you first met and ending with today. Above the line, list all the *good memories* you have had together in your marriage. Below the line, list all the *painful memories*.

Good Memories

When We First Met _____ Today

Painful Memories

Thank the Lord aloud in the presence of each other for the good memories that have been especially meaningful in your relationship.

   "Lord, I thank You for _____(name the good memory)_____."

After thanking the Lord aloud for the good memories of your marriage, pray together the following prayer. Then pray silently for a few moments, allowing the Lord to help you recall the painful experiences and traumatic events of your marriage.

Dear Heavenly Father,

Sometimes pain has come to us through circumstances, sometimes from other people, sometimes from each other. Whatever the cause, surface in our minds all the pain that You want us to deal with at this time. Let us get in touch with the emotional core of hurt, heartache, trauma and threat that has damaged our marriage. Show us where we have allowed a root of bitterness to spring up, causing trouble and defiling many. In Jesus' precious name, we pray. Amen.

Caution: This step is not a time for blame-casting, but for pain-sharing.

On separate sheets of paper, individually make a list of painful memories that the Lord brings to your mind. Use real names, places and dates as much as possible. It is nearly impossible to get in touch with the emotional core of pain without using people's names and recalling specific events. It is easy for spouses to pick up one another's offenses, causing us to turn bitter toward those whom, we perceive, have wrongly influenced our spouses—even when our spouses don't see it. Jealousy can also create bitterness.

One word of caution! Everything is to be spoken in love and respect. This is not a time for malicious talk. It is a time to bring healing to damaged emotions and to free ourselves from our pasts. Simply record what happened and how you felt about it. Each spouse can say "Amen" when finished. Understand that forgiveness is not forgetting. Forgiveness may lead to forgetting, but trying to forget only complicates forgiveness. Before you start the forgiveness process, please recall these ten steps to forgiveness:

1. Allow yourself and your spouse to feel the pain, hurt, resentment, bitterness and hate (see Matthew 5:4).
2. Submit to God, recalling how Christ forgave you (see Matthew 18:21-35; Ephesians 4:32; Colossians 3:13; James 4:7,8).
3. Ask for Christ's grace and power to forgive (see Luke 11:9,10).
4. Agree to live with the unavoidable consequences of the other person's sin against you (see Colossians 3:13; Ephesians 5:21).
5. Release the offense. Tear up the moral, personal or relational debt that the other person owes you (see Matthew 6:12).
6. Never bring up a past offense again as a weapon against your spouse (see Romans 12:17).
7. Keep forgiving when your emotions recycle the pain or when the other person keeps offending you (see Matthew 18:21,22).
8. Reject the sinful act and tolerate it no longer (see Romans 12:21).
9. Turn the vengeance over to God and over to God's human authorities (see Romans 12:19,20).
10. Replace the old resentful feelings with the forgiving love of Christ (see Ephesians 4:31,32).

Do not make forgiveness more difficult than it already is. Some things we don't have to do:

1. We don't have to feel good about the person who hurt us—either before or after we forgive.
2. We don't have to tell the offender or other people about our resentful feelings unless the Holy Spirit guides us to do so. Matthew 5:23-26 does tell us to seek forgiveness and be reconciled to those we have offended as the Holy Spirit would guide.
3. We don't have to wait until we feel like forgiving. We can choose to obey God's Word right now.

Each person is to lift the painful memories before the Lord, asking for courage to face the pain honestly and for grace to forgive fully. Releasing the offenses results in relieving the pain.

Item by item, individually, forgive each person you recall and release the offenses as follows:

Lord, I forgive _____(name)_____ for _____(specifically identify all offenses and painful memories)_____.

Prayerfully focus on each person until every remembered pain has surfaced. Be sure to include your husband or wife and every painful memory in your marriage. Both spouses should also ask the Lord's forgiveness and forgive themselves as needed. Bitterness hardens the heart, but forgiveness softens it. After you have completed the above, pray the following prayer, then say the declaration that follows together aloud:

Dear Heavenly Father,
  We thank You for Your unconditional love and forgiveness. It is Your kindness and patience that have led us to repentance. In the name of Jesus and with His kindness and tenderness, we forgive every person who has ever hurt us, our family or our marriage. We forgive each other for the pain that has come through weakness, poor judgment and outright sin. We accept Your forgiveness of ourselves for the pain and damage caused in our marriage.
  By Your grace bring healing, help and hope to those who have hurt us and to those who have been hurt by us. We bless them all in the name of our Lord Jesus Christ, who taught us, "Love your enemies, do good to those who hate you, bless those who curse you, pray for those who mistreat you" (Luke 6:27,28). According to Your Word, we pray for those who have hurt us. In the precious name of Jesus Christ, amen.

Together make the following declaration:

By the authority of the Lord Jesus Christ who is seated at the heavenly Father's right hand, we assume our responsibility to resist the devil. We declare that we are crucified, buried, made alive, raised up and seated with Christ at the right hand of God. In union with Christ and with His authority we command Satan to release any foothold in our lives or any influence on our marriage. Satan, in the all-powerful name of the crucified, risen and reigning Lord Jesus Christ, leave our presence and our marriage. Do not come back. Take away with you all of your lingering effects upon our memories, our relationships, our present thoughts and our future together.

STEP 6

Unmask Satan's Deceptions

Finally be strong in the Lord and in His mighty power. Put on the armor of God so that you can take your stand against the devil's schemes. For our struggle is not against flesh and blood, but against the rulers, against the authorities, against the powers of this dark world and against the spiritual forces of evil in the heavenly realms (Ephesians 6:10-12).

A. Winning the battle for the mind (see 2 Corinthians 10:3-5)

B. Identifying continuing patterns of defeat (see 1 John 5:18-21)

C. Praying at all times in the Spirit (see Ephesians 6:18)

D. Committing to the Lord all with which you've been entrusted as a good steward (see 1 Corinthians 4:1-3)

The goal of Satan is to discredit the work of Christ and tear apart your marriage and family. His primary weapons are deception, temptation and accusation. He also uses harassment, discouragement and disillusionment. When we buy his little lies, we turn against God and each other. Our homes become battlegrounds instead of proving grounds. The tongue is the instrument Satan uses the most. We either become tongue-tied and refuse to speak the truth in love or we allow the tongue to become a destructive weapon. Our desire is for every member of the family to be a part of the building crew, rather than the wrecking crew.

If only one member of the family pays attention to the Holy Spirit, it will have strengthening effects upon every other member. On the other hand, if only one member of the family pays attention to a deceiving spirit, it will have weakening effects upon every other member as well. The purpose of this Step is to unmask the evil one's deceptions and stand against his attacks in the power of the Holy Spirit.

Satan uses real people to mount his attacks. These attacks may come from deceived or evil people inside or outside our families; for example, a friend or coworker may lead your spouse into an adulterous affair. The attacks may come through relatives or neighbors who use their tongues as destructive weapons. They may come from people who give us bad counsel to leave our marriage or abandon our children. They may even come through satanists who use occult rituals or blood sacrifices in an evil attempt to destroy our families and, therefore, our testimonies.

Ask the Lord to show you the nature of these attacks so you can stand against them and be united as one family under the lordship of Christ.

Pray the following prayer together:

Dear Heavenly Father,

We stand under Your authority. We give thanks that You are our hiding place, our protection, and our refuge. We clothe ourselves and our marriage with the Lord Jesus Christ and with the full armor of God. We choose to be strong in You, Lord, and in the power of Your might. We stand firm in our faith, submit to You, God, and resist the devil. Open our eyes to see the attacks of the evil one against us, our marriage and our family. Give us spiritual discernment to become aware of Satan's schemes, not ignorant of them. Open our eyes to the reality of the spiritual world in which we live. We ask You for the ability to discern spiritually so we can judge rightly between good and evil. As we wait silently before You, reveal to us the attacks of Satan against us, our marriage, our family and our ministries in order that we may stand against them and expose the father of lies. In Jesus' discerning name, we pray. Amen.

As a couple, make a list of whatever God brings to your minds. Look for patterns that seem to repeat themselves, such as conflicts that always break out before church or family devotions. Think of any unresolved conflicts in your marriage that keep reoccurring:

1. Repeating thoughts that cause you to close your spirit toward God and each other (see 1 Timothy 4:1; 2 Corinthians 10:3-5).

2. Recurring times or situations that cause distraction, confusion and disorientation in your marriage and home, usually during family discussions, devotions and times surrounding church or ministry opportunities (see 1 Thessalonians 2:18).

3. Improper stewardship (see 1 Corinthians 4:1,2):
   a. Sins that were tolerated in the home

   b. Anti-Christian objects brought into the home

Sinful activities need to be renounced. Attacks that come from the enemy because of our obedience to Christ need to be understood so we can recognize them and stand against them in the future. As a family, we need to understand how we wrestle not against flesh and blood, but against the powers of darkness (see Ephesians 6:12). We don't want to be blindfolded warriors who strike out at ourselves or one another. When you tear down a satanic stronghold that has been established in your family, you will have some resistance.

Make the following declaration aloud, then pray the following prayer:

Declaration

As children of God who have been delivered from the power of darkness and translated into the kingdom of God's dear Son, we submit to God and resist the devil. We cancel out all demonic working that has been passed on to us from our ancestors. We have been crucified and raised with our Lord Jesus Christ, and we now sit enthroned with Him in heavenly places. We renounce all satanic assignments that are directed toward us, our marriage, our family and our ministry. We cancel every curse that Satan and his deceived, misguided, evil workers have put on us and our marriage. We announce to Satan and all his forces that Christ became a curse for us when He died on the cross. We reject any and every way in which Satan may claim ownership of us. We belong to the Lord Jesus Christ who purchased us with His own blood. We reject all other occultic rituals and blood sacrifices whereby Satan may claim ownership of us, our marriage and our children. We declare ourselves to be eternally and completely signed over and committed to the Lord Jesus Christ. By the authority we have in Jesus Christ, we now command every familiar spirit and every enemy of the Lord Jesus Christ to leave our presence and our home forever. We commit ourselves to our heavenly Father to do His will from this day forward.

Prayer

Dear Heavenly Father,

We come to You as Your children, purchased by the blood of the Lord Jesus Christ. You are the Lord of the universe and the Lord of our lives. We yield our rights to You as the Lord of our marriage. We submit our bodies to You as instruments of righteousness, living sacrifices, that we may glorify You in our bodies and in our marriage. We reserve the sexual use of our bodies for each other only. We now ask You to fill us with Your Holy Spirit. We commit ourselves to the renewing of our minds in order to prove that Your will is good, perfect and acceptable for us. We commit ourselves to take every thought captive to the obedience of Christ. All this we do in the name and authority of the Lord Jesus Christ. Amen.

Next, you need to commit your home to the Lord.

Have you brought any foreign objects into your home that could serve as idols or objects that were ever used for non-Christian religious purposes? These could provide grounds for Satan to have access to your home.

Are there any pornographic videos, magazines or books, or occult or false religion materials?

Anything else that needs to be cleansed from your home?

Ask the Lord to reveal any such sins or articles in your home. Covenant before the Lord to remove all these items from your home and burn or destroy them. Then commit your home to the Lord as follows:

Dear Heavenly Father,

We acknowledge that You are the Lord of all. All things You have created are good and You have charged us to be good stewards of all that You have entrusted to us. Thank You for what You have provided for our family. We claim no ownership of what You have entrusted to us. We dedicate our home to You, our living quarters, our work space and all the property, possessions and finances that you have entrusted to us. We promise to remove from our home anything and everything that displeases you.

We renounce any attacks, devices or ceremonies of the enemy or his people designed to claim any ownership of that with which we have been entrusted. We have been bought and purchased by the blood sacrifice of our Lord Jesus Christ. We claim our home for our family as a place of spiritual safety and protection from the evil one. We renounce anything and everything that has taken place in our home by us, or by those who lived in our house before us, that does not please our heavenly Father. We ask for Your divine protection around our home and our family. We desire to honor You in all our ways. Thank You for Your protection.

Lord, you are the King of our lives and our marriage and we exalt You. May all that we do bring honor and glory to You. In Jesus' holy name, we pray. Amen.

Then declare:

As children of God, seated with Christ in the heavenly places, we command every evil spirit to leave our presence and our home. We renounce all attacks against our house, property, possessions and our very selves. We announce to Satan and all his workers that our marriage, our family and all that our Heavenly Father has entrusted to us belongs to the Lord Jesus Christ. We submit completely to the direction and guidance of the Holy Spirit.

STEP 7

Renew Christian Marriage

All who marry, whether Christian or not, become part of God's creation order of marriage (see Genesis 1:26-28; 2:18-25). A *creation order* is a God-given longing built into the fabric of human life. As a result of this God-given longing, every culture and all people groups on earth practice marriage in some form. No exceptions! Violating marriage breaks the order of creation and always brings terrible consequences.

When one partner (or both) knows Jesus Christ as Lord and Savior, their marriage becomes "sanctified," or set apart as holy, part of God's new Christian order (see 1 Corinthians 7:14). They commit themselves to Christ's new creation in marriage and enter a marriage covenant before God and one another. Christian marriage far exceeds a mere social contract. Marriage as a social contract is only a legal agreement between two parties. Christian marriage is a lifelong covenant with binding vows, spoken before God and human witnesses. If the vows are broken, they bring God's judgment. If they are kept, they bring God's rewards.

Satan's lie is that we are married singles, bound only by a human relationship and a social contract. That means marriage can be broken whenever either party feels the partners have "irreconcilable differences." In Christ, there are no irreconcilable differences. We have been reconciled to Him, and we have been given the ministry of reconciliation.

God's truth is that the marriage vows bind us into the organic union of Christian marriage, a new creation that lasts until the death of one of the spouses. A contract can be canceled, but a new creation lasts a lifetime. Contracts can be broken or renegotiated, but a new creation either grows toward fulfillment or is violated.

Living in obedience to God's Word in Christian marriage (or any other part of life) brings the Lord's shelter of protection (see Psalm 91). It results in God's blessings, including children who are set apart for God's purposes (see 1 Corinthians 7:14). By God's grace His blessings extend not only to those who are faithful to Him, but also to their descendants for many generations to come (see Exodus 20:6; Deuteronomy 7:9; Luke 1:50). Violating marriage brings God's curse, not only upon ourselves, but also upon our descendants for three or four generations (see Exodus 34:7; Numbers 14:18; Jeremiah 32:18).

Make the following declaration aloud together:

> We submit ourselves and our marriage to God, and we resist the devil. Satan, we renounce you in all your works and all your ways. In the all-powerful name of the Lord Jesus Christ, we command you to leave our marriage. Take all of your deceitful spirits, evil demons and fallen angels with you, and go to the place where the Lord Jesus Christ sends you. Leave us and our marriage and don't come back. Take with you all of your temptations to violate our marriage vows. Take with you all of your accusing and demeaning thoughts we could have against each other. Take with you all of your deceptions that contradict God's written Word. The Lord Jesus Christ has torn down your demonic authority, and we stand against your influence and activity toward our lives and our marriage.
>
> You are a defeated foe, disarmed of your weapons, and made a public spectacle by the cross of Christ (see Colossians 2:15). Greater is He that is in us than he that is in the world (see 1 John 4:4). The prince of this world now stands condemned (see John 16:11). Christ has the supremacy over every evil throne, power, rule or authority (see Colossians 1:16). Jesus shared our humanity so that by His death He might destroy him who holds the power of death—that is, the devil (see Hebrews 2:14). We resist you by the authority of Christ and because we are alive in Him; therefore, you must flee from us (see James 4:7).

Pray the following aloud:

Heavenly Father,

We gladly acknowledge that You created marriage and family life for Your glory. Thank You for designing marriage as a *creation order*, woven into the fabric of human society. We commit ourselves anew to a covenant of Christian marriage with all its blessings.

We renounce the lie of the devil that we are married singles, bound only by a human relationship and a social contract. We recall that our marriage is binding as long as we both shall live. We acknowledge that we can never violate our marriage vows without bringing lasting damage upon ourselves, our children and our descendants for three or four generations to come.

We confess that we have not perfectly lived up to our marriage vows. We confess that we have not always lived as one in Christ. We have fallen short of Your perfect will by our own selfishness and sin. We gladly accept Your forgiveness of our sins through the blood of Christ on the cross (see 1 John 2:1,2). By grace through faith we receive Christ's abundant life into our hearts and His holiness into our marriage (see John 10:10; 1 Corinthians 7:14).

We crucify our own fleshly lusts and sinful desires which tempt us to ignore or violate our marriage vows (see 1 Peter 2:11; Galatians 5:24). We clothe ourselves and our marriage with the Lord Jesus Christ and His armor of light (see Romans 13:12-14; Galatians 3:26,27). We give ourselves to live by the Spirit in daily obedience to Christ (see Galatians 5:16; 1 Peter 1:2).

We announce that in Christ we have all the spiritual blessings we need to live out our new creation. We affirm that we are one in Christ Jesus—one marriage, one flesh, one family (see Ephesians 1:3; 3:14,15; Genesis 2:24; Mark 10:6-9). We submit ourselves and our marriage to the ownership of our heavenly Father, to the lordship of Jesus Christ and to the power of the Holy Spirit. From this day forward, we ask You to use our marriage to display Your splendor before our children. We invite You to work through us to show Your glory in the midst of a corrupt and wicked generation. In Jesus' glorious name, amen.

When you were first married, you spoke vows that said, "I take you as my lawful, wedded wife (or husband)." In this renewal of vows, become a giver instead of a taker. Please note the slight change in wording from "I *take you* as my wedded wife (or husband)" to "I *give myself to you* to be your husband (or wife)." As you hold hands and face each other, first the husband and then the wife repeat the following vows. In a group setting, a minister of the gospel can lead this renewal of marriage vows.

" I, _____, give myself to you, _____, to be your wedded _____(husband or wife)_____, to have and to hold from this day forward, for better or for worse, for richer or for poorer, in sickness and in health, to love and to cherish, until death do us part, according to God's holy Word; and hereto, I pledge you my faithfulness."

Living Free in Christ

Intimacy and freedom must be maintained. You have won a very important battle in an ongoing war. Freedom is yours as long as you keep choosing truth and standing firm in the strength of the Lord. If more painful memories should surface or if you become aware of lies that you have been believing, renounce them and choose the truth. Some couples have found it helpful to go through these Steps again.

If you haven't already done so, please read *Victory over the Darkness* and *The Bondage Breaker*. If you are a parent, we suggest reading *The Seduction of Our Children*. *Walking in the Light* was written to help people understand God's guidance so they are able to discern counterfeit guidance. In order to maintain your freedom, we suggest the following:

1. Become active together in a Christ-centered church, a small Christian group and a ministry for Christ. Build healthy allies for your marriage. Step outside of yourselves for Christ.

2. Study your Bibles daily, pray and be sensitive to the leading of the Holy Spirit. We also suggest reading one chapter together every day of *Living Free in Christ* for the next thirty-six days. Then use the devotional, *Daily in Christ* by Neil and Joanne Anderson.

3. Review and apply your personal freedom in Christ. Remind yourselves of your identity in Christ, winning the battle for the mind and processing the personal Steps to Freedom in Christ (on pages 15-38) as an ongoing personal inventory. The Lord uses marriage to reveal each layer of the onion of our selfishness which He wants to peel off.

4. Take every thought captive to the obedience of Christ. Assume responsibility for private thoughts, reject the lie, choose the truth and stand firm in your identity in Christ.

5. Don't drift away! It is very easy to get lazy in your thoughts and revert back to old habit patterns of thinking. Share struggles openly with each other. See the following suggested daily prayer.

6. Don't expect your spouse to fight your battles. While you can help each other, no one else can think, pray, or read the Bible for you.

7. If serious problems still prevail, seek out a competent Christian pastor or counselor who is committed to the biblical institution of marriage and not just to the individual apart from marriage.

Pray daily with confidence as follows:

Dear Heavenly Father,
We honor You as our sovereign Lord. We acknowledge that You are always present with us. You are the only all-powerful and all-wise God. You are kind and loving in all Your ways. We love You. We thank You that we are united together with Christ and we are spiritually alive in Him. We choose not to love the world, and we crucify the flesh and all its sinful desires.

We thank You that we are children of God, new creations in Christ Jesus, full of eternal life in Christ. We ask You to fill us with Your Holy Spirit that we may live our lives free from sin. We declare our dependence upon You, and we take our stand against Satan and all his lying ways. We choose to believe the truth and we refuse to be discouraged or to give up hope on our marriage. You are the God of all hope, and we are confident that You will meet our needs as we seek to live according to Your Word. We express with confidence that we can live a responsible life and be faithful in our marriage through Christ who strengthens us. We ask these things in the precious name of our Lord and Savior, Jesus Christ. Amen.

DECLARATION

We now take our stand in Christ and we put on the whole armor of God. In union with Christ, we command Satan and all his evil spirits to depart from us. We submit our bodies to God as living sacrifices and renew our minds by the living Word of God in order that we may prove that the will of God is good, acceptable and perfect.

Additional resources to be used with the Steps for married couples:
See the bibliography for complete information on each resource.

Books:

The Christ-Centered Marriage and *Study Guide*

Victory over the Darkness and *Study Guide*

The Bondage Breaker and *Study Guide*

The Seduction of Our Children

Spiritual Protection for Your Children

A Way of Escape

Running the Red Lights

Walking in the Light

Living Free in Christ

Daily in Christ

Audio/Visual Series:

"The Christ-Centered Marriage Video Seminar"

"Resolving Personal Conflicts"

"Resolving Spiritual Conflicts"

We Are One in Christ

WE ARE ACCEPTED IN CHRIST

John 1:12	We are God's children.
John 15:15	We are Christ's friends.
Romans 5:1	We have been justified.
1 Corinthians 6:17	We are united with the Lord and one with Him in spirit.
1 Corinthians 6:20	We have been bought with a price. We belong to God.
1 Corinthians 12:27	We are members of Christ's Body.
Ephesians 1:1	We are saints.
Ephesians 1:5	We have been adopted as God's children.
Ephesians 2:18	We have direct access to God through the Holy Spirit.
Colossians 1:14	We have been redeemed and forgiven of all our sins.
Colossians 2:10	We are complete in Christ.

WE ARE SECURE IN CHRIST

Romans 8:1,2	We are free from condemnation.
Romans 8:28	We are assured that all things work together for good.
Romans 8:31-34	We are free from any condemning charges against us.
Romans 8:35-39	We cannot be separated from the love of God.
2 Corinthians 1:21	We have been established, anointed and sealed by God.
Colossians 3:3	We are hidden with Christ in God.
Philippians 1:6	We are confident that the good work God has begun in us will be perfected.
Philippians 3:20	We are citizens of heaven.
2 Timothy 1:7	We have not been given a spirit of fear, but of power, love and a sound mind.
Hebrews 4:16	We can find grace and mercy in time of need.
1 John 5:18	We are born of God and the evil one cannot touch us.

WE ARE SIGNIFICANT IN CHRIST

Matthew 5:13,14	We are the salt and light of the earth.
John 15:1,5	We are a branch of the true vine, a channel of His life.
John 15:16	We have been chosen and appointed to bear fruit.
Acts 1:8	We are personal witnesses of Christ.
1 Corinthians 3:16	We are God's temple.
2 Corinthians 5:17-21	We are ministers of reconciliation.
2 Corinthians 6:1	We are God's coworkers (see 1 Corinthians 3:9).
Ephesians 2:6	We are seated with Christ in the heavenly realm.
Ephesians 2:10	We are God's workmanship.
Ephesians 3:12	We may approach God with freedom and confidence.
Philippians 4:13	We can do all things through Christ who strengthens us.

The purpose of the Steps to Beginning Your Marriage Free is to go beyond the personal Steps to Freedom in Christ by helping engaged couples resolve issues from the past that could create conflicts in their future marriage. Assuming responsibility and resolving your own issues before the Lord is the best way to prepare for marriage!

This appendix assumes that you have already read *The Christ-Centered Marriage*. In addition, reading *Victory over the Darkness* and *The Bondage Breaker* or attending a Living Free in Christ conference will help you resolve personal and spiritual conflicts and instruct you in living the Christian life by faith in the power of the Holy Spirit. The conference is available on video or audiocassette from Freedom in Christ Ministries. We encourage you to work through the Steps to Freedom in Christ before proceeding with the following Steps to Beginning Your Marriage Free.

Are you willing to allow God to show you anything He desires? Is it your desire to walk in the light and speak the truth in love? Then you are ready to work through this process. Set aside a day and find a quiet place where you will not be disturbed. If your current courtship relationship is experiencing difficulty, we suggest that you have a responsible person whom you trust assist you in this process.

Before You Begin the Process

In order to resolve conflicts, you have to address many issues that can seem negative. Therefore, begin by reflecting on the encouraging issues. Answer the following questions and later share your answers with your fiancé/fiancée:

What three character qualities do you most appreciate about your fiancé/fiancée?

1.

2.

3.

What three things does your fiancé/fiancée do that you really appreciate?

1.

2.

3.

Begin with this prayer of commitment:

Dear Heavenly Father,

I love You and thank You for Your grace, truth, love, power, forgiveness and blessings in Christ. I can love my fiancé/fiancée because You first loved me. I can forgive my fiancé/fiancée because I have been forgiven, and there can be a mutual acceptance because You have accepted us. I desire nothing more than to know and do Your will. I ask for Your divine guidance and protection during this time of seeking freedom for my future marriage.

I buckle on the belt of Your truth, put on the breastplate of Your righteousness and commit myself to the gospel of peace. I hold up the shield of faith and stand against the flaming arrows of the enemy. I commit myself to take every thought captive in obedience to You. I put on the helmet of salvation which assures me of Your forgiveness, Your life, and my freedom in You. I put off the old self and put on the new self which is being renewed in Your image. I take the sword of the Spirit, the spoken Word of God, to defend myself against the father of lies.

I acknowledge my dependence on You and understand that apart from Christ I can do nothing. I pray that You will grant me genuine repentance and living faith. I desire Your plans for my future marriage, for it to be a beautiful picture of Your relationship with the Body of Christ. I ask You to fill me with Your Holy Spirit, lead me into all truth and set me free in Christ. In Jesus' precious name, I pray. Amen.

STEP 1

Establish God's Priority for Marriage

Ask the Lord to reveal to you if you are prepared to leave your father and mother and be bonded only to your fiancé/fiancée.

Remember the words of Jesus:

> "Anyone who loves his father or mother more than me is not worthy of me; anyone who loves his son or daughter more than me is not worthy of me" (Matthew 10:37).

This does not mean you shouldn't honor your father and mother, but it does mean that you can have only one Lord in your life. It means your *spiritual* heritage must take precedence over your *natural* heritage.

> For this reason a man will leave his father and mother and be united to his wife, and they will become one flesh. The man and his wife were both naked, and they felt no shame (Genesis 2:24,25).

LEAVING

In what ways could you be holding on to some unhealthy ties that are keeping you from committing yourself fully to the Lord and to your fiancé/fiancée? Those ties could be physical, emotional, mental, spiritual or financial.

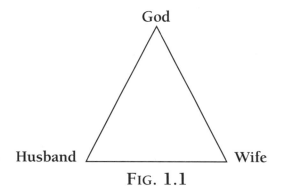

FIG. 1.1

CLEAVING (SEE FIG. 1.1)

Ask the Lord to reveal to you the ways that you have not yet left your father and mother so you can cleave (be faithful) only to your fiancé/fiancée after you marry.

Pray:

Dear Heavenly Father,
I humbly submit myself to You and ask for Your divine guidance. I ask that You reveal to my mind the ways that I might allow my physical heritage to be more important than my spiritual heritage. Show me anything in my life that might take on a greater sense of importance to me than my relationship with You. I also ask You to show me in which ways I am not willing to honorably leave my father and mother—physically, spiritually, mentally, emotionally or financially. I desire to be spiritually bonded to You in order that I may be fully bonded to my fiancé/fiancée in marriage. In Jesus' name, I pray. Amen.

181

You should sit silently before the Lord and honestly consider your relationship to God and to your own parents. Do not consider the relationship that your fiancé/fiancée has with his or her own parents. Let the Lord be the judge, and allow your fiancé/fiancée to assume responsibility for his or her relationship with his or her own parents.

Consider How You Relate to Your Parents

In the space provided, answer the questions and write down any thoughts that come to your mind regarding these issues.

1. Is my relationship with God the most important relationship in my life?

2. Is my relationship with my fiancé/fiancée the second most important relationship in my life?

3. Does the approval of relatives mean more to me than the approval of God?

4. Am I still trying to live up to the expectations of my relatives?

5. Would I be willing to sever any relationship that would threaten my relationship with God even if it included my fiancé/fiancée or others of my physical family?

Consider How You Honor Your Parents

Leaving father and mother cannot mean dishonoring them. Being disrespectful to your parents cannot lead to freedom. Consider the following questions:

1. Have you gone against your parents' counsel in planning to get married?

2. If so, have you prayerfully tried to reconcile your differences and receive their blessing?

3. In what ways have you been disrespectful of your parents?

In what ways have you not shown appreciation?

4. Write down any ways that you are still bonded to your own parents or stepparents in an ungodly way.

Physically

Spiritually

Mentally

Emotionally

Financially

When you have finished your list, privately confess your issues to God.

Later share with your fiancé/fiancée what you have learned. If it has affected your relationship with your fiancé/fiancée in a negative way, ask him or her for forgiveness. If you have been unduly critical of your future in-laws, you should ask your fiancé/fiancée to forgive you.

Conclude this step with the following prayer:

Dear Heavenly Father,

I thank You for revealing these important issues to me. I rededicate my life to You. My desire in my future marriage is to become one flesh and one spirit in Christ. May Your Holy Spirit bond us together in love for You. Show me how I can rightly relate to my earthly parents and other relatives. Thank You for Your forgiveness for any way that I have dishonored my parents, and show me how I can honor them according to Your will. In Jesus' precious name, I pray. Amen.

> **A note for those who have been married previously:** You may need to ask the Lord if there remains any unhealthy bonding between former spouses and their families. The process would be the same as above.

STEP 2

Break Cycles of Abuse

In this Step, first ask the Lord to reveal to your mind the family sins and iniquities that have been passed on to you from previous generations. Second, ask the Lord to reveal sins and wrong patterns of behavior that may affect your future marriage. Before you begin the first part, however, realize that most Christian families are just doing the very best they can, and it would be wrong to see *only* their sins and iniquities.

What habits, customs, traditions and values have you observed in your fiancé's/fiancée's family that you really appreciate?

Later, take the time to encourage your fiancé/fiancée by sharing your answer to the previous question.

Because of one man, Adam, sin entered into the world and consequently all have sinned. This transmission of sin has affected every generation and every people group of the world. The fact that there are generational cycles of abuse is a well-attested social phenomena. Here is an opportunity to find freedom in Christ by breaking the progression of ancestral sins and by making a concerted effort to stop the cycles of abuse. If we do not face these issues, we will teach what we have been taught, discipline any children we may have the way we have been disciplined, and relate to our future spouses the way our parents related to each other. Scripture teaches that those who are fully trained will be like their teachers. Childhood training isn't just based on what was said; it's also based on what was modeled. Family values are caught more than taught.

When we were born physically alive but spiritually dead, we had neither the presence of God in our lives nor the knowledge of His ways. We have been programmed by sin to live our lives independent of God. During those formative years of our lives, we learned how to cope, survive and succeed without God. When we came to Christ, nobody pushed the *clear* button in that marvelous computer we call the mind. That is why Paul says we must no longer be conformed to this world, but be transformed by the renewing of our minds (see Romans 12:2).

We have all developed many defense mechanisms to protect ourselves. Denial, projection, blaming and many other self-protective behaviors are no longer necessary now that we are in Christ. We are accepted for who we are and that gives us the freedom to be real and honest. Jesus is our defense. We can walk in the light and speak the truth in love. We can't fix our pasts, but we can be free from them by the grace of God. Just trying not to be like our parents or other role models in our lives is still letting those people determine who we are and what we are doing. Thank God for the good lessons learned, but let the Lord renew your mind, and become free from what was not right in your past.

Strongholds have been erected in your mind by the environment in which you were raised and the traumatic experiences in your past. Those strongholds affect your temperament and the way you relate to your fiancé/fiancée and future children. Strongholds result in deeply set patterns of behavior that will remain unless we renew our minds according to the Word of God.

Ah, Sovereign Lord, you have made the heavens and the earth by your great power and outstretched arm. Nothing is too hard for you. You show love to thousands but bring the punishment for the fathers' sins into the laps of their children after them (Jeremiah 32:17,18).

IDENTIFYING GENERATIONAL SINS

Start this Step by asking the Lord to reveal to your mind the iniquities and family sins of your ancestors passed on spiritually and environmentally.

Pray the following prayer:

Dear Heavenly Father,
You are the only perfect parent I have. Thank You for my natural parents who brought me into this world. I acknowledge that they were not perfect, nor was my family and community where I grew up. I ask that You reveal to my mind the dysfunctional patterns and family sins of my ancestors that have been going on for generations. Reveal to me the strongholds in my mind that have kept me from fully honoring You and embracing the truth. Give me the grace to face the truth and not to be defensive. Only You can meet my deepest needs of acceptance, security, significance and a sense of belonging. I thank You that You have made me a new creation in Christ. I desire to be free from my past so I can be all that You want me to be. In Jesus' name, I pray. Amen.

Allow the Lord to reveal any and all family sins of your ancestors. Considering your own upbringing and family heritage, honestly answer the following questions:

1. What sins seemed to be repeated over and over again in your family, such as lying, criticizing, drinking, compulsive gambling, cheating, pride, bitterness, adultery, divorce, incest, sexual abuse, etc.?

2. How did your family deal with conflict?

   How do you now deal with it?

3. How did each member of your family communicate? Can you speak the truth in love?

4. How did your parents discipline their children?

How will you discipline your children?

5. Where did your parents get their significance?

Security?

Acceptance?

Where do you get your significance? Security? Acceptance?

6. Did your parents exhibit the spiritual fruit of self-control or were they controllers or enablers? Which are you?

7. What was their religious preference?

What non-Christian beliefs—cultic or occultic—or idols did they embrace? (An idol can be anything that has greater prominence in their lives than does Christ.)

8. What lies did they believe?

How has this affected you?

9. What other ancestral sins has God revealed to your mind?

Later share what you have learned from your list with your fiancé/fiancée. Knowing that you are willing to face these issues will give you and your fiancé/fiancée a lot more hope for the future. Remember, "there is now no condemnation for those who are in Christ Jesus" (Romans 8:1), and we are to accept one another as Christ has accepted us (see Romans 15:7). Mutual sharing allows both of you to understand and accept each other.

We are not responsible for our parents' sins, but because our parents sinned, we have been taught, trained and disciplined in ways that may not be healthy. Denial and cover-up will only perpetuate the sins of our ancestors and affect us and our future children. It is our responsibility to face these issues and stop the cycle of abuse so it is not passed on to the next generation. The Lord instructs us to confess our iniquity and the iniquity of our forefathers (see Leviticus 26:40).

Pray the following prayer for every family sin of your ancestors that you have written down.

> **Dear Heavenly Father,**
> I confess _____(name every sin)_____ as sinful and displeasing to You. Thank You for Your **forgiveness. I now turn from those sins, reject them and ask You to break their hold on my future marriage. In Jesus' name, I pray. Amen.**

CURRENT PATTERNS IN COURTSHIP

We are to confess not only the family sins of our ancestors but also our own sins. Individual sins are dealt with in the personal Steps to Freedom in Christ. However, dating/courting relationships also have corporate sins which must be confessed and forsaken. Corporate sins are patterns of behavior in dating/courting relationships that are displeasing to God and contrary to His revealed will. They do not differ from individual sins in nature.

Sin is still sin whether practiced by an individual or by a couple. A pattern of sinfulness within a dating/courting relationship should be dealt with before you get married or it will continue on into marriage.

Examples of corporate sins in dating/courting relationships might be:

1. Engaging together in sinful activities that displease God or damage others;

2. Taking part together in non-Christian religious rituals or any cult or occult ceremonies or practices;

3. Agreeing together on any sin: covering up for each other, lying, theft, fornication, divorce, drunkenness, child abuse, etc.;

4. Withholding tithes and offerings from God;

5. Falling into patterns of gossip, slander, filthy language or other sins of the tongue in conversations with each other;

6. Tolerating sinful behavior in your families and friends, especially while they live under your roof, such as swearing, foul language, sex outside of marriage, gambling, alcohol, drugs or anything that contradicts God's written Word;

7. Reading or viewing pornographic material or anything produced by psychics, mediums, occult practitioners, cults or false religions.

Pray the following prayer:

Dear Heavenly Father,
As I seek You, bring to my mind all the corporate sins that I have committed in my courting relationship and family. Remind me of the sins of my ancestors and their families. Open my eyes to any tendency to repeat the same dysfunctional patterns. Give me discernment to identify and renounce corporate sins with my fiancé/fiancée that I have tolerated or have not dealt with adequately. Then grant me Your grace that I may confess them, renounce them and turn away from them so I may commit myself never to return to them. In Jesus' cleansing name, I pray. Amen.

Identify any corporate sins the Holy Spirit has brought to your mind and write them down on a separate sheet of paper. Confess all that the Lord has revealed to you. Once you have completed this Step, destroy the paper on which you have written these sins.

At a later time, ask your fiancé's/fiancée's forgiveness for the ways that your involvement in these sins has hurt him or her and damaged your relationship together. If your fiancé/fiancée is reluctant to participate with you in this sharing, then share with him or her how the Lord has convicted you in what you have been doing. With firmness and love say that you are no longer willing to be a part of these actions. Should your fiancé/fiancée not accept you for making a stand for righteousness' sake, then it is best to find that out before you are married.

When finished, make the following declaration aloud:

> **I confess and renounce my own corporate sins and all those sins of my ancestors. I declare by the grace of God that I am a new creation in Christ. I commit myself and my future marriage to the Lord Jesus Christ. I take my place in Christ and by His authority I command Satan to flee from me and my relationship with my fiancé/fiancée (and our family relationships). I belong to God and am a part of His family and under His protection. I put on the armor of God and commit myself to stand firm in my relationship to my heavenly Father.**

Satan's grip from generational sins and cycles of abuse can be broken instantly. However, it will take time to renew our minds and overcome patterns of the flesh. An experienced pastor or committed Christian counselor can often help in this process. We must accept one another and build up one another. Growth in character will also take time and we must be patient with each other. Unconditional love and acceptance frees individuals so they can accept themselves and grow in the grace of the Lord.

Conclude this step with the following prayer:

> **Dear Heavenly Father,**
>
> Thank You for Your unconditional love and acceptance. I give myself to You. Enable me by Your grace to accept my fiancé/fiancée as You have accepted me, and to be merciful as You have been merciful. Show me how we can build up, encourage and forgive each other. I acknowledge that I have not attained the full stature of Christ, but I desire to be like You in my future marriage and in all I do.
>
> I face up to my own corporate sins, as well as the family sins of my ancestors. I honestly confess my participation in them and agree that this behavior is unacceptable to You. I disown them and repudiate them. In Jesus' name, I break all the influence of their dysfunctional patterns upon me and my future marriage. I cancel out all advantages, schemes and other works of the devil that have been passed to me from my ancestors. I break any foothold or stronghold built from the enemy's influence and I give my heart to You and commit to the renewing of my mind.
>
> I invite the Holy Spirit to apply the shed blood of the Lord Jesus on Calvary's cross to my corporate sins and to my ancestral sins. Through God's grace, by faith, I claim the work of Christ in His death and resurrection as my ransom from sin, release from guilt and removal of shame. In Jesus' precious name, I pray. Amen.

STEP 3

Balance Rights and Responsibilities

In this Step ask the Lord to reveal to your mind any ways that you have not related to your fiancé/fiancée in a godly way.

"Do nothing out of selfish ambition or vain conceit, but in humility consider others better than yourselves. Each of you should look not only to your own interests, but also to the interests of others. Your attitude should be the same as that of Christ Jesus" (Philippians 2:3-5). "Who are you to judge someone else's servant? To his own master he stands or falls. And he will stand, for the Lord is able to make him stand" (Romans 14:4).

The following is a list of the languages of love from *The Five Love Languages* by Gary Chapman. If you do not remember what each language means, you may want to read or review chapter 8 in *The Christ-Centered Marriage* before completing this activity. Read the list and write 1 beside the way you tend to show love to others; write 2 beside the way you like to have love shown to you; write 3 beside the way your fiancé/fiancée shows love to you; and write 4 beside the way you tend to show love to your fiancé/fiancée.

_____ Gifts
_____ Service
_____ Time
_____ Touch
_____ Words

What personal needs do you feel are not being met in your life? (For example, you don't feel loved, accepted, appreciated, etc.)

Caution: Do not attack your fiancé's/fiancée's character or suggest what he or she should or should not do. That is his or her responsibility.

Complete the following statements to reinforce your fiancé's/fiancée's attempts to love you:

1. I really feel loved when he or she does or says…

2. I really feel accepted when he or she does or says…

3. I really feel respected when he or she does or says…

4. I really feel appreciated when he or she does or says…

Scripture teaches that we are to be submissive to one another's needs, which include loving, accepting and respecting one another. Pray the following prayer, asking the Lord to reveal any ways that self-centered living and demanding your own rights have kept you from assuming your responsibilities to love and accept your fiancé/fiancée.

> **Dear Heavenly Father,**
>   **Thank You for Your full and complete love and acceptance. Thank You that the unselfish sacrifice of Christ's death on the cross and His resurrection have met my greatest need for forgiveness and life. I ask You to reveal to my mind any ways that I have been selfish in my relationship with my fiancé/fiancée. Show me how I have not loved, accepted or respected him or her in the fear of Christ. Show me how I have been angry, jealous, insecure, manipulative or controlling. In Jesus' name, I pray. Amen.**

Sit silently before the Lord and allow Him to reveal any and all ways that you have not in word or deed...

1. Loved your fiancé/fiancée as you should have (see Ephesians 5:22; Titus 2:4,5).

2. Accepted your fiancé/fiancée as you should have (see Romans 15:7).

3. Respected your fiancé/fiancée as you should have (see Ephesians 5:33).

4. Appreciated your fiancé/fiancée as you should have (see 1 Peter 3:1-9).

5. Trusted God to bring conviction and self-control in your fiancé/fiancée (see John 16:8; Galatians 5:23).

When you have completed the above, verbally confess what the Lord has shown you.

Later ask your fiancé's/fiancée's forgiveness for not being what God called you to be. Don't overlook the times and ways that you have communicated rejection, disrespect or shown lack of appreciation. Now share your own personal needs that you feel are not being met (without attacking the other person's character or telling him or her what he or she should or shouldn't do). Then share the times and the ways that your fiancé/fiancée has shown love, acceptance, respect and appreciation to you.

Conclude this Step with the following prayer of commitment:

Dear Heavenly Father,
I have fallen short of Your glory and have not lived up to my responsibilities. I have been selfish and self-centered. Thank You for Your forgiveness. I commit myself to an increasing pattern of love, acceptance and respect for my fiancé/fiancée. In Jesus' name, I pray. Amen.

STEP 4

Break Sexual Bondage

> **Note:** Before you begin Step Four, *individual* freedom from sexual bondage must be achieved. You should have already dealt with your personal issues in "Step Six: Bondage vs. Freedom" in the Steps to Freedom in Christ (pp. 29-32).
>
> As mentioned in the introduction, everyone is strongly encouraged to work through the individual Steps to Freedom in Christ for the complete process.

Sexual purity:

For this is the will of God, your sanctification; that is, that you abstain from sexual immorality; that each of you know how to possess his own vessel in sanctification and honor, not in lustful passion, like the Gentiles who do not know God (1 Thessalonians 4:3-5, *NASB*).

Sexual need:

The husband should fulfill his marital duty to his wife, and likewise the wife to her husband. The wife's body does not belong to her alone but also to her husband. In the same way, the husband's body does not belong to him alone but also to his wife. Do not deprive each other except by mutual consent and for a time, so that you may devote yourselves to prayer (1 Corinthians 7:3-5).

Sexual honor:

Marriage should be honored by all, and the marriage bed kept pure, for God will judge the adulterer and all the sexually immoral (Hebrews 13:4).

Sexual lust:

"But I tell you that anyone who looks at a woman lustfully has already committed adultery with her in his heart" (Matthew 5:28).

A person cannot personally resolve a problem of lust; only Christ can break that bondage. Be sure to read Chapter 10 in *The Christ-Centered Marriage* before you proceed. Many have found great encouragement by reading *A Way of Escape* (Neil Anderson) and *Running the Red Lights* (Charles Mylander) which share how Jesus Christ is the answer for those struggling with sexual bondage. Individual sexual freedom must be achieved first before you can meet one another's sexual needs in marriage.

Consider areas where you may have opened the door to the enemy and brought bondage to your relationship. These questions need to be honestly answered and forgiveness sought.

1. In what ways have you not been honest in your relationship with your fiancé/fiancée?

2. What have you been doing together that you now think is wrong?

3. How has your conscience been violated or how have you violated the conscience of the other person?

At a later time, be sure you cover any forgiveness issues with your fiancé/fiancée. The best way to find out if you have violated the other person's conscience is to ask!

Complete this step with the following prayer:

Dear Heavenly Father,

I stand before You acknowledging that You know the thoughts and intentions of my heart. I desire to be sexually free before You. I acknowledge that I have sinned and thank You for Your forgiveness and cleansing. I now give my body to You and reserve its sexual use for marriage only. Fill me with Your Holy Spirit and bond us together in love in the right way and at the right time. May my sexual relationship be holy in Your sight. In Jesus' name, I pray. Amen.

Then declare aloud:

In the name and authority of the Lord Jesus Christ, I command Satan to leave my presence. I present my body to the Lord Jesus Christ and reserve its sexual use for my future marriage only.

If you have been sexually involved with your fiancé/fiancée prior to marriage, pray the following aloud:

Dear Heavenly Father,

I know that You desire for me to be free from sexual bondage and to be righteously responsive and respectful of my fiancé's/fiancée's needs. Free me from my lust and show me how we can relate to each other in honest love and respect. I now ask You to reveal to my mind any way that I have sexually sinned in our relationship. Give me the grace to face the truth. In Jesus' precious name, I pray. Amen.

Sit silently before the Lord and allow Him to guide you. Ask Him to cover these next few minutes with grace. Sex is a very intimate expression of love and can be a tremendous cause for guilt and insecurity when experienced outside the will of God.

STEP 5

Release Old Hurts

Forgiveness is what sets us free from our past. It is routinely necessary in any relationship because we don't live with perfect people. Resentment and bitterness will tear us apart. Forgiveness is the first step in reconciliation, which is essential for bonding together. We also need to forgive others so Satan cannot take advantage of us (see 2 Corinthians 2:10,11). We are to be merciful just as our heavenly Father is merciful (see Luke 6:36). We are to forgive as we have been forgiven (see Ephesians 4:32).

Start this step by making a time line, beginning with the day you first met your fiancé/fiancée and ending with today. Above the line, list all the good memories that you have had together. Below the line, list all the painful memories.

Good Memories

When We First Met _____ Today

Painful Memories

Thank the Lord for the good memories that have been especially meaningful in your relationship:

> Lord,
> I thank you for _____ **(name the good memory)** _____ .

After thanking the Lord aloud for the good memories, pray the following prayer:

> **Dear Heavenly Father,**
> Sometimes pain has come to me through circumstances, sometimes from other people, sometimes from my fiancé/fiancée. Whatever the cause, surface in my mind all the pain that You want me to deal with at this time. Let me get in touch with the emotional core of my hurt and heartache, trauma and threats that has damaged my relationship with my fiancé/fiancée. Show me where I have allowed a root of bitterness to spring up, causing trouble and defiling many. In Jesus' precious name, I pray. Amen.

Spend a few moments in silent prayer, allowing the Lord to help you recall the painful experiences and traumatic events of your dating/courting relationship.

List the names of all those who have hurt you in any way, including all those for whom you have bad feelings:

Using a separate sheet of paper, make a list of the painful memories the Lord brings to your mind. Use real names, places and dates as much as possible. It is nearly impossible to get in touch with the emotional core of pain without using people's names and recalling specific events.

It is easy to pick up each other's offenses. It is also easy to turn bitter toward those whom you perceive have wrongly influenced your fiancé/fiancée, even when he or she doesn't see it. Jealousy can also create bitterness.

Realize that this is a time to bring healing to damaged emotions so you can be free from your past. Simply record what happened and how you felt about it. Understand that forgiveness is not forgetting. Forgiveness may lead to forgetting, but trying to forget only complicates forgiveness. Before you start the forgiveness process, please recall these ten steps to forgiveness:

1. Allow yourself to feel the pain, hurt, resentment, bitterness and hate (see Matthew 5:4).
2. Submit to God, recalling how Christ forgave you (see Matthew 18:21-35; Ephesians 4:32; Colossians 3:13; James 4:7,8).
3. Ask for Christ's grace and power to forgive (see Luke 11:9,10).
4. Agree to live with the unavoidable consequences of the other person's sin against you (see Ephesians 5:21; Colossians 3:13).
5. Release the offense. Tear up the moral, personal or relational debt owed you (see Matthew 6:12).
6. Never bring up a past offense again as a weapon against your fiancé/fiancée (see Romans 12:17).
7. Keep forgiving when your emotions recycle the pain or when the other person keeps offending you (see Matthew 18:21,22).
8. Reject the sinful act and tolerate it no longer (see Romans 12:21).
9. Turn the vengeance over to God and over to God's human authorities (see Romans 12:19,20).
10. Replace the old resentful feelings with the forgiving love of Christ (see Ephesians 4:31,32).

Do not make forgiveness more difficult than it already is. Some things we don't have to do:

1. We don't have to feel good about the person who hurt us—either before or after we forgive.
2. We don't have to tell the offender or other people about our resentful feelings unless the Holy Spirit guides us to do so. Jesus tells us in Matthew 5:23-26 to seek forgiveness and be reconciled to those we have offended as the Holy Spirit would guide.
3. We don't have to wait until we feel like forgiving. We can choose to obey God's Word right now.

Lift your painful memories before the Lord, asking for courage to face the pain honestly and for the grace to forgive fully. Releasing the offense results in relieving the pain.

Item by item, forgive each person you recall, and release the offense as follows:

> Lord,
>   I forgive _____ (name) _____ for _____ (specifically identify all offenses and painful memories) _____ .

Prayerfully focus on each person until every remembered pain has surfaced. Be sure to include your fiancé/fiancée and every painful memory in your courtship. You should also accept God's forgiveness of yourself as needed. Bitterness hardens the heart, but forgiveness softens it.

After you have completed the above, pray the following prayer aloud:

> **Dear Heavenly Father,**
>   I thank You for Your unconditional love and forgiveness. It is Your kindness and patience that have led me to forgiveness. In the name of Jesus and with His kindness and tenderness, I forgive every person who has ever hurt me or my family. I forgive my fiancé/fiancée for the pain that has come through weakness, poor judgment or outright sin. I accept Your forgiveness for the pain and damage caused in my relationship with him (or her).
>   By Your grace bring healing, help and hope to those who have hurt me and to those who have been hurt by me. I bless them all in the name of our Lord Jesus Christ, who taught us, "Love your enemies, do good to those who hate you, bless those who curse you, pray for those who mistreat you" (Luke 6:27,28). According to Your Word, I pray for those who have hurt me. In the precious name of Jesus Christ, amen.

Make the following declaration aloud:

> By the authority of the Lord Jesus Christ, who is seated at the heavenly Father's right hand, I assume my responsibility to resist the devil. I declare that I am crucified, buried, made alive, raised up and seated with Christ at the right hand of God. In union with Christ and with His authority, I command Satan to release any and all footholds in my life or any influence on my relationship with my fiancé/fiancée as we contemplate our future marriage. Satan, in the all-powerful name of the crucified, risen and reigning Lord Jesus Christ, leave my presence. Do not come back. Take away with you all of your lingering effects upon our memories, our relationships, our present thoughts and our future together.

STEP 6

Unmask Satan's Deceptions

Finally, be strong in the Lord and in his mighty power. Put on the full armor of God so that you can take your stand against the devil's schemes. For our struggle is not against flesh and blood, but against the rulers, against the authorities, against the powers of this dark world and against the spiritual forces of evil in the heavenly realms (Ephesians 6:10-12).

The goal of Satan is to discredit the work of Christ and tear apart your *relationship,* future marriage and family. His primary weapons are deception, temptation and accusation. He also uses harassment, discouragement and disillusionment. When we buy his little lies, we turn against God and each other. Our homes can become battlegrounds instead of proving grounds. In our relationships, our desire should be that we're a vital part of the building crew, rather than the wrecking crew. The tongue, however, is the instrument Satan uses the most. We either become tongue-tied and refuse to speak the truth in love, or we allow the tongue to become a destructive weapon.

If only one member of a family pays attention to the Holy Spirit, it can have strengthening effects upon every other member. On the other hand, if only one member of a family pays attention to a deceiving spirit, it can have weakening effects upon every other member as well. The purpose of this Step is to unmask the evil one's deceptions and stand against his attacks in the power of the Holy Spirit.

Satan uses real people to mount his attacks. They may come from deceived or evil people inside or outside our families. For example, a friend or coworker may lead your fiancé/fiancée into a sexual affair. The attacks may come through relatives or neighbors who use their tongues as destructive weapons. They may come from people who give us bad counsel concerning marriage. They may even possibly come through satanists who use occultic rituals or blood sacrifices in an evil attempt to destroy our families and, therefore, our testimonies.

Ask the Lord to show you the nature of these attacks so you can stand against them, united as one under the lordship of Christ.

Pray the following prayer:

> **Dear Heavenly Father,**
> I stand under Your authority. I give thanks that You are my hiding place, my protection and my refuge. In the name of Jesus, I clothe myself with the full armor of God. I choose to be strong in You, Lord, and in the power of Your might. I stand firm in my faith, I submit to You and I resist the devil.
> Open my eyes that I may see the attacks of the evil one against me, my family, and my future marriage. Give me spiritual discernment to become aware of Satan's schemes, not ignorant of them. Open my eyes to the reality of the spiritual world in which I live. I ask You for the ability to discern spiritually so I can judge rightly between good and evil.
> As I wait silently before You, reveal to me the attacks of Satan against me, my family, my future marriage and my ministry in order that I may stand against them and expose the father of lies. In Jesus' discerning name, I pray. Amen.

Make a list of whatever God brings to your mind. Look for patterns that seem to repeat themselves, such as conflicts that always break out before church, prayer or discussions on spiritual things. Think of any unresolved conflicts which keep recurring that may be due to one of the following three areas:

. Repeating thoughts that cause you to close your spirit toward God and your fiancé/fiancée (see 2 Corinthians 10:3-5; 1 Timothy 4:1):

. Recurring times or situations that cause distraction, confusion and disorientation in your relationship and home (usually during discussions, devotions and times surrounding church or ministry opportunities; see 1 Thessalonians 2:18):

. Improper stewardship (see 1 Corinthians 4:1,2):
   a. Sins that were tolerated in your home:

   b. Anti-Christian objects brought into your home:

inful activities need to be renounced. Attacks that come from the enemy because of our obedience to Christ need to be understood so we can recognize them and stand against them in the future. You need to understand how you wrestle not against flesh and blood, but against the powers of darkness (see Ephesians 6:12). Don't be like a blindfolded warrior who strikes out at himself or others. When you tear down a satanic stronghold, you will have some resistance. In order to walk free from past influences and present attacks, verbally make the following declaration:

> As a child of God who has been delivered from the power of darkness and translated into the kingdom of God's dear Son, I submit to God and resist the devil. I cancel out all demonic working that has been passed on to me from my ancestors. I have been crucified and raised with my Lord Jesus Christ, and now sit enthroned with Him in heavenly places. I renounce all satanic assignments that are directed toward me, my family, my ministry or my future marriage. I cancel every curse that Satan and his deceived, misguided evil workers have put on me and on God's plan for my future marriage. I announce to Satan and all his forces that Christ became a curse for me when He died on the cross.
>
> I reject any and every way in which Satan may claim ownership of me. I belong to the Lord Jesus Christ who purchased me with His own blood. I reject all other occultic rituals and blood sacrifices whereby Satan may claim ownership of me and God's plan for my future marriage. I declare myself to be eternally and completely signed over and committed to the Lord Jesus Christ.

By the authority I have in Jesus Christ, I now command every enemy of the Lord Jesus Christ to leave my presence, my memory and my present thoughts. I commit myself to our heavenly Father to do His will from this day forward.

Then pray:

Dear Heavenly Father,
   I come to You as Your child, purchased by the blood of the Lord Jesus Christ. You are the Lord of the universe and the Lord of my life. I yield my rights to You as the Lord of my future marriage. I submit my body to You as an instrument of righteousness, a living sacrifice, that I may glorify You in my body and in my future marriage. I reserve the sexual use of my body for marriage only. I now ask You to fill me with Your Holy Spirit. I commit myself to the renewing of my mind in order to prove that Your will is good, perfect and acceptable for me. I commit myself to take every thought captive to the obedience of Christ. All this I do in the name and authority of the Lord Jesus Christ. Amen.

Next, you need to commit the place you live to the Lord.

Have you brought any foreign objects into your home that could serve as idols or objects that were ever used for non-Christian religious purposes? These could provide grounds for Satan to have access to your home.

Are there any pornographic videos, magazines or books, occult or false religion materials?

Is there anything else that needs to be cleansed from your home? Ask the Lord to reveal any such sins or articles in your home.

Covenant before the Lord to remove all these items from your home and burn or destroy them. Then commit your home in prayer to the Lord as follows:

Dear Heavenly Father,
   I acknowledge that You are the Lord of all. All things You have created are good. You have charged me to be a good steward of all that You have entrusted to me. Thank You for what You have provided for me. I claim no ownership of what You have entrusted to me. I dedicate my future home to You, my present living quarters, my work space, and all the property, possessions and finances You have entrusted to me. I promise to remove from my home anything and everything that displeases You.

I renounce any attacks, devices or ceremonies of the enemy or his people designed to claim any ownership of that with which I have been entrusted. I have been bought and purchased by the blood sacrifice of the Lord Jesus Christ. I claim my current home and my future home as a place of spiritual safety and protection from the evil one. I renounce anything and everything not pleasing to our heavenly Father which has taken place in my home by me or by those who have lived here before me. I ask for Your divine protection around my home. I desire to honor You in all my ways. Thank You for Your protection.

Lord, You are the King of my life and I desire the plans that You have for my future marriage. May all that I do bring honor and glory to You. In Jesus' holy name, I pray. Amen.

Then declare aloud:

As a child of God, seated with Christ in the heavenly places, I command every evil spirit to leave my presence and my home. I renounce all attacks against my house, property, possessions and my very life. I announce to Satan and all his workers that God's plan for my future marriage, family and all that my heavenly Father has entrusted to me belongs to the Lord Jesus Christ. I submit completely to the direction and guidance of the Holy Spirit.

STEP 7

Christian Marriage

All who marry, whether Christian or not, become part of God's creation order of marriage (see Genesis 1:26-28; 2:18-25). A *creation order* is a God-given longing built into the fabric of human life. As a result of this God-given longing, every culture and people group on earth practice marriage in some form. No exceptions! Violating marriage breaks the order of creation and always brings terrible consequences.

When one partner (or both) knows Jesus Christ as Lord and Savior, their marriage becomes a sanctified— or set apart as holy—part of God's new Christian order (see 1 Corinthians 7:14). They commit themselves to Christ's new creation in marriage and enter a marriage covenant before God and one another. Christian marriage far exceeds a mere social contract. Marriage as a social contract is only a legal agreement between two parties. Christian marriage is a lifelong covenant with binding vows, spoken before God and human witnesses. If the vows are broken, they bring God's judgment. If they are kept, they bring God's rewards.

Satan's lie is that people who marry are really married singles, bound only by a human relationship and a social contract. That means marriage can be broken whenever either party feels the partners have "irreconcilable differences." In Christ, there are no irreconcilable differences. We have been reconciled to Him and we have been given the ministry of reconciliation.

God's truth is that marriage vows bind us into the organic union of Christian marriage, a new creation that lasts until the death of one of the spouses. A contract can be canceled, but a Christian covenant lasts a lifetime. Contracts can be broken or renegotiated, but a new creation in Christ either grows toward fulfillment or is violated.

Living in obedience to God's Word in Christian marriage, as in any other part of life, brings the Lord's shelter of protection (see Psalm 91). It results in God's blessings, including children who are set apart for God's purposes (see 1 Corinthians 7:14). By God's grace, His blessings extend not only to those who are faithful to Him, but also to their descendants for many generations to come (see Exodus 20:6; Deuteronomy 7:9; Luke 1:50). Violating marriage vows brings God's curse, not only upon ourselves, but also upon our descendants for three or four generations (see Exodus 34:7; Numbers 14:18; Jeremiah 32:18).

Declare aloud:

> I submit myself to God's plan for my future marriage. Satan, I renounce you in all your works and all your ways. In the all-powerful name of the Lord Jesus Christ, I command you to leave me. Take all your deceitful spirits, evil demons and fallen angels with you, and go to the place where the Lord Jesus Christ sends you. Leave my fiancé/fiancée and me and don't come back. Take with you all of your temptations. Take with you all of your accusing and demeaning thoughts that have been raised up against the knowledge of God and toward us. Take with you all of your deceptions that contradict God's written Word. The Lord Jesus Christ has torn down your demonic authority and I stand against your influence and activity toward my life and my future marriage.
>
> You are a defeated foe, disarmed of your weapons and made a public spectacle by the cross and resurrection of Christ (see Colossians 2:15). He (God) that is in me is greater than you who are in the world (see 1 John 4:4). You, as prince of this world, now stand condemned (see John 16:11). Christ has the supremacy over every evil throne, power, rule or authority (see Colossians 1:16). Jesus shared our humanity so that by His death He might destroy him who holds the power of death—that is, the devil (see Hebrews 2:14). I resist you by the authority of Christ and because I am alive in Him; therefore, you must flee from me (see James 4:7).

Pray aloud:

Dear Heavenly Father,

I gladly acknowledge that You created marriage and family life for Your glory. Thank You for designing marriage as a creation order, woven into the fabric of human society. I commit myself anew to honor the covenant of Christian marriage with all its blessings.

I renounce the lie of the devil that we are to be nothing more than married singles, bound only by a human relationship and a social contract. I choose to believe that marriage is binding as long as we both shall live. I acknowledge that we can never violate our marriage vows without bringing lasting damage upon ourselves and our future descendants for three or four generations to come.

I confess that I have fallen short of Your perfect will by my own selfishness and sin. I gladly accept Your forgiveness of my sins through the blood of Christ on the cross (see 1 John 2:1,2). By grace through faith I receive Christ's abundant life into my heart and His holiness into my life (see John 10:10; 1 Corinthians 7:14).

I crucify my own fleshly lusts and sinful desires which tempt me to ignore or violate my future marriage vows (see Galatians 5:24; 1 Peter 2:11). I clothe myself and Your plans for my coming marriage with the Lord Jesus Christ and His armor of light (see Romans 13:12-14; Galatians 3:26,27). I give myself to live by the power of the Holy Spirit in daily obedience to Christ (see Galatians 5:16; 1 Peter 1:2).

I announce that in Christ I have all the spiritual blessings I need to live out my new creation and the Christian covenant of marriage. I affirm that I can become one in Christ Jesus—one marriage, one flesh, one family (see Genesis 2:24; Mark 10:6-9; Ephesians 1:3; 3:14,15). I submit myself and God's plan for my future marriage to the ownership of my heavenly Father, to the Lordship of Jesus Christ, and to the power of the Holy Spirit. From this day forward, I ask You to use Your plans for my future marriage to display Your splendor before our families and friends. I invite You to work through us to show Your glory in the midst of a corrupt and wicked generation. In Jesus' glorious name, amen.

Living Free in Christ

Know that both marriage intimacy and freedom must be maintained. In gaining your freedom, you have won a very important battle in an ongoing war. And freedom is yours as long as you keep choosing truth and standing firm in the strength of the Lord. If more painful memories should surface, or if you become aware of lies that you have been living, renounce them and choose the truth. If you haven't already done so, please read *Victory over the Darkness* and *The Bondage Breaker*. *Walking in the Light* was written to help people understand God's guidance so they are able to discern counterfeit guidance. In order to maintain your freedom, we suggest the following:

1. Become active in a Christ-centered church, a small Christian group and a ministry for Christ. Build healthy allies for your coming marriage. Step outside of yourself for Christ.

2. Study your Bible daily, pray and be sensitive to the leading of the Holy Spirit. We also suggest reading one chapter of *Living Free in Christ* together every day for the next 36 days. Then use the devotional, *Daily in Christ*, by Neil and Joanne Anderson.

3. Review and apply your personal freedom in Christ. Remind yourself of your identity in Christ, winning the battle for the mind and processing the Steps to Freedom in Christ as an ongoing personal inventory. Realize that the Lord will use marriage to reveal more layers of our selfishness which He wants to peel off like the layers of an onion.

4. Take every thought captive to the obedience of Christ. Assume responsibility for private thoughts, reject the lie, choose the truth and stand firm in your identity in Christ.

5. Don't drift away! It is very easy to get lazy in your thoughts and revert back to old habits or patterns of thinking. Share struggles openly with each other. See the suggested daily prayer.

6. Don't expect your fiancé/fiancée to fight your battles. While you can help each other, no one else can think, pray or read the Bible for you.

7. If serious problems surface in your relationship, seek out a competent Christian pastor or counselor who is committed to the biblical institution of marriage and not just to the individual apart from marriage.

Pray daily with confidence as follows:

Dear Heavenly Father,

I honor You as my sovereign Lord. I acknowledge that You are always present with me. You are the only all-powerful and all-wise God. You are kind and loving in all Your ways. I love You. I thank You that I am united with Christ and am spiritually alive in Him. I choose not to love the world and I crucify the flesh and all its sinful desires.

I thank You that I am a child of God, a new creation in Christ Jesus, dead to sin but alive to God. I ask You to fill me with Your Holy Spirit that I may live my life free from sin. I declare my dependence upon You and take my stand against Satan and all his lying ways. I choose to believe the truth. You are the God of all hope and I am confident that You will meet my needs as I seek to live according to Your Word. I express with confidence that I can live a responsible life and be faithful in my coming marriage through Christ who strengthens me. I pray these things in the precious name of my Lord and Savior, Jesus Christ. Amen.

Declaration:

I now take my stand in Christ and put on the whole armor of God. In union with Christ, I command Satan and all his evil spirits to depart from me. I submit my body to God as a living sacrifice and I renew my mind by the living Word of God in order that I may prove that the will of God is good, acceptable and perfect.

Additional resources to be used with the Steps for engaged couples:
See the bibliography for complete information on each resource.
Books:
The Christ-Centered Marriage and *Study Guide*
Victory over the Darkness and *Study Guide*
The Bondage Breaker and *Study Guide*

Audio/Visual Series
"The Christ-Centered Marriage Video Seminar"
"Resolving Personal Conflicts"
"Resolving Spiritual Conflicts"

In Christ

I Am Accepted

John 1:12	I am God's child.
John 15:15	I am Christ's friend.
Romans 5:1	I have been justified.
1 Corinthians 6:17	I am united with the Lord, and I am one spirit with Him.
1 Corinthians 6:20	I have been bought with a price. I belong to God.
1 Corinthians 12:27	I am a member of Christ's Body.
Ephesians 1:1	I am a saint.
Ephesians 1:5	I have been adopted as God's child.
Ephesians 2:18	I have direct access to God through the Holy Spirit.
Colossians 1:14	I have been redeemed and forgiven of all my sins.
Colossians 2:10	I am complete in Christ.

I Am Secure

Romans 8:1,2	I am free from condemnation.
Romans 8:28	I am assured that all things work together for good.
Romans 8:31-34	I am free from any condemning charges against me.
Romans 8:35-39	I cannot be separated from the love of God.
2 Corinthians 1:21,22	I have been established, anointed and sealed by God.
Colossians 3:3	I am hidden with Christ in God.
Philippians 1:6	I am confident that the good work God has begun in me will be perfected.
Philippians 3:20	I am a citizen of heaven.
2 Timothy 1:7	I have not been given a spirit of fear, but of power, love, and a sound mind.
Hebrews 4:16	I can find grace and mercy to help in time of need.
1 John 5:18	I am born of God and the evil one cannot touch me.

I Am Significant

Matthew 5:13,14	I am the salt and light of the earth.
John 15:1,5	I am a branch of the true vine, a channel of His life.
John 15:16	I have been chosen and appointed to bear fruit.
Acts 1:8	I am a personal witness of Christ.
1 Corinthians 3:16	I am God's temple.
2 Corinthians 5:17-21	I am a minister of reconciliation for God.
2 Corinthians 6:1	I am God's coworker (see 1 Corinthians 3:9).
Ephesians 2:6	I am seated with Christ in the heavenly realm.
Ephesians 2:10	I am God's workmanship.
Ephesians 3:12	I may approach God with freedom and confidence.
Philippians 4:13	I can do all things through Christ who strengthens me.

Advance Preparation

Before you attempt to go through this procedure, please read the book, *Setting Your Church Free*. This outline will guide you through the process, but has few of the whys and hows. Explanations and biblical background are found in the book. You will gain an understanding of what the process intends to accomplish and all the advance preparation needed: when to schedule the event, how to prepare the participants, how to set up the room, etc. You will also learn how the facilitator conducts the process, what the participants do and the role of the recorder.

It is vital for the participants to experience personal freedom in Christ prior to engaging in the Setting Your Ministry Free event. All of the participants must have recently gone through the personal Steps to Freedom in Christ. Each participant should have a copy of these Steps to Setting Your Ministry Free as well.

We recommend a day of fasting and prayer by the participants and their prayer partners prior to the event. Ask for prayer partners to intercede in prayer before and during this time together.

It is essential that 100 percent of the board members and selected key staff members be present the first time a church or ministry group goes through the process. Consider postponing if even one member cannot attend. The process works best when every member is present and is greatly weakened if even one is missing. Because ministry leaders and staff members need to be a part of the process, we recommend that an unbiased outside facilitator lead your group through these Steps. Although the time may vary with different groups, the Setting Your Ministry Free event will require at least a full day.

CAUTION: Other ministries have found that it does *not* work well to try to involve the whole ministry directly in the Prayer Action Plan which will be developed at the conclusion of these Steps. People feel judged and condemned if they have not been through the process themselves. We recommend a summary report to the rest of the ministry in which the leaders who went through the process take responsibility for what they learned, e.g.,"We haven't been the leaders we should be, but we are committing ourselves to pray and take action." A sermon series works well in most churches. Other ministries might use a devotional series.

Implementation works best if the leaders pray the Prayer Action Plan until it becomes a part of their lives and their thinking. Think of it as a letter from Jesus—not new revelation—but conviction and guidance from the Holy Spirit that your ministry must obey. Expect resistance since this is a spiritual battle.

Beginning the Retreat

Pray the following personal renewal prayer once silently and then aloud together:

Dear Heavenly Father,

Open my eyes to see Your truth. Give me ears to hear and a compelling desire to respond in faith to what the Lord Jesus Christ has already done for me.

I confess Jesus Christ—crucified, risen and reigning—as my one and only Lord and Savior. I renounce any past involvement with non-Christian religions or experiences. I announce that Christ died on the cross for me and for my sins and rose again bodily from the dead for my justification and redemption.

I confess that the Lord Jesus Christ rescued me from the dominion of darkness and transferred me into His kingdom of light. I renounce Satan in all his works and all his ways. I announce that Jesus Christ is my Lord, Savior, Teacher and Friend. I give myself to obey everything that He commanded. I yield myself fully to Christ to do whatever He wants me to do, to be whatever He wants me to be, to give up whatever He wants me to give up, to give away whatever He wants me to give away, to become whatever He wants me to become.

I confess, reject, renounce and utterly disown every sin in which I have ever been involved. I announce that in Christ I have received redemption, the forgiveness of sins. I accept His reconciliation to the heavenly Father and I am thankful that I have peace with God.

As an expression of my faith in Christ's forgiveness of me, I forgive every person who has ever hurt, abused or taken advantage of me. I give up my right to seek revenge and I choose to let God settle the score as the final Judge who metes out perfect justice.

I open all the doors of my life to the Lord Jesus Christ and ask Him to take control of every part of my being. I gladly accept the filling and leading of the Holy Spirit into every part of my life. I surrender myself to live in union with the Lord Jesus Christ from this moment until I stand before the judgment seat of Christ and hear my name read from the Lamb's Book of Life.

Thank you, Heavenly Father, for uniting me with the Lord Jesus Christ and with all those who truly belong to You and live under Your gracious reign. In Jesus' powerful name, amen.

Processing these Steps is not business as usual. It will require that you move out of your comfort zone in a meaningful way and engage in a form of prayer that may not be your ministry's usual custom. In many countries Christians pray aloud, all together at the same time. If you have not done this before, stand in a circle holding hands, praying aloud at the same time. Ask the Lord to fill you with His Holy Spirit, guide you and your ministry and protect you from the evil one. Claim Christ's resources against Satan and his evil forces. Conclude this time by saying the Lord's Prayer together.

Bible Study

LETTERS TO THE SEVEN CHURCHES

Read the letters to the seven churches in Revelation 2—3. It is helpful to take turns, having seven of the participants read one letter apiece. Then all the participants look for the following items in the descriptions of the churches:

- Note the love of the risen Lord Jesus for His churches and His encouragement to them. Christ wants all of His churches to become free. Count how many times Jesus uses "I" in each letter. The major emphasis in these seven letters is on the near presence of the living Christ among the churches.

- Note that each church has an angel (see Revelation 1:9-20). In Revelation 1:16, Jesus holds the stars (angels) in His right hand. Two common functions of angels in the book of Revelation are (1) to praise and worship God and (2) to carry out the judgments and promises of Christ.
- Note that each letter begins with "I know your deeds."
- Note the corporate sins of the churches in Revelation 2—3. Many Christians are not used to thinking about corporate sins, although the concept is taught in Nehemiah 9, Daniel 9 and Revelation 2—3.
- Note the phrases that indicate Satan's attacks or opposition to the churches (see Revelation 2:9,10,13,24; 3:9).
- Note the Lord's judgments for disobedience and promises for obedience.
- Note the repeated phrase "to him who overcomes." In the New Testament, "overcomes" is a word most often used for the Christian's battle against the world, the flesh and the devil.

You may want to divide the participants into seven groups, one for each church. As you ask the questions, have the groups respond spontaneously. Not all seven groups have to respond to each question.

During this Setting Your Ministry Free event, each person needs to be sensitive to God's leading. To each of the churches in Revelation 2—3, John writes, "He who has an ear, let him hear what the Spirit says to the churches." If the Lord Jesus wrote a letter to your ministry, would you obey Him? Or would some hindrance keep you from really applying His message and making the necessary changes?

Pray together the following prayer, then read aloud the renunciations that follow:

Dear Heavenly Father,

Open our eyes to see Your truth and our ears to hear what Your Holy Spirit is saying to our ministry. We acknowledge that the Lord Jesus Christ is the Head of our ministry, and we renounce any claim of ownership on our part. Lord, this is Your ministry, not ours, and You are the Head. We renounce any independent spirit and declare our full dependence upon You.

We come together to discern Your will for our ministry. We renounce any and all desires or attempts to exert our own wills through arguing, manipulating or intimidating. You are light and in You there is no darkness at all. We choose to walk in the light in order to have fellowship with You and with one another. We ask You to fill us with Your Holy Spirit and guide us through these Steps to our ministry's freedom. Set us free to fulfill Your purpose for our being here.

Lead us not into temptation but deliver us from the evil one. Because we are seated with Christ in the heavenlies and because the church is commissioned to go into all the world and make disciples of all nations, we take our stand against the evil one and all his forces. We gladly submit to You, Heavenly Father, and obey Your command to resist the devil. We ask You to ban the adversary from our presence so we will be free to know Your will and choose to obey it. In Jesus' precious name, amen.

The first renunciation is an ancient declaration of the Early Church. The others are based on Revelation 2—3. Although they may not precisely fit your ministry, they are a biblical example of corporate sins all ministries should avoid. Make the following declaration together:

MINISTRY RENUNCIATIONS

We renounce	We announce
We renounce you, Satan, in all your works and in all your ways.	We announce that Christ is Lord of our lives and choose to follow only His ways.
We renounce forsaking our first love.	We announce that Christ is our first love because He first loved us and gave Himself as an atoning sacrifice for our sins.
We renounce tolerating false teaching.	We announce that God's truth is revealed to us through the living and written Word of God.
We renounce overlooking non-Christian beliefs and practices among our people.	We announce that Christ is our true identity and the only way to salvation and fellowship with God.
We renounce tolerating sexual immorality among some of our people.	We announce that our sexuality is God's gift, and that sexual intercourse is to be enjoyed only within the marriage of one man and one woman.
We renounce our reputation of being alive when we are dead.	We announce that Christ alone is our Resurrection and our Life.
We renounce our incomplete deeds—starting to do God's will and then not following through.	We announce that Christ is the Head of His Body, the Church, and that as His members we find freedom and strength to finish the work He has given us to do.
We renounce disobedience to God's Word, including the Great Commandment and the Great Commission.	We announce that God energizes us to desire and to do His will so we can obey Christ.
We renounce our lukewarmness, being neither hot nor cold for Christ.	We announce that Christ is our refining fire who disciplines us for our own good so that our faith may prove genuine.
We renounce our false pride in financial "security" that blinds us to our actual spiritual needs.	We announce that Christ is our true wealth, security and insight, and outside of Him we are wretched, pitiful, poor, blind and naked.

What if the Lord Jesus were to write a letter to your ministry? What would He commend? What would He rebuke? Although you cannot have a letter with the authority of Scripture, you can ask the Holy Spirit to help you discern how the Head of the Church views your ministry. He can help you apply scriptural truths to your lives and to your ministry.

Discerning the Lord's View of Our Ministry

Note: You will need sheets of poster board, flip charts or butcher paper and felt-tip pens for recording responses. If you have not already done so, appoint a recorder to take notes of all the lists that are compiled by the group.

STEP 1

Our Ministry's Strengths

In this first Step, you are seeking to discern the strengths of your ministry. Pray together the following prayer, then follow with a few moments of silent prayer. Allow the Lord to impress upon your hearts what you are doing right. The facilitator will close the time in prayer.

Dear Heavenly Father,

Thank You for calling and choosing us as shepherds and servant leaders in this ministry. Thank You for this ministry and what You have done through it. Thank You for the people who serve You.

Show us what the living Lord Jesus commends in our ministry. Remind us of what we are doing right and the strengths You have given to our ministry. As we wait silently before You, show us our good works that glorify our Father in heaven. We ask this in the wonderful name of Jesus. Amen.

This Step has two parts. In the first part, the facilitator asks the group to share the ministry's strengths as the Holy Spirit brings them to mind. Each participant should help identify as many strengths of the ministry as possible.

The second part takes place after all of the strengths are shared. The facilitator asks the group to summarize the greatest strengths God has given to your ministry. Good questions to ask here are: "What are the things we always do best?" "What works for us every time?" "How has God uniquely gifted us as a ministry?" Keep this list short, having only the greatest strengths identified, normally five to seven items.

The facilitator will write on the poster board, flip chart or butcher paper the greatest strengths, beginning each one with "We thank God for...." Write them in complete sentences and save the statements for the final summary in the Prayer Action Plan (Step Six).

Conclude this Step by praying in unison the following prayer:

Dear Heavenly Father,

Thank You for the strengths You have given to us and to our ministry. Thank You for gracing us with Your presence and for working through the gifts, talents and service of Your people. We know that apart from Christ we can do nothing, so we gladly acknowledge that every good and perfect gift is from above. Continue to equip us to be good stewards of these strengths, as well as responsible managers of all the relationships and the resources You have given us. In Jesus Christ our Lord, we pray. Amen.

STEP 2

Our Ministry's Weaknesses

In Step Two, the group will ask the Holy Spirit to help discern the weaknesses of your ministry. What are your shortcomings, faults and failures? What are you not doing well? What should your ministry be doing that is not being done?

Pray together the following prayer. Then spend a couple of minutes in silent prayer, allowing the Lord to impress upon your hearts the weaknesses of your ministry:

Dear Heavenly Father,

    We have not fully utilized the gifts, talents and strengths that You have made available to us. We slip into patterns of thinking and acting that displease You. We fall short of Your best and of all that You intend for us. We ask You to open our eyes so we may see our weaknesses as You do. We wait silently before You in the powerful name of Jesus. Amen.

The facilitator will ask the group to list the weaknesses that the Holy Spirit brings to your minds. Participants should express their own opinions. This is not a time for any objection or defensiveness from others. Absolute accuracy is not essential this early in the process. You are not trying to identify your greatest weaknesses (as with strengths in Step One), but simply listing them for future reference.

When you have finished listing your ministry's weaknesses, pray the following prayer together:

Dear Heavenly Father,

    You know our weaknesses, as well as our strengths, and You love us just the same. We confess and renounce the times we have placed our confidence in ourselves instead of You. We now choose to put no confidence in our flesh, and we declare our dependence upon You. We are confident that the good work You have begun in us will be completed.

    Show us how we can strengthen our weaknesses and live with our limitations. May Your power be made perfect in our weakness. Thank You for Your forgiveness and Your gracious presence in our lives. In Jesus' strong name, we pray. Amen.

STEP 3

Memories

In this Step, you are asking the Lord to remind you of both the best memories and the traumatic events in your ministry's past. If yours is an older ministry, consider it decade by decade, beginning in the earliest recalled or researched past. What happened in the 1930s, 40s, 50s, 60s, 70s, 80s, 90s? If yours is a younger ministry, you may want to divide its history into halves or thirds. What happened in our first five years? The last five years?

Make two lists for this Step, one titled "Good Memories" and the other titled "Painful Memories." List all of the good memories first. The good memories are fun to recall and an occasion for thanksgiving to God for His blessings upon His people.

Begin with the following prayer, and follow it with a few moments of silence:

Dear Heavenly Father,
 Thank you for the wonderful experiences we have shared together that have built such special memories. We thank You for Your blessings upon us and for all the good times You have given us. With joy and thanksgiving, we ask You to bring the good memories of our ministry to our minds. With grateful hearts, we pray in the name of Jesus. Amen.

When the list of good memories is complete, the facilitator will ask the participants to lift them before the Lord in thanksgiving and praise. Begin with the following words:

Lord,
 I thank You for _____ (name the good memory) _____ .

After thanking the Lord for the good memories throughout the ministry's past, pray together the following prayer. Then follow with a few moments of silent prayer, allowing the Lord to reveal to your mind the painful experiences of your ministry's past:

Dear Heavenly Father,
 We thank You for the riches of Your kindness, forbearance and patience, knowing that Your kindness has led us to repentance. We acknowledge that we have not extended that same patience and kindness toward those who have offended us. We have not acted gracefully and wisely in all our past dealings.
 Sometimes pain has come to others even when we were using our best judgment in following You. Sometimes the actions and attitudes of others have deeply wounded us. Show us where we have allowed a root of bitterness to spring up, causing trouble and defiling many. As we wait silently before You, bring to our minds all the painful memories of our ministry's past. In Jesus' compassionate name, we pray. Amen.

Make another list of painful memories. Use real names. It is nearly impossible to get in touch with the emotional core of pain without using people's names. Everything said here is to be spoken with respect. Carefully avoid placing blame or making disparaging remarks. Absolute confidentiality must be assured. No person should share this confidential information outside the group. Ask the recorder *not* to write down the painful memories section. After the process is finished, you will want to destroy this large sheet of painful memories in front of the whole group.

You can't fix the past, but you can free yourself from it by facing it, forgiving and seeking forgiveness. Once again the group interacts and the facilitator writes the names of those responsible for the painful memories on the sheets up front. Then each person is to individually and privately forgive these people from their hearts, asking for courage to face the pain honestly and for grace to forgive fully. Releasing offenses results in relieving the pain and bondage to the past. In 2 Corinthians 2:5-11, Paul urged the church to forgive the one who caused sorrow to the church. They were to comfort the offender and reaffirm their love for him (or her). Paul saw this as a test of their obedience. You must forgive in order that no advantage be taken of your ministry by Satan. Item by item, individually and silently, forgive each person and release the offenses as follows:

> Lord,
>   I forgive _____ (name the person) _____ for _____ (specifically name every painful memory) _____.

Prayerfully focus on each individual until every remembered pain has surfaced. Each person should also acknowledge and receive God's forgiveness as needed. Forgiveness sets you free from the past. When every head is lifted from this time of silent prayer, proceed with the following declaration and prayer.

DECLARATION

> By the authority of the Lord Jesus Christ who is seated at Your right hand, we assume our responsibility to resist the devil. In Jesus' all-powerful name, we retake any ground that Satan may have gained in our lives and in our ministry through these painful memories. Because we are seated with Christ in the heavenly realms, we command Satan to leave our presence and our ministry.

PRAYER

> Dear Heavenly Father,
>   We forgive each and every person who has hurt us or our ministry. We forgive as the Lord forgave us.
>   We release our resentments and regrets into Your hands. You alone can heal our broken hearts and bind up our wounds. We ask You to heal the pain in our hearts and in the corporate memory of our ministry. We have allowed a root of bitterness to spring up and defile many. We also confess the times we did not seek to resolve these painful memories according to Your Word. Thank You for Your forgiveness.
>   We commit ourselves to think of these memories, whenever we may happen to recall them, from the vantage point of our union with Christ. We will recall Your forgiveness and healing.
>   May Your grace and mercy guide us as we seek to live out our calling as spiritual leaders. We ask You, Heavenly Father, to fill us with Your Holy Spirit. We surrender full control of our ministry to our crucified, risen and reigning Head.
>   We ask You to bring healing to those who have hurt us. Also bring healing to those who may have been hurt by us. Bless those who curse us and give rich and satisfying ministries to all who belong to You but have gone away from us. We bless them all in the name of our Lord Jesus Christ who taught us to "love your enemies, do good to those who hate you, bless those who curse you, pray for those who mistreat you" (Luke 6:27,28). According to Your Word, we pray for those who have hurt us.

Before you say "Amen," all the participants should pray individually and audibly as the Lord leads by lifting spontaneous prayers before the Lord for each individual listed earlier by saying:

214

We forgive...

We release...

We bless...

In Jesus' name, we pray. Amen.

Reminder: After the process is finished, you will want to destroy the large sheet of painful memories in front of the whole group.

STEP 4

Corporate Sins

In this fourth Step, you are going to identify corporate sins. Individual sins that do not corporately affect the ministry will not be a part of this process as they must be dealt with individually. Corporate sins need not involve the whole ministry, but they must involve a significant group within the ministry.

Pray together the following prayer. Then follow with a few moments of silent prayer. Ask the Lord to impress upon your minds the past and present corporate sins of your ministry or of any significant group within it:

> Dear Heavenly Father,
> As we seek Your face, bring to our minds all the corporate sins that we, or any significant group within our ministry, have committed. Like Ezra and Daniel, we stand before You ready to repent of the sins of our spiritual ancestors in this ministry. We also ask for Your discernment to identify and renounce our own sins. As we wait silently before You, bring to our minds all the corporate sins that we, and the spiritual leaders before us, have tolerated or not adequately dealt with. Then grant us the grace that we may confess, renounce and forsake them. In Jesus' forgiving name, we pray. Amen.

The facilitator will now ask you to share your ministry's corporate sins. Usually this Step starts slowly but gradually gains momentum. Unlike the first Steps, the facilitator will seek discernment from the group. Write on the sheets only those corporate sins that have group consensus. From this Step onward, group discernment is vital, rather than listing each person's ideas. Be patient and wait for general agreement.

Pray the following prayer aloud together for *each corporate sin* you have listed:

> Heavenly Father,
> We confess _____ (name one sin each time) _____ as sinful and displeasing to our Lord Jesus Christ. We turn from it, forsake it and renounce it. Thank You for Your forgiveness. In Jesus' name, we pray. Amen.

When every corporate sin has been confessed and renounced, pray the following together:

> Heavenly Father,
> As spiritual leaders in our ministry, we acknowledge that these corporate sins are unacceptable to You. We renounce every use of our corporate body as an instrument of unrighteousness by ourselves and by those who have gone before us. We reject and disown all the sins of our ancestors. We cancel out all advantages, schemes and other works of the devil that have been passed on to our ministry from them.
> By the authority of Christ, the Head of His Body, the Church, we demolish every Satanic foothold and stronghold in our ministry gained because of our own corporate sins. We retake all ground given to the adversary in our ministry, in our related organizations and in our life together as colaborers in this ministry. We release control of that territory to the Holy Spirit.
> We invite the Holy Spirit to cleanse us, renew us, fill us and lead us into all truth. Cause us to obey Your truth so that our ministry will be free to serve You.
> We submit ourselves and our ministry to the sovereignty and ownership of the heavenly Father, the lordship and fullness of Christ and the presence and power of the Holy Spirit. By your grace

and according to Your Word, we acknowledge that we are fellow citizens with the saints and we belong to God's household. We affirm that the Church has been built upon the foundation of the apostles and prophets, Christ Jesus Himself being the Chief Cornerstone. We praise our Lord Jesus Christ for His Headship of our ministry and see ourselves as His Body, bride and building.

"Now to him who is able to do immeasurably more than all we ask or imagine, according to his power that is at work within us, to him be glory in the church and in Christ Jesus throughout all generations, for ever and ever! Amen" (Ephesians 3:20,21).

At this point the facilitator will invite everyone to search his or her own heart. Ask the Holy Spirit to reveal your participation in your ministry's corporate sins. Each person, as directed by the Holy Spirit, should then pray aloud, confessing personal involvement in these corporate sins.

It is off-limits to confess someone else's sins.

After this prayer time, you may want to talk during the break with anyone in the room with whom you need to reconcile, make amends or ask forgiveness. These can be powerful moments of healing hurts and conflicts within the group.

STEP 5

Attacks of Spiritual Enemies

Step Four dealt with the ground given over to Satan because of what your ministry or its people have done wrong. Step Five has a different focus. The attacks you are going to identify in this Step come because of the things your ministry and your leaders are doing right.

Pray together the following prayer; then follow with a few moments of silent prayer. Ask the Lord to help you discern accurately the nature of Satan's attacks on your ministry, its leaders and its people because of what you are doing right.

> Dear Heavenly Father,
>
> We thank You for our refuge in Christ. We choose to be strong in the Lord and in His mighty power. In Christ Jesus, we put on the full armor of God. We choose to stand firm and be strong in our faith. We accept the truth that our struggle is not against flesh and blood, but against the spiritual forces of evil in the heavenly realms.
>
> We desire to be aware of Satan's schemes, not ignorant of them. Open our eyes to the reality of the spiritual world in which we live. We ask You for the ability to discern spiritually so we can rightly judge between good and evil.
>
> As we wait silently before You, reveal to us the attacks of Satan against us, our spiritual leaders, our people and our ministry in order that we may stand against them and expose the father of lies. In Jesus' discerning name, we pray. Amen.

Once again the *group* needs to discern the spiritual attacks, not just list an individual's ideas. It takes a little longer to reach group consensus, but it is far better than listing only the ideas of one person.

When the list is complete, renounce each attack, one by one, as follows:

> In the name and authority of our Lord Jesus Christ, we renounce Satan's attacks of (*or by, on, with, through*)   (list each of the identified attacks one at a time). We resist them and come against them in Jesus' all-powerful name. Together we declare, "The Lord rebuke you, the Lord bind you" from any present or future influence on us.

Testimonies of some former satanists and cult members indicate that certain deceived or wicked people are deliberately out to destroy effective Christian ministries. Use the following declaration to break the influence of any of these attacks against your ministry, its leaders or its people, and then conclude this Step with the closing prayer:

DECLARATION

We announce that all authority has been given to Jesus in heaven and on earth. As leaders of this ministry and members of the Body of Christ, we reject and disown all influence and authority of demonic powers and evil spirits that cause resistance to Christ's work. As children of God, we have been delivered from the power of darkness and brought into the kingdom of God's dear Son.

Because we are seated with Christ in the heavenly realms, we renounce all satanic assignments that are directed toward our ministry. We cancel every curse that deceived or wicked people have put on us. We announce to Satan and all his forces that Christ became a curse for us when He died on the cross.

We renounce any and all sacrifices by satanists or anyone else who would claim false ownership of us, our ministry, our leaders or our people. We announce that we have been bought and purchased by the blood of the Lamb. We accept only the sacrifice of Jesus whereby we belong to Him.

PRAYER

Dear Heavenly Father,

We worship You and You alone. You are the Lord of our lives and the Lord of our ministry. We offer our bodies to You as living sacrifices, holy and pleasing to God. We also present our ministry to You as a sacrifice of praise.

We pray for Your protection of our ministry's spiritual leaders, members of our corporate body and their families. Grant us the wisdom and grace to deal with heretics and spiritual wolves. We pray for discernment in order to judge between good and evil. We dedicate all our facilities to You, including property, offices, equipment and transportation.

Lord Jesus Christ, You are the Head of this ministry and we exalt You. May all that we do bring honor and glory to You. In Jesus' holy name, we pray. Amen.

STEP 6

Prayer Action Plan

Place four large sheets of paper side by side on the wall. All of the previous sheets should also be visible. On the first sheet write "We renounce." On the next write "We announce," and then "We affirm" and "We will" on the other sheets. Turn to page 228 of these Steps for an example and how the wording begins for each item.

You are now ready to synthesize everything you have discerned in the last five Steps. Especially look for recurring patterns that can be put together.

Renounce evil (attacks, corporate sins, conflicts, weaknesses). For example, "We renounce division among us." "We renounce" is our response to Jesus who requires that we "repent."

Next, announce the positive biblical opposite of what you renounced, worded in terms of your resources in Christ: "We announce that in Christ we have the unity of the Spirit." "We announce" is our response to Jesus who charges us "to remember."

Then, affirm in emotional language a scriptural promise or truth that encourages and motivates you in regard to the same item: "We affirm that in the depth of our hearts we are all one in Christ Jesus" (see Galatians 3:26-28). "We affirm" is our response to Jesus who tells us to "hold on."

Finally, commit to an action step you will take: "We will talk to the right person in the right spirit when conflicts arise." "We will" is our response to Jesus who requires us to "obey."

Your goal in this crucial statement is to make the shortest list possible without leaving out any major pattern of bondage within your ministry. You will want to set your ministry free by using this list as a prayer and action guide in removing the advantages of the evil one. Therefore, it holds special importance. Pray the following prayer together and spend a few moments silently seeking God's wisdom. Ask for the Holy Spirit's discernment, unity, and even the right words and order of items.

> **Dear Heavenly Father,**
> **We thank You for opening our eyes to see the strengths, weaknesses, good memories, painful memories, corporate sins and spiritual attacks of evil enemies. Thank You for helping us grasp our spiritual battle with demonic powers.**
> **Provide us with discernment into the true condition of our ministry. You know our ministry intimately. Give us Your plan of action. Teach us to pray it with Your power.**
> **We ask for Your divine guidance in formulating this Prayer Action Plan. We thank You that the Holy Spirit helps us in our weakness because we don't really know how or what to pray. Give us unity. Grant us wisdom. Supply us with the right words and Your order of subjects for us to list.**
> **Open our eyes to the truth of Your Word. Convict us of the need to follow through with what You cause us to see. In Jesus' all-wise name, we pray. Amen.**

For each subject, work across the four sheets: "We renounce," "We announce," "We affirm" and "We will," before going on to the next item. Fatigue is a factor now, so call upon the Holy Spirit for divine energy to make sense out of all the lists on the sheets (see Colossians 1:29).

When you have finished the list, ask all the participants to stand, face the four sheets, hold hands and pray the Prayer Action Plan aloud. This prayer is essential and should be repeated at subsequent board and staff meetings and by individual leaders at home. It is not uncommon to have items added to the list in the subsequent days and months.

Some strategies for implementing the Prayer Action Plan are as follows:
- Pray through it on a daily basis for 40 days.
- Pray through it together in each of your regular meetings.

STEP 7

Leadership Strategy

Your Prayer Action Plan is like a letter from Jesus to your ministry. In it He calls you to repent ("We renounce"), to remember ("We announce"), to hold on ("We affirm"), and to obey ("We will"). With this view of your ministry, how does the Lord want you to implement the Prayer Action Plan?

Pray together the following prayer, followed by moments of silent prayer. In spite of fatigue from this process, ask the Lord to impress upon your minds and hearts how, as leaders, the Prayer Action Plan can be implemented in your ministry in the days ahead.

Dear Heavenly Father,

We come before You in worship, adoration and thanksgiving. Thank You for revealing to us Your view of our ministry. Show us if there is anything else that is keeping our ministry in bondage. We commit ourselves to renounce it, stand against it in Christ, hold fast to Your promises and obey Your will.

We ask You to reveal what we should do with our Prayer Action Plan. Unveil to us the practical steps that You want us as leaders to take. Make Your will for us known in order that we may fully obey Your direction for our ministry. In Jesus' powerful name, we pray. Amen.

After praying your Prayer Action Plan for 40 days:

- Preach through it in a sermon series or use it for devotions at staff meetings.
- Take other groups of leaders in your ministry through the Setting Your Ministry Free process.
- Discuss in future meetings specific ways to obey each action point (see the Strategy Questionnaire in the book *Setting Your Church Free,* page 289).
- Present a summary report to your whole ministry and ask them to forgive the leadership for not being all that God has called them to be.
- Recruit committed intercessors to pray for your leadership team and their follow-through of the leadership strategy.

The facilitator will list on the sheets the action points reached by group consensus.

At this point, name one person who will hold the group accountable for following through on this Leadership Action Plan.

Conclude the session by praying together the following:

Dear Heavenly Father,

Thank You, Lord, that we can call You our heavenly Father. Thank You for Your love and acceptance of us. Thank You for all You have done for us today. Thank You for hearing our prayers, forgiving our corporate sins and setting us free from the damaging influence of Satan's schemes against our ministry.

Thank You for opening our eyes to see and our ears to hear. Now give us a heart to obey. We commit ourselves to follow through on the Leadership Action Plan You have given us. Teach us to pray and apply this plan as You have directed.

We praise You for uniting us with the Lord Jesus Christ. We praise You that the Son of God came to destroy the works of the devil. We ask for Your protection for our marriages, our families and our ministry. Keep us from scandal. We love You and commit ourselves to become the people You have called us to be. Empower us to walk in the light and to speak the truth in love. Show us how our ministry can work cooperatively with the whole Body of Christ. We desire to be united together in one spirit.

"Now to the King eternal, immortal, invisible, the only God, be honor and glory for ever and ever. Amen" (1 Timothy 1:17).

After Completing the Seven Steps

Appoint someone to destroy the sheet for "Step Three: Painful Memories." Ask the recorder or a secretary to compile all the other lists for the participants in this retreat. Compile the Prayer Action Plan on a single sheet for easy use by the participants. Place the leadership strategy steps on the reverse side of the sheet. Follow the format below.

OUR GREATEST STRENGTHS

. _____

. _____

. _____

. _____

. _____

OUR PRAYER ACTION PLAN

We renounce...	We announce...	We affirm...	We will...
1.	1.	1.	1.
2.	2.	2.	2.
3.	3.	3.	3.
4.	4.	4.	4.
5.	5.	5.	5.

Some groups enjoy a fellowship meal together at the close of this time. Plan in advance what you will do to celebrate!

Additional resources to be used with the Steps for your ministry:
See the bibliography for complete information on each resource.

Books:

Setting Your Church Free

Helping Others Find Freedom in Christ

Helping Others Find Freedom in Christ Training Manual and *Study Guide*

Audio/Visual Series:

"Setting Your Church Free"

"Helping Others Find Freedom in Christ Video Training Program"

"Spiritual Conflicts and Counseling"

Appendix

Confidential Personal Inventory

I. PERSONAL INFORMATION

Name _____   Age _____   Telephone _____

Address _____

Church Affiliation: Present _____

                        Past _____

Education: Highest grade completed _____

               Degree(s) earned _____

Marital Status _____

Previous History of Marriage/Divorce _____

Vocation: Present _____

              Past _____

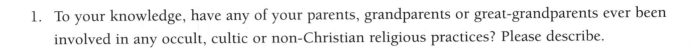

II. FAMILY HISTORY

A. Religious

1. To your knowledge, have any of your parents, grandparents or great-grandparents ever been involved in any occult, cultic or non-Christian religious practices? Please describe.

2. Briefly describe your parents' Christian experience (i.e., if they were believers, did they profess and live their Christianity?).

B. Marital Status

1. Are your parents presently married or divorced? Describe their relationship.

2. Was your father clearly the head of the home or was there a role reversal where your mother ruled the home? Explain.

3. How did your father treat your mother?

4. To your knowledge, was there ever an adulterous affair in your parents' or grandparents' relationships? Any incestuous relationships?

5. Were you adopted or raised by foster parents or legal guardians?

C. Sibling Data

1. Please identify the sex and age of your sibling(s) and place yourself in the birth order.

2. Please describe the emotional atmosphere in your home while you were growing up. Include a brief description of your relationship with your parents and sibling(s).

D. Health

1. Are there any addiction problems in your family history (alcohol, drugs, etc.)? Please describe.

2. Is there any history of mental illness? Please describe.

3. Please indicate if you have any history of the following recurring ailments in your family:

   ❏ Tuberculosis   ❏ Cancer

   ❏ Heart disease   ❏ Ulcers

   ❏ Diabetes   ❏ Glandular problems

   ❏ Other(s) _____

4. How would you describe your family's concern for:

   a. Diet:

b. Exercise:

c. Rest:

E. Moral Climate

Rate the moral atmosphere in which you were raised during the first 18 years of your life by circling one number in each category on the following chart:

	Overly Permissive	Permissive	Average	Strict	Overly Strict
Clothing	5	4	3	2	1
Sex	5	4	3	2	1
Dating	5	4	3	2	1
Movies	5	4	3	2	1
Music	5	4	3	2	1
Literature	5	4	3	2	1
Free will	5	4	3	2	1
Drinking	5	4	3	2	1
Smoking	5	4	3	2	1
Church attendance	5	4	3	2	1

III. HISTORY OF PERSONAL HEALTH

A. Physical

1. Describe your eating habits. Do you lean toward eating only junk food or only eating healthy food; do you eat regularly or sporadically; is your diet balanced; etc.?

2. Do you have any addictions or cravings that cause you difficulty in controlling your intake of sweets, drugs, alcohol or food in general? Explain.

3. Are you presently under any kind of medication for either physical or psychological reasons? Explain.

4. Do you have any problems sleeping? Describe your sleeping patterns (i.e., do you have restful sleep?). Are you having any recurring nightmares or other sleep disturbances?

5. Does your schedule allow for regular periods of rest and relaxation?

6. Have you ever experienced any type of trauma (i.e., history of abuse: physical, emotional or sexual; involvement in a severe accident; death of family member; etc.)? Explain.

B. Mental

1. Describe briefly your earliest memory.

2. Do you have periods or blocks of time in your past that you can't remember? Please describe your experiences.

3. Please indicate any of the following which you have or are presently struggling with:

❑ daydreaming	❑ lustful thoughts	❑ inferiority
❑ inadequacy	❑ worry	❑ doubts
❑ fantasizing	❑ obsessive thoughts	❑ insecurity
❑ dizziness	❑ headaches	❑ compulsive thoughts
❑ blasphemous thoughts		

4. Do you spend much time wishing you were somebody else or fantasizing that you are somebody else or possibly imagining yourself living at a different time, place or under different circumstances? Explain.

5. How many hours of TV do you watch per week? _____

   List your five favorite programs.

6. How many hours do you spend a week reading? _____

   What do you primarily read (newspaper, magazines, books, etc.) and on what topics?

7. How much time do you spend listening to music? _____

   What type(s) of music do you listen to?

8. Would you consider yourself to be an optimist or a pessimist (i.e., do you have a tendency to see the good in people and life, or the bad)?

9. Have you ever thought that maybe you were "cracking up" and do you presently fear that possibility? Explain.

10. Do you have regular devotions in the Bible? When and to what extent?

11. Do you find prayer mentally difficult? Explain.

12. When attending church or other Christian ministries, are you plagued with foul thoughts, jealousies or other mental harassments? Explain.

C. Emotional

1. Please indicate which of the following emotions you have experienced or are presently having difficulty controlling:

❏ frustration
❏ anger
❏ anxiety
❏ loneliness
❏ worthlessness
❏ depression
❏ hatred
❏ bitterness

❏ fear of dying
❏ fear of losing your mind
❏ fear of committing suicide
❏ fear of hurting loved ones
❏ fear of going to hell
❏ fear of abandonment
❏ fear of _____
   _____

2. Which of the above listed emotions do you feel are sinful? Why?

3. Concerning your emotions, whether positive or negative, please indicate which of the following best describes you:

❏ readily express my emotions
❏ express some of my emotions, but not all
❏ readily acknowledge their presence, but reserved in expressing them
❏ tendency to suppress my emotions

❑ find it safest not to express how I feel

❑ tendency to disregard how I feel since I cannot trust my feelings

❑ consciously or subconsciously deny them since it is too painful to deal with them

4. Is there someone in your life whom you know that you could be emotionally honest with right now (i.e., you could tell this person exactly how you feel about yourself, life and other people)?

5. How important is it that we are emotionally honest before God, and do you feel that you are? Explain.

IV. SPIRITUAL HISTORY

A. If you were to die tonight, do you know where you would spend eternity?

B. Suppose you did die tonight and appeared before God in heaven and He were to ask you "By what right should I allow you into My presence?" How would you answer Him?

C. First John 5:11-12 says, "God has given us eternal life, and this life is in his Son. He who has the Son has life; he who does not have the Son of God does not have life."

1. Do you have the Son of God in you (see 2 Corinthians 13:5)?

2. When did you receive Him (see John 1:12)?

3. How do you know that you have received Him?

D. Are you plagued with doubts concerning your salvation? Please explain.

E. Are you presently enjoying fellowship with other believers and, if so, where and when?

F. Are you under authority of a local church where the Bible is preached, and do you regularly support it with your time, talent and treasure? If not, why?

Non-Christian Spiritual Experience Inventory

Check any of the following with which you or your ancestors have had any involvement. Place a check mark beside each one in which you have participated in, whether for fun, out of curiosity or in earnest.

❑ Psychic readings
❑ Card laying
❑ Crystal ball
❑ Palm reading
❑ Tea leaves
❑ Tarot cards
❑ Attended or participated in a seance
❑ Attended or participated in a spiritualist meeting
❑ Ouija board
❑ Magic Eight Ball
❑ Automatic (spirit) writing
❑ Levitation
❑ Table lifting
❑ Read or followed horoscopes
❑ Astrology
❑ Clairvoyance
❑ Telepathy
❑ ESP
❑ Speaking in a trance
❑ Mystical meditation
❑ Astral projection/travel
❑ Magical charming
❑ Fetishism (objects of worship/idols)
❑ Cabala/kabala
❑ Materialization
❑ Metaphysics
❑ Self-realization
❑ Witchcraft
❑ Sorcery
❑ Mental suggestion
❑ Dream interpretation
❑ I Ching
❑ Been hypnotized
❑ Practiced self-hypnosis
❑ Practiced yoga
❑ Practiced water-witching (dowsing) rod/pendulum
❑ Other _____

❑ Christian Science
❑ Unity
❑ The Way International
❑ Unification Church
❑ Mormonism
❑ Church of the Living Word
❑ The Local Church
❑ Worldwide Church of God (H. W. Armstrong)
❑ Children of God
❑ Jehovah's Witnesses
❑ Unitarianism
❑ Masonic orders
❑ Swedenborgianism
❑ Zen Buddhism
❑ Hare Krishna
❑ Bahaism
❑ Rosicrucianism
❑ New Age
❑ Inner Peace Movement
❑ Spiritual Frontiers Fellowship
❑ Transcendental Meditation
❑ EST/The Forum
❑ Eckankar
❑ Mind control philosophies
❑ Science of the Mind
❑ Science of Creative Intelligence
❑ Theosophical Society
❑ Islam
❑ Black Muslim
❑ Hinduism
❑ Other _____
_____
_____

Non–Christian Spiritual Experience Inventory (Continued)

Have you ever…

❏ Had a spirit guide?

❏ Read or possessed occult literature, especially the *Satanic Bible*, *Book of Shadows*, *Secrets of the Psalms*, *Sixth and Seventh Books of Moses*?

❏ Read or studied parapsychology?

❏ Practiced black or white magic?

❏ Possessed occult or pagan religious objects which were made for use in pagan temples or religious rites or in the practice of magic, sorcery, witchcraft, divination or spiritualism?

❏ Seen or been involved in Satan worship?

❏ Sought healing (either as a child or as an adult) through magic conjuration, charming, psychic healing or New Age medicine?

❏ Tried to locate a missing person or object by consulting someone with psychic powers?

❏ Encountered ghosts or materializations of persons known to be dead?

❏ Entered into a blood pact with another person?

❏ Been the object of sexual attacks by demons—incubi, succubi?

❏ Been involved with heavy metal or allied kinds of rock music?

❏ Heard voices in your mind or had compulsive thoughts that were foreign to what you believe?

❏ Had periods in childhood or the present when you cannot remember what happened?

1. Have you ever attended a New Age or parapsychology seminar, consulted a medium, spiritist or channeler? Explain.

2. Do you or have you ever had an imaginary friend or spirit guide offering you guidance or companionship? Explain.

3. Have you ever heard voices in your mind or had repeating and nagging thoughts that were foreign to what you believe or feel, like there was a dialogue going on in your head? Explain.

4. What other spiritual experiences have you had that would be considered out of the ordinary such as sensing an evil presence in your room at night as a child?

5. Have you been a victim of satanic ritual abuse? Explain.

Bibliography

Books

Anderson, Neil T. *The Bondage Breaker*. Eugene, Ore.: Harvest House, 1990, 1993.

_____. *The Bondage Breaker Study Guide*. Eugene, Ore.: Harvest House, 1992, 1993.

_____. *Breaking Through to Spiritual Maturity*. Ventura, Calif.: Gospel Light, 1992.

_____. *Helping Others Find Freedom in Christ*. Ventura, Calif.: Regal Books, 1995.

_____. *Living Free in Christ*. Ventura, Calif.: Regal Books, 1993.

_____. *Released from Bondage*. Nashville, Tenn.: Thomas Nelson Publishers, 1993.

_____. *Victory over the Darkness*. Ventura, Calif.: Regal Books, 1990.

_____. *Victory over the Darkness Study Guide*. Ventura, Calif.: Regal Books, 1994.

_____. *Walking in the Light*. Nashville, Tenn.: Thomas Nelson Publishers, 1992.

_____. *A Way of Escape*. Eugene, Ore.: Harvest House, 1994.

_____. *What God Says About Me*. Ventura, Calif.: Gospel Light, 1998.

_____ with Anderson, Joanne. *Daily in Christ*. Eugene, Ore.: Harvest House, 1993.

_____ and McGee, Jr., Tom. *Helping Others Find Freedom in Christ Training Manual and Study Guide*. Ventura, Calif.: Gospel Light, 1995.

_____ and Miller, Rich. *Awesome God*. Eugene, Ore.: Harvest House, 1996.

_____ and Miller, Rich. *Know Light, No Fear*. Nashville, Tenn.: Thomas Nelson Publishers, 1996.

_____ and Miller, Rich. *Leading Teens to Freedom in Christ*. Ventura, Calif.: Regal Books, 1997.

_____ and Miller, Rich. *Reality Check*. Eugene, Ore.: Harvest House, 1996.

_____ and Mylander, Charles. *The Christ-Centered Marriage*. Ventura, Calif.: Regal Books, 1996.

_____ and Mylander, Charles. *The Christ-Centered Marriage Study Guide*. Ventura, Calif.: Gospel Light, 1997.

_____ and Mylander, Charles. *Setting Your Church Free*. Ventura, Calif.: Regal Books, 1994.

_____ and Park, Dave. *The Bondage Breaker Youth Edition*. Eugene, Ore.: Harvest House, 1993.

_____ and Park, Dave. *The Bondage Breaker Youth Edition Study Guide*. Eugene, Ore.: Harvest House Publishers, 1995.

_____ and Park, Dave. *Busting Free!* Ventura, Calif.: Gospel Light, 1994.

_____ and Park, Dave. *Extreme Faith*. Eugene, Ore.: Harvest House, 1996.

_____ and Park, Dave. *Purity Under Pressure*. Eugene, Ore.: Harvest House, 1995.

_____ and Park, Dave. *Stomping Out the Darkness*. Ventura, Calif.: Regal Books, 1993.

_____ and Park, Dave. *Stomping Out the Darkness Study Guide*. Ventura, Calif.: Gospel Light, 1994.

_____ and Park, Dave. *Ultimate Love*. Eugene, Ore.: Harvest House, 1996.

_____ and Quarles, Mike and Julia. *Freedom from Addiction*. Ventura, Calif.: Regal Books, 1996.

_____ and Quarles, Mike and Julia. *Freedom from Addiction Workbook*. Ventura, Calif.: Gospel Light, 1997.

_____ and Russo, Steve. *The Seduction of Our Children*. Eugene, Ore.: Harvest House, 1991.

_____ and Saucy, Robert. *The Common Made Holy*. Eugene, Ore.: Harvest House Publishers, 1997.

_____ and Saucy, Robert. *The Common Made Holy Study Guide*. Eugene, Ore.: Harvest House Publishers, 1997.

_____ and Towns, Elmer L. *Rivers of Revival*. Ventura, Calif.: Regal Books, 1997.

_____ and Vander Hook, Pete and Sue. *Spiritual Protection for Your Children*. Ventura, Calif.: Regal Books, 1996.

Miller, Rich. *To My Dear Slimeball*. Eugene, Ore.: Harvest House, 1995.

Park, Dave. *The Common Made Holy Youth Edition*—work in progress.

Warner, Tim. *Spiritual Warfare*. Wheaton, Ill.: Crossway Books, 1991.

Audio/Visual Resources

Anderson, Neil T. "The Christ-Centered Marriage Video Seminar" (includes *The Christ-Centered Marriage* book, *The Christ-Centered Marriage Study Guide*, two copies of *Steps to Setting Your Marriage Free*, two copies of *The Steps to Freedom in Christ* and two videocassettes).

_____. "Free in Christ" (audiocassette). Hope Resources, 1997.

_____. "Resolving Personal Conflicts" (eight audio or four videocassettes). La Habra, Calif.: Freedom in Christ Ministries, 1993.

_____. "Resolving Spiritual Conflicts" (eight audio or four videocassettes). La Habra, Calif.: Freedom in Christ Ministries, 1993.

_____. "Helping Others Find Freedom in Christ Video Training Program" (includes six copies of *The Steps to Freedom in Christ* and two three-hour videocassettes). Ventura, Calif.: Gospel Light, 1995.

_____ "The Seduction of Our Children" (six audiocassettes or five videocassettes). La Habra, Calif.: Freedom in Christ Ministries, 1992.

_____. "Spiritual Conflicts and Counseling" (eight audio or four videocassettes). La Habra, Calif.: Freedom in Christ Ministries, 1993.

_____ and Mylander, Charles. "Setting Your Church Free" (eight audio or four videocassettes). La Habra, Calif.: Freedom in Christ Ministries, 1992.

_____ and Park, Dave. "Busting Free! Video Seminar" (two videocassettes). Ventura, Calif.: Gospel Light, 1997.

_____ and Quarles, Mike and Julia. "Freedom from Addiction Video Study" (includes six copies of *The Steps to Freedom in Christ*, *Freedom from Addiction* book, and *Freedom from Addiction Workbook*). Ventura, Calif.: Gospel Light, 1997.

Freedom in Christ Resources

Part One: *Resolving Personal Conflicts*

Victory over the Darkness
by Neil Anderson

Start here! This best-seller combined with *The Bondage Breaker* will show you how to find your freedom in Christ. Realize the power of your identity in Christ!

Paperback $10.95 • 239 pp. B001
Study Guide • Paper $8.95 • 153 pp. G001

Who I Am in Christ
by Neil Anderson

36 readings and prayers based on scriptural passages that assure us of God's love and our security and freedom in His kingdom.

Paperback $14.95 • 288 pp. B033

Daily in Christ
by Neil and Joanne Anderson

This uplifting 365-day devotional will encourage, motivate and challenge you to live *Daily in Christ*. There's a one-page devotional and brief heartfelt prayer for each day. Celebrate and experience your freedom all year.

Paperback $11.95 • 365 pp. B010

Breaking Through to Spiritual Maturity
by Neil Anderson

This is a dynamic Group Study of *Victory over the Darkness* and *The Bondage Breaker*. Complete with teaching notes for a 13-week (or 26-week) Bible study, with reproducible handouts. Ideal for Sunday School classes, Bible studies and discipleship groups.

Paperback $16.95 • 151 pp. G003

Victory over the Darkness Video & Audio
by Neil Anderson

In this, the first half of his "basic training" seminar, Neil Anderson explores how to resolve personal conflicts through discovering one's identity in Christ, embracing the ministry of reconciliation, experiencing emotional freedom and more.

Videotape Set $69.95 • 8 lessons V031
Audiotape Set $14.95 • 8 lessons A031
Workbook $4 • Paper 20pp. W009

Part Two: *Resolving Spiritual Conflicts*

The Bondage Breaker
by Neil Anderson

This best-seller combines the definitive process of breaking bondages with the *Steps to Freedom in Christ*. Read this with *Victory over the Darkness* and you will be able to resolve your personal and spiritual conflicts.

Paperback $10.95 • 302 pp. B002
Study Guide • Paper $6.95 • 139 pp. G002

The Steps to Freedom in Christ
by Neil Anderson

This is a handy version of *The Steps to Freedom in Christ*, the discipleship counseling process from *The Bondage Breaker*. It is ideal for personal use or for helping another person who wants to find his or her freedom.

Booklet $4 • 36 pp. G004

The Steps to Freedom in Christ Video
by Neil Anderson

In this special video experience, Dr. Neil Anderson personally leads you or a loved one through the bondage-breaking Steps to Freedom in Christ in the privacy of your living room. Includes *The Steps to Freedom in Christ* booklet.

Videotape $19.95 • 70 minutes V010

Spiritual Warfare
by Dr. Timothy Warner

This concise book offers balanced, biblical insights on spiritual warfare, with practical information and ammunition for winning the spiritual battle. Every reader will benefit by learning from the author's extensive experience.

Paperback $10.95 • 160 pp. B007

The Bondage Breaker Video & Audio
by Neil Anderson

In this, the second half of his "basic training" seminar, Neil Anderson explores how to resolve spiritual conflicts through the authority and protection God provides, living free in Christ, training believers to resist temptation and more.

Videotape $69.95 • 360 minutes VO32
Audiotape $34.95 • A032
Workbook $4 • Paper 20pp. W010

Freedom in Christ Conferences

Do you know that Freedom in Christ conducts conferences?

If you are interested in a Living Free in Christ Adult Conference with Dr. Neil T. Anderson and FIC staff or Stomping Out the Darkness Student Conference, call us today at 865-342-4000.

Bring a Freedom in Christ Conference to your city by calling 865-342-4000

Available at your local Christian bookstore or from
Freedom in Christ
9051 Executive Park Drive, Suite 503
Knoxville, TN 37923

Customer Service: (866) IN CHRIST (462-4747)
Fax: (865) 342-4001   Phone: (865) 342-4000
Internet: www.ficm.org
E-mail: info@ficm.org

043786

Freedom in Christ Resources

Part Three: *Discipleship Counseling*

Helping Others Find Freedom in Christ
by Neil Anderson

This book provides comprehensive, hands-on biblical discipleship counseling training for lay leaders, counselors and pastors, equipping them to help others.
Paperback $14.95 • 297 pp. B015
Training Manual and Study Guide $11.95

Helping Others Find Freedom in Christ Video Training Program

This Video Training Program is a complete training kit for churches and groups who want to establish a freedom ministry using *The Steps to Freedom in Christ*. Includes four 45-minute video lessons.
Video Training Program $39.95 • V015

Freedom from Addiction
by Neil Anderson and Mike and Julia Quarles

A book like no other on true recovery! This unique Christ-centered model has helped thousands break free from alcoholism, drug addiction and other addictive behaviors. The Quarles's amazing story will encourage every reader!
Paperback $16.95 • 356 pp. B019

Freedom from Addiction Video Study
by Neil Anderson and Mike and Julia Quarles

A dynamic resource for recovery group leading pastors and Christian counselors. A step-by-step study that changes lives. Includes video study, paperback and workbook.
Video Study $89.95 • V019

Discipleship Counseling
by Neil Anderson

This series presents advanced counseling insights and practical, biblical answers to help others find their freedom in Christ. It is the full content from Dr. Anderson's advanced seminar of the same name.
Videotape Set $99.95 • 8 lessons V033
Audiotape Set $44.95 • 8 lessons A033
Workbook $5 • Paper 24pp. W011

Setting Your Church Free
by Neil Anderson and Charles Mylander

This powerful book reveals how pastors and church leaders can lead their entire churches to freedom by discovering the key issues of both corporate bondage and corporate freedom. A must-read for every church leader.
Paperback $15.95 • 352 pp. B013

Part Four: *Church Leadership*

Setting Your Church Free Video Conference
by Neil Anderson and Charles Mylander

This leadership series presents the powerful principles taught in *Setting Your Church Free*. Ideal for church staffs and boards to study and discuss together. The series ends with the steps to setting your church free.
Videotape Set $69.95 • 8 lessons V006
Audiocassette Set $40 • 8 lessons A006
Additional workbooks $6 • paper 42 pp. W006
Corporate Steps $2 • G006

Topical Resources

God's Power at Work in You
by Neil Anderson and Robert Saucy

Anderson and Saucy deal with the dangerous common misconceptions that hinder spiritual growth, including: How can we overcome sin and resist temptation? What is God's role in helping us stay pure? What is our role? What is the key to consistent victory?
Paperback $10.95 B032

Released from Bondage
by Neil Anderson

This book shares true stories of freedom from obsessive thoughts, compulsive behaviors, guilt, satanic ritual abuse, childhood abuse and demonic strongholds, combined with helpful commentary from Dr. Anderson.
Paperback $12.95 • 258 pp. B006

Rivers of Revival
by Neil Anderson and Elmer Towns

Answers what many Christians are asking today: "What will it take to see revival?" Examines the fascinating subject of personal revival and past and current evangelistic streams that could help usher in global revival.
Hardcover $18.95 • 288 pp. B023

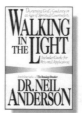

Walking in the Light
by Neil Anderson

Everyone wants to know God's will for his life. Dr. Anderson explains the fascinating spiritual dimensions of divine guidance and how to avoid spiritual counterfeits. Includes a personal application guide for each chapter.
Paperback $12.95 • 234 pp. B011

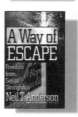

A Way of Escape
by Neil Anderson

Talking about sex is never easy. This vital book provides real answers for sexual struggles, unwanted thoughts, compulsive habits or a painful past. Don't learn to just cope; learn how to resolve your sexual issues in Christ.
Paperback $10.95 • 238 pp. B014